Edited by Nancy C. DeJoy, Collin Craig,
Steven T. Lessner, and Bonnie J. Williams

Reading and Writing Literacies

A Custom Publication for
Michigan State University

Cover Art: Courtesy of Ben Rubinstein

Ben Rubinstein is a MSU Professional Writing alumnus. Ben is a
graphic designer who can be reached at benrubinstein@gmail.com.

Pearson Learning Solutions, 501 Boylston Street, Suite 900, Boston,
MA 02116
A Pearson Education Company
www.pearsoned.com

Printed in the United States of America

1 2 3 4 5 6 7 8 9 10 XXXX 16 15 14 13 12 11

000200010270787979

CT/FC

ISBN 10: 1-256-30726-2
ISBN 13: 978-1-256-30726-6

Contents

Electronic Readings 1

Introduction 3

Lived Literacies

Lived Literacies: Introduction 9

Welcome to St. Paul's
Lorene Cary 10

Reading Ourselves and the World Around Us
Alberto Manguel 15

Growing Up
Russell Baker 18

Mother Tongue
Amy Tan 26

Hearing Voices
Linda Hogan 33

The Struggle to be an All-American Girl
Elizabeth Wong 38

From Silence to Words: Writing as Struggle
Min-zhan Lu 41

Only Daughter
Sandra Cisneros 56

CONTENTS

African American Women Talkin' that Talk
Denise Troutman 60

Lived Literacies: External Resources 88

Cultural Literacies

Cultural Literacies: Introduction 91

School vs. Education
Russell Baker 92

How We Listen to Music
Aaron Copland 95

The Myth of the Latin Woman: I Just Met a Girl
Named María
Judith Ortiz Cofer 101

The Merits of Meritocracy
David Brooks 107

Children, Wired: For Better and For Worse
Daphne Bavelier, C. Shawn Green, and Matthew W. G. Dye 113

Fighting for Our Lives
Deborah Tannen 139

The Rhetoric of Celebrity Cookbooks
Christine M. Mitchell 161

The Song Decoders
Rob Walker 177

Cultural Literacies: External Resources 189

Disciplinary Literacies

Disciplinary Literacies: Introduction 193

Winning Hearts and Minds in War on Plagiarism
Scott Jaschik 194

Learning the Language
Perry Klass 202

CONTENTS

Policing Race and Class
David Cole 206

The Truth Wears Off: Is There Something
Wrong With the Scientific Method?
Jonah Lehrer 216

Disciplinary Literacies: External Resources 228

Remixing/Technological Literacies

Remixing/Technological Literacies: Introduction 231

For Some, the Blogging Never Stops
Katie Hafner and Tim Gnatek 232

I Think, Therefore IM
Jennifer Lee 237

Finding One's Own Space in Cyberspace
Amy Bruckman 242

Remixing/Technological Literacies: External Resources 253

Revising Literacies

Revising Literacies: Introduction 257

Writing Is my Passion
bell hooks 258

Professions for Women
Virginia Woolf 262

A Letter to America
Margaret Atwood 268

White Privilege: Unpacking the Invisible Knapsack
Peggy McIntosh 272

Reflection on My EFL Experiences
Ramesh Kumar Pokharel 278

Revising Literacies: External Resources 281

Appendix 1: RAIDS 282

Electronic Readings
These readings are available online

Lived Literacies
The Screenwriter's Tale by Jennifer Lawler
Indian Education
  Sherman Alexie
"I Just Wanna Be Average"
  Mike Rose
You Are What You Like
  Christiane Gelitz

Cultural Literacies
Football Red and Baseball Green: The Heroics and
  Bucolics of American Sport by Murray Ross
Poetry for Everyday Life
  David Brooks
Book of Rhymes
  Ben Detrick and Jonathan Mannion
Love Supreme
  Adam Haslett
Culture Jamming
  Kalle Lasn
A Generation's Vanity, Heard Through Lyrics
  John Tierney
From Spaghetti and Meatballs through Hawaiian
Pizza to Sushi: The Changing Nature
of Ethnicity in American Restaurants
  Liora Gvion and Naomi Trostler

Disciplinary Literacies
One Carpenter's Life by Larry Haun
Learning to Read Biology: One Student's Rhetorical
  Development in College by Christina Haas

1

The Nature of Reading and Writing at Work by
  William Diehl and Larry Mikulecky
To Tug Hearts, Music First Must Tickle the Neurons
  Pam Belluck
Method
  Robert Coles
Peer Review Improves Undergraduate
Science Writing Skills
  Debra Conte
Group Peer Review as an Active Learning Strategy
in a Research Course
  Sue Odom, Betty Glenn, Susan Sanner,
  and Kathleen A. S. Cannella
Ethics and the Limits of Scientific Freedom
  Peter Singer
The Knife
  Richard Selzer

Remixing/Technological Literacies
Teaching Visual Literacy in a Multimodal Age by
  Glenda Rakes
For Some, The Blogging Never Stops
  You, The DJ by Sasha Frere-Jones
Popular Music in School: Remixing the Issues by
  Robert H. Woody

Revising Literacies
Literacy in Three Metaphors by Sylvia Scribner
Stories, Not Information: Transforming Information
  Literacy by Jeff Purdue
Being an Ally by Helen Fox
The Nobel Lecture by Toni Morrison
How Do I Write a Text for College?
Making the Transition from High School Writing
  Patty Strong

Introduction

While making decisions about what texts to include in this reader we had long conversations about what we have learned from our first-year writing students over the past few years. We wanted to help students make successful transitions to writing, reading, and researching in higher education in America. (We also forced ourselves to limit selections so that teachers and students can add additional texts appropriate for their particular contexts.) Some of the readings included here have worked well in the past, others are new readings that we selected because they open spaces for students to make valuable contributions to our understanding of literacy in the contexts of their lives. Each of the readings included, then, opens up conversations about literacy that invite students to make the conceptual shift from thinking of themselves as consumers of knowledge to understanding themselves as participants who make important contributions to their communities. Sometimes, those contributions change the way we think, other times they may also change practices (like the student project that inspired teachers to include undergraduate students in professional presentations). Our students tell us that the transition away from education as the consumption of knowledge (and tests that measure the quality of your consumption) and toward education as a participatory activity that sets expectations for new contributions is challenging, exciting, uneven, frustrating, and rewarding—usually all at once!

We know that these challenges and opportunities occur because as students adjust to life in higher education and choose their majors, they are introduced to multiple ways of making knowledge that require them to think about language and learning in different ways. As a way of helping teachers and learners focus on these new challenges and opportunities we chose readings that demonstrate an understanding of literacy as a broad and flexible concept that can help us understand ourselves, one another, and our worlds in engaged— and engaging—ways. From our own experiences we know that we live in evolving cultures that constantly shape how we "read" and function in the world. Our selections demonstrate how diverse communities gain access to and use multiple literacies for multiple aims. We hope that our decision to organize around the themes of personal, cultural, disciplinary, technological, and revisionary forms of literacy inspires teachers and students to contribute their own stories, ideas, critical analyses, and suggestions for how we might all work to use language to improve our own lives and the lives of all of the members of the diverse communities to which we belong. We hope that, taken collectively, the readings in this book encourage writing and researching that helps us all see our own and each other's potential for successful, meaningful lives as literate people in higher education and beyond.

We aimed to create a reading experience that was relevant to each of the types of literacy we use to organize the sections of this book. But we also selected readings that can be used to look at more than one type of literacy. For example, Elizabeth Wong's "The Struggle to Be an All American Girl" demonstrates lived experiences with learning English as a Chinese student (her personal literacy); but she also revises her values about American culture when she is faced with learning how to merge her American and Chinese identities (cultural literacy). Sylvia Scribner's "Literacy in Three Metaphors" revises some major assumptions about literacy as merely reading and writing; but it does so in a way that meets the expectations for writing in her discipline. Similarly, the videos from TED.com that are listed at the end of each section are appropriate for use with the essays in that section. However, they can also be used in combination with readings from other sections. Shereen El Feki's talk "Culture in the Arab World" is listed in the Remixing/Technological section, but it could also be used as you explore Cultural Literacies. We group readings and other resources thematically because we want our readers to be able to see consistencies and differences across literacy themes. We encourage you to rearrange them as you go because we want you to create your own connections across your writing assignments.

We invite you to think about the types of writing and researching that you can generate with this Reader and encourage you to contemplate how you might participate in conversations that are situated in multiple contexts. As you explore these readings think about what you might add to these conversations. For example:

- How does your own literacy history lead to suggestions about how to enhance other students' transitions to higher education?
- What are language practices that are crucial in your everyday life?

- How do some of the literacy artifacts in your life indicate a larger set of values?
- What are the writing, reading, and researching practices most common in fields connected to your major? How might you create a literacy plan that prepares you to be successful in that major and related careers?
- How do technologies enhance and/or inhibit forms of literacy not usually studied in school, but vital to our happiness outside of school?
- How might you use inquiry into literacy as a strategy toward developing new knowledge and revising existing ideas?
- How might you use that inquiry to enter multiple conversations?

We know that these are big questions. But we also know that asking them together will result in richer relationships, better conversations, and more effective responses to our worlds than we could ever create alone.

Nancy
Collin
Steve
Bonnie

Lived Literacies

Lived Literacies: Introduction

The readings in this section invite you to explore the ways that literacy and the values and practices associated with literacy affect our lived experiences of self, other and world. They help you to get some ideas about how specific literacy experiences, practices, attitudes, etc. affect how we see ourselves, others and our worlds. As you read, pay attention to the invention strategies used by the writers. For example, in "Mother Tongue," Amy Tan reflects on her experiences by creating a contrast between how she uses language with and for her mother and how she uses language in her life as a writer and presenter. Reflecting on contrasts is an invention strategy you might use to explore your own literacy history. In "The Screenwriter's Tale," Jennifer Lawler observes the ways that people react to her life as a writer who does not stick to academic writing even though she is an academic. Observing and analyzing people's reaction to difference is an invention strategy that helps Lawler understand these reactions and communicate their significance. You might want to use observation (of difference or another reaction) as an invention strategy as you explore possible focuses for your own literacy narrative. Don't worry about finding all of the invention strategies or worry about if the ones you see are the "right" ones. At this point, just concentrate on reading as part of the writing process, a part that can help you discover new ways to go about generating ideas and trying new invention strategies.

Welcome to St. Paul's

Lorene Cary

Lorene Cary studied in England after graduating from the University of Pennsylvania (M.A., 1978). She has worked for Time *and* TV Guide *and taught at and served as a member of the Board of Trustees of St. Paul's, an exclusive boarding school she attended. This essay describes her arrival at St. Paul's, which until a few years earlier had been all-white and all-male. Excerpted from* Black Ice *(1991), a story about her experiences at St. Paul's, the essay reveals the many life changes she encountered as an African-American girl in a very different, almost all-white, almost all-male world.*

My family and I stood in the Rectory just a year and a half after Lee's first tea. Unlike her, I was armed with the experience of a proper, on-campus interview, and I was escorted by attractive young parents and a cuddly kid sister. Unlike Ed Shockley, I was not afraid that the white boys were going to catch me alone in the woods one night and beat me up. But for the first time, I had a whiff, as subtle as the scent of the old books that lined the wall, of my utter aloneness in this new world. I reached into myself for the head-to-the-side, hands-on-hips cockiness that had brought me here and found just enough of it to keep me going.

My dormitory was around the corner from the Rectory, over a bridge and across the road from the library. Inside, just off the common room, steps led to the open doorway of the housemaster. He, too, was on hand to greet us.

I wasn't sure about Mr. Hawley. He had a round face whose top half was nearly bald and whose bottom half was covered with a full, tweed-colored beard. Between the top and bottom halves a pair of glasses perched on a small nose and caught the light. He made a funny face when he spied my sister: "And look what you brought along! We've got a couple of those creatures running around somewhere. I'll see if they've been run over yet by some station wagon gone berserk."

I was later to learn that all the intelligence and will, all the imagination and mischief in that face was revealed in the pale eyes behind the glasses, but on this first meeting, I could only bring myself to concentrate on the beard and the Kriss Kringle mouth.

Mr. Hawley, it turned out, had family in Philadelphia, so we talked about the city, and my parents described for him just exactly where we lived.

Like other St. Paul's buildings, the Hawleys' house had alcoves, staircases, and a courtyard, that presented to me a facade of impenetrable, almost European, privacy. The housemaster's home was directly accessible from the dormitory, but only by going from the vestibule into the common room, then up stairs, through a heavy wooden door, into a hallway, and another, inner door. Once in the living room, I could see through the windows that we were across the street from the gray granite library, but I would not have known it had the drapes been pulled. The architecture that I so admired from the outside did not yield itself up to me from within as I had expected. I now felt disconcerted, as I had in the Rectory. Mr. Hawley wanted to know just how far one would drive along Baltimore Pike to get to Yeadon, and I, standing in his living room, had no idea where his kitchen might be.

Mrs. Hawley, a short, soft-spoken woman, appeared from the rear hallway. Like her husband, she said ironic things, but more gently. Startlingly blond children came with her, one peeking from behind her skirt.

Mr. Hawley directed us to my room and showed my father where to park by the back door so that we could unload more handily. We carried my things up from a basement entrance. Doors whooshed open and closed as other girls and their families came and went, and the halls echoed with the sounds of mothers' heels.

My room faced east. In the afternoon it seemed dull and empty and dark.

"This'll be lovely when you get it all fixed up," my mother said, by which I assumed that it looked dull to her, too.

Fine dust had settled contentedly over the sturdy oak bureau and cloudy mirror, over the charming, squat little oak desk and chair and in the corners of the closet. White people, as we said, were not personally fastidious (any black woman who'd ever been a maid could tell you that, and some did, in appalling detail, so I'd heard stories). I was determined to give the place a good wash.

The casement windows matched those elsewhere on campus. My father opened one, tightened the wing nut to hold the sash in place, and stood looking out into the meadow. Then he peeked into the room next door, which was still empty, and recalled how, at Lincoln University, the first students to arrive scavenged the best furniture in the dormitory. "If there's any furniture you don't like, better speak now," he joked. "I guess you wouldn't want to do that here."

I checked the room next door, and pronounced, with laughter but not conviction, that I'd gotten a fair bargain.

The room seemed crowded with all of us about. I found myself chattering on, very gaily, about where I would put my things. What with the windows at one end, the narrow bed against one wall, the bureau, the desk, the radiator, the closet, the door leading into the next room, the door leading in, and the economy of my possessions, there were few options, realistically, for interior design.

Still, I could not stop buzzing. So long as we stood crowded together in the room, my sister jumping on the naked mattress, my mother wondering about smoking a cigarette, my father by the open window clenching his jaw and rubbing the back of his neck, and me burbling and babbling as if words were British soldiers marching in pointless columns, bright and gay, with flags and bright brass buttons on crimson-colored breasts, on and on and on into battle; so long as we had nothing to do except to wait for the next thing to do; so long as the intolerable closeness remained and the intolerable separation loomed to be made, so long would this adrenaline rush through me, anarchic, atavistic, compelling.

Outside the move-in continued. Convinced that I was missing yet another ritual of initiation, I ran down the hall to check the bulletin board. As I stood reading, an Asian boy propelled himself into the vestibule. He introduced himself without smiling and asked me my name. Then, addressing me by the name I gave, he asked whether or not I lived in Simpson House.

"Listen," he said. "There's a girl upstairs. She's just moved in. Her name is Fumiko, and she's from Japan. She can hardly speak any English at all. She understands a lot, but she really needs someone to go and make her feel welcome."

"Do you speak Japanese?"

"Of course not." (He was Chinese-American.) He appeared to be reevaluating me. "Look, is anyone else around?"

"I don't know. I've just arrived myself."

"Well, welcome! Look, we've been helping her, but she needs a girl in her own house, and guys can't come in. Maybe you can tell some of the other girls. Really, she's only just come to the country."

Reluctantly, I agreed. I went to the room on the second floor that the boy had described, and found her. I introduced myself. We tried hard to pronounce each other's names, and we laughed at our mistakes. Fumiko was taller than I. She kept suppressing bows. We agreed to meet again later.

I returned to my family much calmer than I'd left, and I told them about my new friend. Now my mother seemed agitated. Just before we left for dinner, she began to tell me what items of clothing should go into which drawer.

"You always put underwear in the top. See, it's the shallowest one. Big, bulky things like sweaters and jeans go down at the bottom. But, now, please don't just jam your things in. I don't want you walking around here with stuff that's all jerked up."

"I know where things go."

"Listen. Skirts, your good pants, all that stuff needs to be hung up. Let's see how this is packed." My mother unzipped one of the suitcases on the bed. "You know, maybe you might want us to take this big one home. I can't see where you have room to store it."

I watched my mother lift layers of underwear delicately from their berths. Her hands, precise, familiar, called up in me a frenzy of possession. "I've got all night to unpack," I said. "Please don't. I should do that."

"I'll just help you get started. Lord, I hope you don't start putting together any of those crazy outfits you concoct at home. I know you think that stuff looks cute, but it doesn't. You didn't pack any of those fishnet stockings, I hope." Mama selected a drawer for panties and one for bras and slips. I'd brought a girdle—hers, of course—that was hidden in the next layer.

"I *really* want to do that myself."

"I'm not taking anything away from you." Her voice rose with maternal indignation.

"Let the child do it herself," my father said.

I knew that they were going to fight. It would be a silent fight, because we were, even in this room, in public, so long as we were on school grounds. I did not see how we would avoid it. We'd been cooped up together, as my parents called it, all day.

Then my mother laughed. "All right, all right, I was just getting you started," she said. "You'd think I was doing something wrong."

We left for dinner, and I closed my door.

Reading Ourselves and the World Around Us*

Alberto Manguel

Alberto Manguel (1948–) was born in Buenos Aires, reared in Israel, and, in 1981, was granted Canadian citizenship. He has edited anthologies of fantasy literature, short fiction by Latin American women, erotica, and ghost and mystery stories. He has also written a novel, News from a Foreign Country Game *(1991) and a nonfiction work,* A History of Reading *(1996), from which the following essay comes. In this brief excerpt, Manguel describes an early memory of literacy, the moment at which he realized that he could read.*

I first discovered that I could read at the age of four. I had seen, over and over again, the letters that I knew (because I had been told) were the names of the pictures under which they sat. The boy drawn in thick black lines, dressed in red shorts and a green shirt (that same red and green cloth from which all the other images in the book were cut, dogs and cats and trees and thin tall mothers), was also somehow, I realized, the stern black shapes beneath him, as if the boy's body had been dismembered into three clean-cut figures: one arm and the torso, **b**; the severed head so perfectly round, **o**; and the limp, low-hanging legs, **y**. I drew eyes in the round face, and a smile, and filled in the hollow circle of the torso. But there was more: I knew that not only did these shapes mirror the boy above them, but they also could tell me precisely what the boy was doing, arms stretched out and legs apart. **The boy runs**, said the shapes. He wasn't jumping, as I might

*Editor's title

Reprinted from *A History of Reading*, by permission of the author.

have thought, or pretending to be frozen into place, or playing a game whose rules and purpose were unknown to me. **The boy runs**.

And yet these realizations were common acts of conjuring, less interesting because someone else had performed them for me. Another reader—my nurse, probably—had explained the shapes and now, every time the pages opened to the image of this exuberant boy, I knew what the shapes beneath him meant. There was pleasure in this, but it wore thin. There was no surprise.

Then one day, from the window of a car (the destination of that journey is now forgotten), I saw a billboard by the side of the road. The sight could not have lasted very long; perhaps the car stopped for a moment, perhaps it just slowed down long enough for me to see, large and looming, shapes similar to those in my book, but shapes that I had never seen before. And yet, all of a sudden, I knew what they were; I heard them in my head, they metamorphosed from black lines and white spaces into a solid, sonorous, meaningful reality. I had done this all by myself. No one had performed the magic for me. I and the shapes were alone together, revealing ourselves in a silently respectful dialogue. Since I could turn bare lines into living reality, I was all-powerful. I could read.

What that word was on the long-past billboard I no longer know (vaguely I seem to remember a word with several As in it), but the impression of suddenly being able to comprehend what before I could only gaze at is as vivid today as it must have been then. It was like acquiring an entirely new sense, so that now certain things no longer consisted merely of what my eyes could see, my ears could hear, my tongue could taste, my nose could smell, my fingers could feel, but of what my whole body could decipher, translate, give voice to, read.

The readers of books, into whose family I was unknowingly entering (we always think that we are alone in each discovery, and that every experience, from death to birth, is terrifyingly unique), extend or concentrate a function common to us all. Reading letters on a page is only one of its many guises. The astronomer reading a map of stars that no longer exist; the Japanese architect reading the land on which a house is to be built so as to guard it from evil forces; the zoologist reading the spoor of animals in the forest; the card-player reading her partner's gestures before playing the winning card; the dancer reading the choreographer's notations, and the public reading the dancer's movements on the stage; the weaver reading the intricate design of a carpet being woven; the organ-player reading various simultaneous strands of music orchestrated on the page: the parent reading the baby's face for signs of joy or fright, or wonder; the Chinese fortune-teller reading the ancient marks on the shell of a tortoise; the lover blindly reading the loved one's body at night, under the sheets; the psychiatrist helping patients read their own bewildering dreams; the Hawaiian fisherman reading the ocean currents by plunging a hand into the water, the farmer reading the weather in the sky—all these share with bookreaders the craft of deciphering and translating signs. Some of these readings are coloured by the knowledge that the thing read was created for this specific purpose by other human beings—music notation or road signs, for instance—or by the gods—the tortoise shell, the sky at night. Others belong to chance.

And yet, in every case, it is the reader who reads the sense; it is the reader who grants or recognizes in an object, place or event a certain possible readability; it is the reader who must attribute meaning to a system of signs, and then decipher it. We all read ourselves and the world around us in order to glimpse what and where we are. We read to understand, or to begin to understand. We cannot do but read. Reading, almost as much as breathing, is our essential function.

Growing Up

Russell Baker

Russell Baker (1925–) was born in a rural town in Virginia and grew up in New Jersey and Maryland. He received his B.A. in English from Johns Hopkins University in 1947 and worked as a reporter for the Baltimore Sun *and then the* New York Times. *In 1962 he began writing his "Observer" column for the* Times, *which was syndicated in over 400 newspapers for more than two decades. His topics range from the mundane everyday annoyances to serious social problems, and his style is generally casual but thoughtful. In 1979 he received the Pulitzer Prize for distinguished commentary; he received the Prize again for his autobiography* Growing Up *(1982), from which the following selection is excerpted. His collections of columns and essays include* All Things Considered *(1965),* Poor Russell's Almanac *(1972),* So This Is Depravity *(1980),* The Rescue of Miss Yaskell and Other Pipe Dreams *(1983), and* There's a Country in My Cellar *(1990). The following excerpt from his autobiography describes, with humor and insight, the moment when he decides he wants to become a writer.*

I began working in journalism when I was eight years old. It was my mother's idea. She wanted me to "make something" of myself and, after a levelheaded appraisal of my strengths, decided I had better start young if I was to have any chance of keeping up with the competition.

The flaw in my character which she had already spotted was lack of "gumption." My idea of a perfect afternoon was lying in front of the radio rereading my favorite Big Little Book, *Dick Tracy Meets*

Reprinted from *Growing Up* (1982), by permission of the author.

Stooge Viller. My mother despised inactivity. Seeing me having a good time in repose, she was powerless to hide her disgust. "You've got no more gumption than a bump on a log," she said. "Get out in the kitchen and help Doris do those dirty dishes."

My sister Doris, though two years younger than I, had enough gumption for a dozen people. She positively enjoyed washing dishes, making beds, and cleaning the house. When she was only seven she could carry a piece of short-weighted cheese back to the A&P, threaten the manager with legal action, and come back triumphantly with the full quarter-pound we'd paid for and a few ounces extra thrown in for forgiveness. Doris could have made something of herself if she hadn't been a girl. Because of this defect, however, the best she could hope for was a career as a nurse or schoolteacher, the only work that capable females were considered up to in those days.

This must have saddened my mother, this twist of fate that had allocated all the gumption to the daughter and left her with a son who was content with Dick Tracy and Stooge Viller. If disappointed, though, she wasted no energy on self-pity. She would make me make something of myself whether I wanted to or not. "The Lord helps those who help themselves," she said. That was the way her mind worked.

She was realistic about the difficulty. Having sized up the material the Lord had given her to mold, she didn't overestimate what she could do with it. She didn't insist that I grow up to be President of the United States.

Fifty years ago parents still asked boys if they wanted to grow up to be President, and asked it not jokingly but seriously. Many parents who were hardly more than paupers still believed their sons could do it. Abraham Lincoln had done it. We were only sixty-five years from Lincoln. Many a grandfather who walked among us could remember Lincoln's time. Men of grandfatherly age were the worst for asking if you wanted to grow up to be President. A surprising number of little boys said yes and meant it.

I was asked many times myself. No, I would say, I didn't want to grow up to be President. My mother was present during one of these interrogations. An elderly uncle, having posed the usual question and exposed my lack of interest in the Presidency, asked, "Well, what *do* you want to be when you grow up?"

I loved to pick through trash piles and collect empty bottles, tin cans with pretty labels, and discarded magazines. The most desirable job on earth sprang instantly to mind. "I want to be a garbage man," I said.

My uncle smiled, but my mother had seen the first distressing evidence of a bump budding on a log. "Have a little gumption, Russell," she said. Her calling me Russell was a signal of unhappiness. When she approved of me I was always "Buddy."

When I turned eight years old she decided that the job of starting me on the road toward making something of myself could no longer be safely delayed. "Buddy," she said one day, "I want you to come home right after school this afternoon. Somebody's coming and I want you to meet him."

When I burst in that afternoon she was in conference in the parlor with an executive of the Curtis Publishing Company. She introduced me. He bent low from the waist and shook my hand. Was it true as my mother had told him, he asked, that I longed for the opportunity to conquer the world of business?

My mother replied that I was blessed with a rare determination to make something of myself.

"That's right," I whispered.

"But have you got the grit, the character, the never-say-quit spirit it takes to succeed in business?"

My mother said I certainly did.

"That's right," I said.

He eyed me silently for a long pause, as though weighing whether I could be trusted to keep his confidence, then spoke man-to-man. Before taking a crucial step, he said, he wanted to advise me that working for the Curtis Publishing Company placed enormous responsibility on a young man. It was one of the great companies of America. Perhaps the greatest publishing house in the world. I had heard, no doubt, of the *Saturday Evening Post?*

Heard of it? My mother said that everyone in our house had heard of the *Saturday Post* and that I, in fact, read it with religious devotion.

Then doubtless he said, we were also familiar with those two monthly pillars of the magazine world, the *Ladies Home Journal* and the *Country Gentleman.*

Indeed we were familiar with them, said my mother.

Representing the *Saturday Evening Post* was one of the weightiest honors that could be bestowed in the world of business, he said. He was personally proud of being a part of that great corporation.

My mother said he had every right to be.

Again he studied me as though debating whether I was worthy of a knighthood. Finally: "Are you trustworthy?"

My mother said I was the soul of honesty.

"That's right," I said.

The caller smiled for the first time. He told me I was a lucky young man. He admired my spunk. Too many young men thought life was all play. Those young men would not go far in this world. Only a young man willing to work and save and keep his face washed and his hair neatly combed could hope to come out on top in a world such as ours. Did I truly and sincerely believe that I was such a young man?

"He certainly does," said my mother.

"That's right," I said.

He said he had been so impressed by what he had seen of me that he was going to make me a representative of the Curtis Publishing Company. On the following Tuesday, he said, thirty freshly printed copies of the *Saturday Evening Post* would be delivered at our door. I would place these magazines, still damp with the ink of the presses, in a handsome canvas bag, sling it over my shoulder, and set forth through the streets to bring the best in journalism, fiction, and cartoons to the American public.

He had brought the canvas bag with him. He presented it with reverence fit for a chasuble. He showed me how to drape the sling over my left shoulder and across the chest so that the pouch lay easily accessible to my right hand, allowing the best in journalism, fiction, and cartoons to be swiftly extracted and sold to a citizenry whose happiness and security depended upon us soldiers of the free press.

The following Tuesday I raced home from school, put the canvas bag over my shoulder, dumped the magazines in, and, tilting to the left to balance their weight on my right hip, embarked on the highway of journalism.

We lived in Belleville, New Jersey, a commuter town at the northern fringe of Newark. It was 1932, the bleakest year of the Depression. My father had died two years before, leaving us with a few pieces of Sears, Roebuck furniture and not much else, and my mother had taken Doris and me to live with one of her younger brothers. This was my Uncle Allen. Uncle Allen had made something of himself by 1932.

As salesman for a soft-drink bottler in Newark, he had an income of $30 a week; wore pearl-gray spats, detachable collars, and a three-piece suit; was happily married; and took in threadbare relatives.

With my load of magazines I headed toward Belleville Avenue. That's where the people were. There were two filling stations at the intersection with Union Avenue, as well as an A&P, a fruit stand, a bakery, a barber shop, Zuccarelli's drugstore, and a diner shaped like a railroad car. For several hours I made myself highly visible, shifting position now and then from corner to corner, from shop window to shop window, to make sure everyone could see the heavy black lettering on the canvas bag that said THE SATURDAY EVENING POST. When the angle of the light indicated it was suppertime, I walked back to the house.

"How many did you sell, Buddy?" my mother asked.

"None."

"Where did you go?"

"The corner of Belleville and Union Avenues."

"What did you do?"

"Stood on the corner waiting for somebody to buy a *Saturday Evening Post*."

"You just stood there?"

"Didn't sell a single one."

"For God's sake, Russell."

Uncle Allen intervened. "I've been thinking about it for some time," he said, "and I've about decided to take the *Post* regularly. Put me down as a regular customer." I handed him a magazine and he paid me a nickel. It was the first nickel I earned.

Afterwards my mother instructed me in salesmanship. I would have to ring doorbells, address adults with charming self-confidence, and break down resistance with a sales talk pointing out that no one, no matter how poor, could afford to be without the *Saturday Evening Post* in the home.

I told my mother I'd changed my mind about wanting to succeed in the magazine business.

"If you think I'm going to raise a good-for-nothing," she replied, "you've got another think coming." She told me to hit the streets with the canvas bag and start ringing doorbells the instant school was out next day. When I objected that I didn't feel any aptitude for salesmanship, she asked how I'd like to lend her my leather belt so she could whack some sense into me, I bowed to superior will and entered journalism with a heavy heart.

My mother and I had fought this battle almost as long as I could remember. It probably started even before memory began, when I was a country child in northern Virginia and my mother, dissatisfied with my father's plain workman's life, determined that I would not grow up like him and his people, with calluses on their hands, overalls on their backs, and fourth-grade educations in their heads. She had fancier ideas of life's possibilities. Introducing me to the *Saturday Evening Post,* she was trying to wean me as early as possible from my father's world where men left with their lunch pails at sunup, worked with their hands until the grime ate into the pores, and died with a few sticks of mail-order furniture as their legacy. In my mother's vision of the better life there were desks and white collars, well-pressed suits, evenings of reading and lively talk, and perhaps—if a man were very, very lucky and hit the jackpot, really made something important of himself—perhaps there might be a fantastic salary of $5,000 a year to support a big house and a Buick with a rumble seat and a vacation in Atlantic City.

And so I set forth with my sack of magazines. I was afraid of the dogs that snarled behind the doors of potential buyers. I was timid about ringing the doorbells of strangers, relieved when no one came to the door, and scared when someone did. Despite my mother's in-structions, I could not deliver an engaging sales pitch. When a door opened I simply asked, "Want to buy a *Saturday Evening Post?*" In Belleville few persons did. It was a town of 30,000 people, and most weeks I rang a fair majority of its doorbells. But I rarely sold my thirty copies. Some weeks I canvassed the entire town for six days and still had four or five unsold magazines on Monday evening; then I dreaded the coming of Tuesday morning, when a batch of thirty fresh *Satur-day Evening Posts* was due at the front door.

"Better get out there and sell the rest of those magazines tonight," my mother would say.

I usually posted myself then at a busy intersection where a traffic light controlled commuter flow from Newark. When the light turned red I stood on the curb and shouted my sales pitch at the motorists.

"Want to buy a *Saturday Evening Post?*"

One rainy night when car windows were sealed against me I came back soaked and with not a single sale to report. My mother beckoned to Doris.

"Go back down there with Buddy and show him how to sell these magazines," she said.

Brimming with zest, Doris, who was then seven years old, returned with me to the corner. She took a magazine from the bag, and when the light turned red she strode to the nearest car and banged her small fist against the closed window. The driver, probably startled at what he took to be a midget assaulting his car, lowered the window to stare, and Doris thrust a *Saturday Evening Post* at him.

"You need this magazine," she piped, "and it only costs a nickel."

Her salesmanship was irresistible. Before the light changed half a dozen times she disposed of the entire batch. I didn't feel humiliated. To the contrary, I was so happy I decided to give her a treat. Leading her to the vegetable store on Belleville Avenue, I bought three apples, which cost a nickel, and gave her one.

"You shouldn't waste money," she said.

"Eat your apple." I bit into mine.

"You shouldn't eat before supper," she said. "It'll spoil your appetite."

Back at the house that evening, she dutifully reported me for wasting a nickel. Instead of a scolding, I was rewarded with a pat on the back for having the good sense to buy fruit instead of candy. My mother reached into her bottomless supply of maxims and told Doris, "An apple a day keeps the doctor away."

By the time I was ten I had learned all my mother's maxims by heart. Asking to stay up past normal bedtime, I knew that a refusal would be explained with, "Early to bed and early to rise, makes a man healthy, wealthy, and wise." If I whimpered about having to get up early in the morning, I could depend on her to say, "The early bird gets the worm."

The one I most despised was, "If at first you don't succeed, try, try again." This was the battle cry with which she constantly sent me back into the hopeless struggle whenever I moaned that I had rung every doorbell in town and knew there wasn't a single potential buyer left in Belleville that week. After listening to my explanation, she handed me the canvas bag and said, "If at first you don't succeed . . ."

Three years in that job, which I would gladly have quit after the first day except for her insistence, produced at least one valuable result. My mother finally concluded that I would never make something of myself by pursuing a life in business and started considering careers that demanded less competitive zeal.

One evening when I was eleven I brought home a short "composition" on my summer vacation which the teacher had graded with an A. Reading it with her own schoolteacher's eye, my mother agreed that it was top-drawer seventh grade prose and complimented me. Nothing more was said about it immediately, but a new idea had taken life in her mind. Halfway through supper she suddenly interrupted the conversation.

"Buddy," she said, "maybe you could be a writer."

I clasped the idea to my heart. I had never met a writer, had shown no previous urge to write, and hadn't a notion how to become a writer, but I loved stories and thought that making up stories must surely be almost as much fun as reading them. Best of all, though, and what really gladdened my heart, was the ease of the writer's life. Writers did not have to trudge through the town peddling from canvas bags, defending themselves against angry dogs, being rejected by surly strangers. Writers did not have to ring doorbells. So far as I could make out, what writers did couldn't even be classified as work.

I was enchanted. Writers didn't have to have any gumption at all. I did not dare tell anybody for fear of being laughed at in the schoolyard, but secretly I decided that what I'd like to be when I grew up was a writer.

Mother Tongue
Amy Tan

Amy Tan was born in Oakland, California in 1952, several years after her mother and father immigrated from China. She was raised in various cities in the San Francisco Bay Area. When she was eight, her essay, "What the Library Means to Me," won first prize among elementary school participants, for which Tan received a transistor radio and publication in the local newspaper. Upon the deaths of her brother and father in 1967 and 1968 from brain tumors, the family began a haphazard journey through Europe, before settling in Montreux, Switzerland, where Tan graduated in her junior year in 1969.

For the next seven years, Tan attended five schools. She first went to Linfield College in McMinnville, Oregon, and there, on a blind date, met her future husband, Lou DeMattei. She followed him to San Jose, where she enrolled in San Jose City College. She next attended San Jose State University, and, while working two part-time jobs, she became an English honors student and a President's Scholar, while carrying a semester course load of 21 units. In 1972 she graduated with honors, receiving a B.A. with a double major in English and Linguistics. She was awarded a scholarship to attend the Summer Linguistics Institute at the University of California, Santa Cruz. In 1973, she earned her M.A. in Linguistics, also from San Jose State University, and was then awarded a Graduate Minority Fellowship under the affirmative action program at the University of California, Berkeley, where she enrolled as a doctoral student in linguistics.

Reprinted from *Threepenny Review* (1990), by permission of the author.

I am not a scholar of English or literature. I cannot give you much more than personal opinions on the English language and its variations in this country or others.

I am a writer. And by that definition, I am someone who has always loved language. I am fascinated by language in daily life. I spend a great deal of my time thinking about the power of language—the way it can evoke an emotion, a visual image, a complex idea, or a simple truth. Language is the tool of my trade. And I use them all—all the Englishes I grew up with.

Recently, I was made keenly aware of the different Englishes I do use. I was giving a talk to a large group of people, the same talk I had already given to half a dozen other groups. The nature of the talk was about my writing, my life, and my book, *The Joy Luck Club*. The talk was going along well enough, until I remembered one major difference that made the whole talk sound wrong. My mother was in the room. And it was perhaps the first time she had heard me give a lengthy speech, using the kind of English I have never used with her. I was saying things like, "The intersection of memory upon imagination" and "There is an aspect of my fiction that relates to thus-and-thus"—a speech filled with carefully wrought grammatical phrases, burdened, it suddenly seemed to me, with nominalized forms, past perfect tenses, conditional phrases, all the forms of standard English that I had learned in school and through books, the forms of English I did not use at home with my mother.

Just last week, I was walking down the street with my mother, and I again found myself conscious of the English I was using, and the English I do use with her. We were talking about the price of new and used furniture and I heard myself saying this: "Not waste money that way." My husband was with us as well, and he didn't notice any switch in my English. And then I realized why. It's because over the twenty years we've been together I've often used that same kind of English with him, and sometimes he even uses it with me. It has become our language of intimacy, a different sort of English that relates to family talk, the language I grew up with.

So you'll have some idea of what this family talk I heard sounds like, I'll quote what my mother said during a recent conversation which I videotaped and then transcribed. During this conversation, my mother was talking about a political gangster in Shanghai who had the same last name as her family's, Du, and how the gangster in his early years wanted to be adopted by her family, which was rich by comparison. Later, the gangster became more powerful, far richer than my mother's family, and one day showed up at my mother's wedding to pay his respects. Here's what she said in part:

"Du Yusong having business like fruit stand. Like off the street kind. He is Du like Du Zong—but not Tsung-ming Island people. The local people call putong, the river east side, he belong to that side local people. That man want to ask Du Zong father take him in like become own family. Du Zong father wasn't look down on him, but didn't take seriously, until that man big like become a mafia. Now important person, very hard to inviting him. Chinese way, came only to show respect, don't stay for dinner. Respect for making big celebration, he shows up. Mean gives lots of respect. Chinese custom. Chinese social life that way. If too important won't have to stay too long. He come to my wedding. I didn't see, I heard it. I gone to boy's side, they have YMCA dinner. Chinese age I was nineteen."

You should know that my mother's expressive command of English belies how much she actually understands. She reads the *Forbes* report, listens to *Wall Street Week*, converses daily with her stockbroker, reads all of Shirley MacLaine's books with ease—all kinds of things I can't begin to understand. Yet some of my friends tell me they understand 50 percent of what my mother says. Some say they understand 80 to 90 percent. Some say they understand none of it, as if she were speaking pure Chinese. But to me, my mother's English is perfectly clear, perfectly natural. It's my mother tongue. Her language, as I hear it, is vivid, direct, full of observation and imagery. That was the language that helped shape the way I saw things, expressed things, made sense of the world.

Lately, I've been giving more thought to the kind of English my mother speaks. Like others, I have described it to people as "broken" or "fractured" English. But I wince when I say that. It has always bothered me that I can think of no way to describe it other than "broken," as if it were damaged and needed to be fixed, as if it lacked a certain wholeness and soundness. I've heard other terms used, "limited English," for example. But they seem just as bad, as if everything is limited, including people's perceptions of the limited English speaker.

I know this for a fact, because when I was growing up, my mother's "limited" English limited *my* perception of her. I was ashamed of her English. I believed that her English reflected the quality of what she had to say. That is, because she expressed them imperfectly her thoughts were imperfect. And I had plenty of empirical evidence to support me: the fact that people in department stores, at banks, and at restaurants did not take her seriously, did not give her good service, pretended not to understand her, or even acted as if they did not hear her.

My mother has long realized the limitations of her English as well. When I was fifteen, she used to have me call people on the phone to pretend I was she. In this guise, I was forced to ask for information or even to complain and yell at people who had been rude to her. One time it was a call to her stockbroker in New York. She had cashed out her small portfolio and it just so happened we were going to go to New York the next week, our very first trip outside California. I had to get on the phone and say in an adolescent voice that was not very convincing, "This is Mrs. Tan."

And my mother was standing in the back whispering loudly, "Why he don't send me check, already two weeks late. So mad he lie to me, losing me money."

And then I said in perfect English, "Yes, I'm getting rather concerned. You had agreed to send the check two weeks ago, but it hasn't arrived."

Then she began to talk more loudly. "What he want, I come to New York tell him front of his boss, you cheating me?" And I was trying to calm her down, make her be quiet, while telling the stockbroker, "I can't tolerate any more excuses. If I don't receive the check immediately, I am going to have to speak to your manager when I'm in New York next week." And sure enough, the following week there we were in front of this astonished stockbroker, and I was sitting there red-faced and quiet, and my mother, the real Mrs. Tan, was shouting at his boss in her impeccable broken English.

We used a similar routine just five days ago, for a situation that was far less humorous. My mother had gone to the hospital for an appointment, to find out about a benign brain tumor a CAT scan had revealed a month ago. She said she had spoken very good English, her best English, no mistakes. Still, she said, the hospital did not apologize when they said they had lost the CAT scan and she had come for nothing. She said they did not seem to have any sympathy when she told them she was anxious to know the exact diagnosis, since her husband and son had both died of brain tumors. She said they would not give her any more information until the next time and she would have to make another appointment for that. So she said she would not leave until the doctor called her daughter. She wouldn't budge. And when the doctor finally called her daughter, me, who spoke in perfect English—lo and behold—we had assurances the CAT scan would be found, promises that a conference call on Monday would be held, and apologies for any suffering my mother had gone through for a most regrettable mistake.

I think my mother's English almost had an effect on limiting my possibilities in life as well. Sociologists and linguists probably will tell you that a person's developing language skills are more influenced by peers. But I do think that the language spoken in the family, especially in immigrant families which are more insular, plays a large role in shaping the language of the child. And I believe that it affected my re-sults on achievement tests, IQ tests, and the SAT. While my English skills were never judged as poor, compared to math, English could not be considered my strong suit. In grade school I did moderately well, getting perhaps B's, sometimes B-pluses, in English and scoring per-haps in the sixtieth or seventieth percentile on achievement tests. But those scores were not good enough to override the opinion that my true abilities lay in math and science, because in those areas I achieved A's and scored in the ninetieth percentile or higher.

This was understandable. Math is precise, there is only one cor-rect answer. Whereas, for me at least, the answers on English tests were always a judgment call, a matter of opinion and personal experience. Those tests were constructed around items like fill-in-the-blank sen-tence completion, Such as, "Even though Tom was _____, Mary thought he was _____." And the correct answer always seemed to be the most bland combinations of thoughts, for example, "Even though Tom was shy, Mary thought he was charming," with the gram-matical structure "even though" limiting the correct answer to some sort of semantic opposites, so you wouldn't get answers like, Even though Tom was foolish, Mary thought he was ridiculous." Well, ac-cording to my mother, there were very few limitations as to what Tom could have been and what Mary might have thought of him. So I never did well on tests like that.

The same was true with word analogies, pairs of words in which you were supposed to find some sort of logical, semantic relationship—

for example, "*Sunset* is to *nightfall* as _____ is to _____."
And here you would be presented with a list of four possible pairs, one
of which showed the same kind of relationship: *red* is to *stoplight, bus*
is to *arrival, chills* is to *fever, yawn* is to *boring*. Well, I could never think
that way. I knew what the tests were asking, but I could not block out
of my mind the images already created by the first pair, "*sunset* is to
nightfall"—and I would see a burst of colors against a darkening sky,
the moon rising, the lowering of a curtain of stars. And all the other
pairs of words—red, bus, stoplight, boring—just threw up a mass of
confusing images, making it impossible for me to sort out something
as logical as saying: "A sunset precedes nightfall" is the same as "a chill
precedes a fever." The only way I would have gotten that answer right
would have been to imagine an associative situation, for example, my
being disobedient and staying out past sunset, catching a chill at night,
which turns into feverish pneumonia as punishment, which indeed did
happen to me.

I have been thinking about all this lately, about my mother's English,
about achievement tests. Because lately I've been asked, as a writer,
why there are not more Asian Americans represented in American literature. Why are there few Asian Americans enrolled in creative writing programs? Why do so many Chinese students go into engineering?
Well, these are broad sociological questions I can't begin to answer.
But I have noticed in surveys—in fact, just last week—that Asian students, as a whole, always do significantly better on math achievement
tests than in English. And this makes me think that there are other
Asian American students whose English spoken in the home might
also be described as "broken" or "limited." And perhaps they also have
teachers who are steering them away from writing and into math and
science, which is what happened to me.

Fortunately, I happen to be rebellious in nature and enjoy the
challenge of disproving assumptions made about me. I became an
English major my first year in college, after being enrolled as pre-med.
I started writing nonfiction as a freelancer the week after I was told by
my former boss that writing was my worst skill and I should hone my
talents toward account management.

But it wasn't until 1985 that I finally began to write fiction. And
at first I wrote using what I thought to be wittily crafted sentences,
sentences that would finally prove I had mastery over the English

language. Here's an example from the first draft of a story that later made its way into *The Joy Luck Club*, but without this line: "That was my mental quandary in its nascent state." A terrible line, which I can barely pronounce.

Fortunately, for reasons I won't get into today, I later decided I should envision a reader for the stories I would write. And the reader I decided upon was my mother, because these were stories about mothers. So with this reader in mind—and in fact she did read my early drafts—I began to write stories using all the Englishes I grew up with: the English I spoke to my mother, which for lack of a better term might be described as "simple"; the English she used with me, which for lack of a better term might be described as "broken"; my translation of her Chinese, which could certainly be described as "watered down"; and what I imagined to be her translation of her Chinese if she could speak in perfect English, her internal language, and for that I sought to preserve the essence, but neither an English nor a Chinese structure. I wanted to capture what language ability tests can never reveal: her intent, her passion, her imagery, the rhythms of her speech and the nature of her thoughts.

Apart from what any critic had to say about my writing, I knew I had succeeded where it counted when my mother finished reading my book and gave me her verdict: "So easy to read."

Hearing Voices

Linda Hogan

Chickasaw native Linda Hogan (1947–) was born to a military family in Denver, Colo. and grew up in Oklahoma. She received an M.A. in 1978 from the University of Colorado at Boulder. Early in her career she supported herself with freelance writing and a variety of jobs, including nurse's aide, dental assistant, library clerk, and waitress. Hogan's writing spans all genres: Among her poetry collections are Seeing Through the Sun *(1985) and* The Book of Medicines *(1993). Her 1981 collection,* Daughters, I Love You, *was inspired by her adoption of two children of Oglaga Lakota heritage. Hogan has also written several novels, including* Mean Spirit *(1991) and* Power *(1999), and the essay collection* Dwellings *(1995), a spiritual exploration of relationships between humans and the natural world. Her work is decidedly feminist, and her focus on environmental and anti-nuclear issues has contributed significantly to the development of contemporary Native American poetry. Hogan's poetry, essays, and short stories have been anthologized widely. She has served as writer-in-residence for the states of Colorado and Oklahoma and has taught at Colorado College, the University of Minnesota, and the University of Colorado. Among her numerous awards are a Guggenheim Fellowship, the Five Civilized Tribes Playwriting Award for* A Piece of the Moon *(1980), and the Wordcraft Circle Writer of the Year Award for her most recent work,* The Woman Who Watches Over the World. A Native Memoir *(2002). In this selection, Hogan explores the nature of her writing, considering herself part of a*

Reprinted from *The Writer on Her Work, Volume II* (1992), by permission of the author.

*larger community of voices including animals, plants, and
the earth itself.*

When Barbara McClintock was awarded a Nobel Prize for
her work on gene transposition in corn plants, the most
striking thing about her was that she made her discoveries
by listening to what the corn spoke to her, by respecting the life of the
corn and "letting it come."

McClintock says she learned "the stories" of the plants. She
"heard" them. She watched the daily green journeys of growth from
earth toward sky and sun. She knew her plants in the way a healer or
mystic would have known them, from the inside, the inner voices of
corn and woman speaking to one another.

As an Indian woman, I come from a long history of people who
have listened to the language of this continent, people who have known
that corn grows with the songs and prayers of the people, that it has a
story to tell, that the world is alive. Both in oral traditions and in
mythology—the true language of inner life—account after account
tells of the stones giving guidance, the trees singing, the corn telling of
inner earth, the dragonfly offering up a tongue. This is true in the
European traditions as well: Psyche received direction from the reeds
and the ants, Orpheus knew the languages of earth, animals, and birds.

This intuitive and common language is what I seek for my writing, work in touch with the mystery and force of life, work that
speaks a few of the many voices around us, and it is important to me
that McClintock listened to the voices of corn. It is important to the
continuance of life that she told the truth of her method and that it
reminded us of where our strength, our knowing, and our sustenance
come from.

It is also poetry, this science, and I note how often scientific theories lead to the world of poetry and vision, theories telling us how
atoms that were stars have been transformed into our living, breathing bodies. And in these theories, or maybe they should be called stories, we begin to understand how we are each many people, including
the stars we once were, and how we are in essence the earth and the universe, how what we do travels clear around the earth and returns. In a
single moment of our living, there is our ancestral and personal history, our future, even our deaths planted in us and already growing

toward their fulfillment. The corn plants are there, and like all the rest we are forever merging our borders with theirs in the world collective.

Our very lives might depend on this listening. In the Chernobyl nuclear accident, the wind told the story that was being suppressed by the people. It gave away the truth. It carried the story of danger to other countries. It was a poet, a prophet, a scientist.

Sometimes, like the wind, poetry has its own laws speaking for the life of the planet. It is a language that wants to bring back together what the other words have torn apart. It is the language of life speaking through us about the sacredness of life.

This life speaking life is what I find so compelling about the work of poets such as Ernesto Cardenal, who is also a priest and was the Nicaraguan Minister of Culture. He writes: "The armadilloes are very happy with this government. . . . Not only humans desired libera-tion/the whole ecology wanted it." Cardenal has also written "The Parrots," a poem about caged birds who were being sent to the United States as pets for the wealthy, how the cages were opened, the parrots allowed back into the mountains and jungles, freed like the people, "and sent back to the land we were pulled from."

How we have been pulled from the land! And how poetry has worked hard to set us free, uncage us, keep us from split tongues that mimic the voices of our captors. It returns us to our land. Poetry is a string of words that parades without a permit. It is a lockbox of words to put an ear to as we try to crack the safe of language, listening for the right combination, the treasure inside. It is life resonating. It is sometimes called Prayer, Soothsaying, Complaint, Invocation, Procla-mation, Testimony, Witness. Writing is and does all these things. And like that parade, it is illegitimately insistent on going its own way, on being part of the miracle of life, telling the story about what hap-pened when we were cosmic dust, what it means to be stars listening to our human atoms.

But don't misunderstand me. I am not just a dreamer. I am also the practical type. A friend's father, watching the United States stage another revolution in another Third World country, said, "Why doesn't the government just feed people and then let the political chips fall where they may?" He was right. It was easy, obvious, even financially more reasonable to do that, to let democracy be chosen because it feeds hunger. I want my writing to be that simple, that clear and direct. Likewise, I feel it is not enough for me just to write, but I need to live it, to be informed by it. I have found over the years that my work has more courage than I do. It has more wisdom. It teaches me, leads me places I never knew I was heading. And it is about a new way of living, of being in the world.

I was on a panel recently where the question was raised whether we thought literature could save lives. The audience, book people, smiled expectantly with the thought. I wanted to say, Yes, it saves lives. But I couldn't speak those words. It saves spirits maybe, hearts. It changes minds, but for me writing is an incredible privilege. When I sit down at the desk, there are other women who are hungry, homeless. I don't want to forget that, that the world of matter is still there to be reckoned with. This writing is a form of freedom most other people do not have. So, when I write, I feel a responsibility, a commitment to other humans and to the animal and plant communities as well.

Still, writing has changed me. And there is the powerful need we all have to tell a story, each of us with a piece of the whole pattern to complete. As Alice Walker says, We are all telling part of the same story, and as Sharon Olds has said, Every writer is a cell on the body politic of America.

Another Nobel Prize laureate is Betty William, a Northern Ireland co-winner of the 1977 Peace Prize. I heard her speak about how, after witnessing the death of children, she stepped outside in the middle of the night and began knocking on doors and yelling, behaviors that would have earned her a diagnosis of hysteria in our own medical circles. She knocked on doors that might have opened with weapons pointing in her face, and she cried out, "What kind of people have we become that we would allow children to be killed on our streets?" Within four hours the city was awake, and there were sixteen thousand names on petitions for peace. Now, that woman's work is a lesson to those of us who deal with language, and to those of us who are dealt into silence. She used language to begin the process of peace. This is the living, breathing power of the word. It is poetry. So are the names of those who signed the petitions. Maybe it is this kind of language that saves lives.

Writing begins for me with survival, with life and with freeing life, saving life, speaking life. It is work that speaks what can't be easily said. It originates from a compelling desire to live and be alive. For me, it is sometimes the need to speak for other forms of life, to take the side of human life, even our sometimes frivolous living, and our grief-filled living, our joyous living, our violent living, busy living our peaceful living. It is about possibility. It is based in the world of matter. I am interested in how something small turns into an image that is large and strong with resonance, where the ordinary becomes beautiful. I believe the divine, the magic, is here in the weeds at our feet, unacknowledged. What a world this is. Where else could water rise up to the sky, turn into snow crystals, magnificently brought together, fall from the sky all around us, pile up billions deep, and catch the small sparks of sunlight as they return again to water?

These acts of magic happen all the time; in Chaco Canyon, my sister has seen a kiva, a ceremonial room in the earth, that is in the center of the canyon. This place has been uninhabited for what seems like forever. It has been without water. In fact, there are theories that the ancient people disappeared when they journeyed after water. In the center of it a corn plant was growing. It was all alone and it had been there since the ancient ones, the old ones who came before us all, those people who wove dog hair into belts, who witnessed the painting of flute players on the seeping canyon walls, who knew the stories of corn. And there was one corn plant growing out of the holy place. It planted itself yearly. With no water, no person to care for it, no overturning of the soil, this corn plant rises up to tell its story, and that's what this poetry is.

The Struggle to Be an All-American Girl

Elizabeth Wong

Elizabeth Wong, a playwright and television writer, grew up in Chinatown in Los Angeles. Although she resisted, her mother insisted that she learn the Chinese language and culture when she was in grade school. Educated at the University of Southern California (1980) and New York University (1991), Wong has worked as a reporter and taught in the theater department at Bowdoin College. In this essay, which was first published in the Los Angeles Times, *Wong recounts her childhood rebellion against learning Chinese and her adult regret of her assimilation into American culture.*

It's still there, the Chinese school on Yale Street where my brother and I used to go. Despite the new coat of paint and the high wire fence, the school I knew 10 years ago remains remarkably, stoically the same.

Every day at 5 P.M., instead of playing with our fourth- and fifth-grade friends or sneaking out to the empty lot to hunt ghosts and animal bones, my brother and I had to go to Chinese school. No amount of kicking, screaming, or pleading could dissuade my mother, who was solidly determined to have us learn the language of our heritage.

Forcibly, she walked us the seven long, hilly blocks from our home to school, depositing our defiant tearful faces before the stern principal. My only memory of him is that he swayed on his heels like a palm tree, and he always clasped his impatient twitching hands behind his back. I recognized him as a repressed maniacal child killer, and knew that if we ever saw his hands we'd be in big trouble.

Reprinted from the *Los Angeles Times*, September 7, 1980, by permission of the author.

We all sat in little chairs in an empty auditorium. The room smelled like Chinese medicine, an imported faraway mustiness. Like ancient mothballs or dirty closets. I hated that smell. I favored crisp new scents. Like the soft French perfume that my American teacher wore in public school.

There was a stage far to the right, flanked by an American flag and the flag of the Nationalist Republic of China, which was also red, white and blue but not as pretty.

Although the emphasis at the school was mainly language—speaking, reading, writing—the lessons always began with an exercise in politeness. With the entrance of the teacher, the best student would tap a bell and everyone would get up, kowtow, and chant, "Sing san ho," the phonetic for "How are you, teacher?"

Being ten years old, I had better things to learn than ideographs copied painstakingly in lines that ran right to left from the tip of a *moc but*, a real ink pen that had to be held in an awkward way if blotches were to be avoided. After all, I could do the multiplication tables, name the satellites of Mars, and write reports on *Little Women* and *Black Beauty.* Nancy Drew, my favorite book heroine, never spoke Chinese.

The language was a source of embarrassment. More times than not, I had tried to disassociate myself from the nagging loud voice that followed me wherever I wandered in the nearby American supermarket outside Chinatown. The voice belonged to my grandmother, a fragile woman in her seventies who could outshout the best of the street vendors. Her humor was raunchy, her Chinese rhythmless, patternless. It was quick, it was loud, it was unbeautiful. It was not like the quiet, lilting romance of French or the gentle refinement of the American South. Chinese sounded pedestrian. Public.

In Chinatown, the comings and goings of hundreds of Chinese on their daily tasks sounded chaotic and frenzied. I did not want to be thought of as mad, as talking gibberish. When I spoke English, people nodded at me, smiled sweetly, said encouraging words. Even the people in my culture would cluck and say that I'd do well in life. "My, doesn't she move her lips fast," they would say, meaning that I'd be able to keep up with the world outside Chinatown.

My brother was even more fanatical than I about speaking English. He was especially hard on my mother, criticizing her, often cruelly, for her pidgin speech—smatterings of Chinese scattered like chop suey in her conversation. "It's not 'What it is,' Mom," he'd say in exasperation. "It's 'What *is* it, what *is* it, what *is* it!'" Sometimes Mom might leave out an occasional "the" or "a," or perhaps a verb of being. He would stop her in mid-sentence: "Say it again, Mom. Say it right." When he tripped over his own tongue, he'd blame it on her: "See, Mom, it's all your fault. You set a bad example."

What infuriated my mother most was when my brother cornered her on her consonants, especially "r." My father had played a cruel joke on Mom by assigning her an American name that her tongue wouldn't allow her to say. No matter how hard she tried, "Ruth" always ended up "Luth" or "Roof."

After two years of writing with a *moc but* and reciting words with multiples of meanings, I finally was granted a cultural divorce. I was permitted to stop Chinese school.

I thought of myself as multicultural. I preferred tacos to egg rolls; I enjoyed Cinco de Mayo[1] more than Chinese New Year.

At last, I was one of you; I wasn't one of them.

Sadly, I still am.

---

[1]Fifth of May, Mexican national holiday marking Mexico's victory over France at Puebla in 1862.

From Silence to Words: Writing as Struggle

Min-zhan Lu

Min-zhan Lu (1946–) was born in China. Lu, who grew up speaking English as well as a number of Chinese dialects, has taught composition and literary criticism at Drake University. She has published both academic articles related to composition issues and articles about her life in China. This article, published in College English *in 1987, relates Lu's challenges acquiring literacy in both China and the United States and how those challenges have affected her writing and teaching.*

Imagine that you enter a parlor. You come late. When you arrive, others have long preceded you, and they are engaged in a heated discussion. . . . You listen for a while, until you decide that you have caught the tenor of the argument; then you put in your oar. Someone answers; you answer him; another comes to your defense; another aligns himself against you, to either the embarrassment or gratification of your opponent, depending upon the quality of your ally's assistance. However, the discussion is interminable. The hour grows late, you must depart. And you do depart, with the discussion still vigorously in progress.

— *Kenneth Burke, The Philosophy of Literary Form*

Men are not built in silence, but in word, in work, in action-reflection.

— *Paulo Freire, Pedagogy of the Oppressed*

Reprinted from *College English* (1987), by permission of National Council of Teachers of English.

My mother withdrew into silence two months before she died. A few nights before she fell silent, she told me she regretted the way she had raised me and my sisters. I knew she was referring to the way we had been brought up in the midst of two conflicting worlds—the world of home, dominated by the ideology of the Western humanistic tradition, and the world of a society dominated by Mao Tse-tung's Marxism. My mother had devoted her life to our education, an education she knew had made us suffer political persecution during the Cultural Revolution. I wanted to find a way to convince her that, in spite of the persecution, I had benefited from the education she had worked so hard to give me. But I was silent. My understanding of my education was so dominated by memories of confusion and frustration that I was unable to reflect on what I could have gained from it.

This paper is my attempt to fill up that silence with words, words I didn't have then, words that I have since come to by reflecting on my earlier experience as a student in China and on my recent experience as a composition teacher in the United States. For in spite of the frustration and confusion I experienced growing up caught between two conflicting worlds, the conflict ultimately helped me to grow as a reader and writer. Constantly having to switch back and forth between the discourse of home and that of school made me sensitive and self-conscious about the struggle I experienced every time I tried to read, write, or think in either discourse. Eventually, it led me to search for constructive uses for such struggle.

From early childhood, I had identified the differences between home and the outside world by the different languages I used in each. My parents had wanted my sisters and me to get the best education they could conceive of—Cambridge. They had hired a live-in tutor, a Scot, to make us bilingual. I learned to speak English with my parents, my tutor, and my sisters. I was allowed to speak Shanghai dialect only with the servants. When I was four (the year after the Communist Revolution of 1949), my parents sent me to a local private school where I learned to speak, read, and write in a new language—Standard Chinese, the official written language of New China.

In those days I moved from home to school, from English to Standard Chinese to Shanghai dialect, with no apparent friction. I spoke each language with those who spoke the language. All seemed quite "natural"—servants spoke only Shanghai dialect because they were servants; teachers spoke Standard Chinese because they were teachers; languages had different words because they were different languages. I thought of English as my family language, comparable to the many strange dialects I didn't speak but had often heard some of my classmates speak with their families. While I was happy to have a special family language, until second grade I didn't feel that my family language was any different than some of my classmates' family dialects.

My second grade homeroom teacher was a young graduate from a missionary school. When she found out I spoke English, she began to practice her English on me. One day she used English when asking me to run an errand for her. As I turned to close the door behind me, I noticed the puzzled faces of my classmates. I had the same sensation I had often experienced when some stranger in a crowd would turn on hearing me speak English. I was more intensely pleased on this occasion, however, because suddenly I felt that my family language had been singled out from the family languages of my classmates. Since we were not allowed to speak any dialect other than Standard Chinese in the classroom, having my teacher speak English to me in class made English an official language of the classroom. I began to take pride in my ability to speak it.

This incident confirmed in my mind what my parents had always told me about the importance of English to one's life. Time and again they had told me of how my paternal grandfather, who was well versed in classic Chinese, kept losing good-paying jobs because he couldn't speak English. My grandmother reminisced constantly about how she had slaved and saved to send my father to a first-rate missionary school. And we were made to understand that it was my father's fluent English that had opened the door to his success. Even though my family had always stressed the importance of English for my future, I used to complain bitterly about the extra English lessons we had to take after school. It was only after my homeroom teacher had "sanctified" English that I began to connect English with my education. I became a much more eager student in my tutorials.

What I learned from my tutorials seemed to enhance and reinforce what I was learning in my classroom. In those days each word had one meaning. One day I would be making a sentence at school: "The national flag of China is red." The next day I would recite at home, "My love is like a red, red rose." There seemed to be an agreement between the Chinese "red" and the English "red," and both corresponded to the patch of color printed next to the word. "Love" was my love for my mother at home and my love for my "motherland" at school; both "loves" meant how I felt about my mother. Having two loads of homework forced me to develop a quick memory for words and a sensitivity to form and style. What I learned in one language carried over to the other. I made sentences such as, "I saw a red, red rose among the green leaves," with both the English lyric and the classic Chinese lyric—red flower among green leaves—running through my mind, and I was praised by both teacher and tutor for being a good student.

Although my elementary schooling took place during the fifties, I was almost oblivious to the great political and social changes happening around me. Years later, I read in my history and political philosophy textbooks that the fifties were a time when "China was making a transition from a semi-feudal, semi-capitalist, and semi-colonial country into a socialist country," a period in which "the Proletarians were breaking into the educational territory dominated by Bourgeois Intellectuals." While people all over the country were being officially classified into Proletarians, Petty-bourgeois, National-bourgeois, Poor-peasants, and Intellectuals, and were trying to adjust to their new social identities, my parents were allowed to continue the upper middle-class life they had established before the 1949 Revolution because of my father's affiliation with British firms. I had always felt that my family was different from the families of my classmates, but I didn't perceive society's view of my family until the summer vacation before I entered high school.

First, my aunt was caught by her colleagues talking to her husband over the phone in English. Because of it, she was criticized and almost labeled a Rightist. (This was the year of the Anti-Rightist movement, a movement in which the Intellectuals became the target of the "socialist class-struggle.") I had heard others telling my mother that she was foolish to teach us English when Russian had replaced English as the "official" foreign language. I had also learned at school that the American and British Imperialists were the arch-enemies of New China. Yet I had made no connection between the arch-enemies and the English our family spoke. What happened to my aunt forced the connection on me. I began to see my parents' choice of a family language as an anti-Revolutionary act and was alarmed that I had participated in such an act. From then on, I took care not to use English outside home and to conceal my knowledge of English from my new classmates.

Certain words began to play important roles in my new life at the junior high. On the first day of school, we were handed forms to fill out with our parents' class, job, and income. Being one of the few people not employed by the government, my father had never been officially classified. Since he was a medical doctor, he told me to put him down as an Intellectual. My homeroom teacher called me into the office a couple of days afterwards and told me that my father couldn't be an Intellectual if his income far exceeded that of a Capitalist. He also told me that since my father worked for Foreign Imperialists, my father should be classified as an Imperialist Lackey. The teacher looked nonplussed when I told him that my father couldn't be an Imperialist Lackey because he was a medical doctor. But I could tell from the way he took notes on my form that my father's job had put me in an unfavorable position in his eyes.

The Standard Chinese term "class" was not a new word for me. Since first grade, I had been taught sentences such as, "The Working class are the masters of New China." I had always known that it was good to be a worker, but until then, I had never felt threatened for not being one. That fall, "class" began to take on a new meaning for me. I noticed a group of Working-class students and teachers at school. I was made to understand that because of my class background, I was excluded from that group.

Another word that became important was "consciousness." One of the slogans posted in the school building read, "Turn our students into future Proletarians with socialist consciousness and education!" For several weeks we studied this slogan in our political philosophy course, a subject I had never had in elementary school. I still remember the definition of "socialist consciousness" that we were repeatedly tested on through the years: "Socialist consciousness is a person's political soul. It is the consciousness of the Proletarians represented by Marxist Mao Tse-tung thought. It takes expression in one's action, language, and lifestyle. It is the task of every Chinese student to grow up into a Proletarian with a socialist consciousness so that he can serve the people and the motherland." To make the abstract concept accessible to us, our teacher pointed out that the immediate task for students from Working-class families was to strengthen their socialist consciousnesses. For those of us who were from other class backgrounds, the task was to turn ourselves into Workers with social-ist consciousnesses. The teacher never explained exactly how we were supposed to "turn" into Workers. Instead, we were given samples of the ritualistic annual plans we had to write at the beginning of each term. In these plans, we performed "self-criticism" on our conscious-nesses and made vows to turn ourselves into Workers with socialist consciousnesses. The teacher's division between those who did and those who didn't have a socialist consciousness led me to reify the no-tion of "consciousness" into a thing one possesses. I equated this in-tangible "thing" with a concrete way of dressing, speaking, and writing. For instance, I never doubted that my political philosophy teacher had a socialist consciousness because she was from a steel-worker's family (she announced this the first day of class) and was a party member who wore grey cadre suits and talked like a philosophy textbook. I noticed other things about her. She had beautiful eyes and spoke Standard Chinese with such a pure accent that I thought she should be a film star. But I was embarrassed that I had noticed things that ought not to have been associated with her. I blamed my obser-vation on my Bourgeois consciousness.

At the same time, the way reading and writing were taught through memorization and imitation also encouraged me to reduce concepts and ideas to simple definitions. In literature and political philosophy classes, we were taught a large number of quotations from Marx, Lenin, and Mao Tse-tung. Each concept that appeared in these quotations came with a definition. We were required to memorize the definitions of the words along with the quotations. Every time I mem-orized a definition, I felt I had learned a word: "The national red flag symbolizes the blood shed by Revolutionary ancestors for our social-ist cause"; "New China rises like a red sun over the eastern horizon." As I memorized these sentences, I reduced their metaphors to dictio-nary meanings: "red" meant "Revolution" and "red sun" meant "New China" in the "language" of the Working class. I learned mechanically but eagerly. I soon became quite fluent in this new language.

As school began to define me as a political subject, my parents tried to build up my resistance to the "communist poisoning" by exposing me to the "great books"—novels by Charles Dickens, Nathaniel Hawthorne, Emily Brontë, Jane Austen, and writers from around the turn of the century. My parents implied that these writers represented how I, their child, should read and write. My parents replaced the word "Bourgeois" with the word "cultured." They reminded me that I was in school only to learn math and science. I needed to pass the other courses to stay in school, but I was not to let the "Red doctrines" corrupt my mind. Gone were the days when I could innocently write, "I saw the red, red rose among the green leaves," collapsing, as I did, English and Chinese cultural traditions. "Red" came to mean Revolution at school, "the Commies" at home, and adultery in *The Scarlet Letter.* Since I took these symbols and metaphors as meanings natural to people of the same class, I abandoned my earlier definitions of English and Standard Chinese as the language of home and the language of school. I now defined English as the language of the Bourgeois and Standard Chinese as the language of the Working class. I thought of the language of the Working class as someone else's language and the language of the Bourgeois as my language. But I also believed that, although the language of the Bourgeois was my real language, I could and would adopt the language of the Working class when I was at school. I began to put on and take off my Working class language in the same way I put on and took off my school clothes to avoid being criticized for wearing Bourgeois clothes.

In my literature classes, I learned the Working-class formula for reading. Each work in the textbook had a short "Author's Biography": "X X X, born in 19— in the province of X X X, is from a Worker's family. He joined the Revolution in 19—. He is a Revolutionary realist with a passionate love for the Party and Chinese Revolution. His work expresses the thoughts and emotions of the masses and sings praise to the prosperous socialist construction on all fronts of China." The teacher used the "Author's Biography" as a yardstick to measure the texts. We were taught to locate details in the texts that illustrated these summaries, such as words that expressed Workers' thoughts and emotions or events that illustrated the Workers' lives.

I learned a formula for Working-class writing in the composition classes. We were given sample essays and told to imitate them. The theme was always about how the collective taught the individual a lesson. I would write papers about labor-learning experiences or school-cleaning days, depending on the occasion of the collective activity closest to the assignment. To make each paper look different, I dressed it up with details about the date, the weather, the environment, or the appearance of the Master-worker who had taught me "the lesson." But as I became more and more fluent in the generic voice of the Working-class Student, I also became more and more self-conscious about the language we used at home.

For instance, in senior high we began to have English classes ("to study English for the Revolution," as the slogan on the cover of the textbook said), and I was given my first Chinese-English dictionary. There I discovered the English version of the term "class-struggle." (The Chinese characters for a school "class" and for a social "class" are different.) I had often used the English word "class" at home in sentences such as, "So and so has class," but I had not connected this sense of "class" with "class-struggle." Once the connection was made, I heard a second layer of meaning every time someone at home said a person had "class." The expression began to mean the person had the style and sophistication characteristic of the bourgeoisie. The word lost its innocence. I was uneasy about hearing that second layer of meaning because I was sure my parents did not hear the word that way. I felt that therefore I should not be hearing it that way either. Hearing the second layer of meaning made me wonder if I was losing my English.

My suspicion deepened when I noticed myself unconsciously merging and switching between the "reading" of home and the "reading" of school. Once I had to write a report on *The Revolutionary Family*, a book about an illiterate woman's awakening and growth as a Revolutionary through the deaths of her husband and all her children for the cause of the Revolution. In one scene the woman deliberated over whether or not she should encourage her youngest son to join the Revolution. Her memory of her husband's death made her afraid to encourage her son. Yet she also remembered her earlier married life and the first time her husband tried to explain the meaning of the Revolution to her. These memories made her feel she should encourage her son to continue the cause his father had begun.

I was moved by this scene. "Moved" was a word my mother and sisters used a lot when we discussed books. Our favorite moments in novels were moments of what I would now call internal conflict, moments which we said "moved" us. I remember that we were "moved" by Jane Eyre when she was torn between her sense of ethics, which compelled her to leave the man she loved, and her impulse to stay with the only man who had ever loved her. We were also moved by Agnes in *David Copperfield* because of the way she restrained her love for

David so that he could live happily with the woman he loved. My standard method of doing a book report was to model it on the review by the Publishing Bureau and to dress it up with detailed quotations from the book. The review of *The Revolutionary Family* emphasized the woman's Revolutionary spirit. I decided to use the scene that had moved me to illustrate this point. I wrote the report the night before it was due. When I had finished, I realized I couldn't possibly hand it in. Instead of illustrating her Revolutionary spirit, I had dwelled on her internal conflict, which could be seen as a moment of weak sentimentality that I should never have emphasized in a Revolutionary heroine. I wrote another report, taking care to illustrate the grandeur of her Revolutionary spirit by expanding on a quotation in which she decided that if the life of her son could change the lives of millions of sons, she should not begrudge his life for the cause of Revolution. I handed in my second version but kept the first in my desk.

I never showed it to anyone. I could never show it to people outside my family, because it had deviated so much from the reading enacted by the jacket review. Neither could I show it to my mother or sisters, because I was ashamed to have been so moved by such a "Revolutionary" book. My parents would have been shocked to learn that I could like such a book in the same way they liked Dickens. Writing this book report increased my fear that I was losing the command over both the "language of home" and the "language of school" that I had worked so hard to gain. I tried to remind myself that, if I could still tell when my reading or writing sounded incorrect, then I had retained my command over both languages. Yet I could no longer be confident of my command over either language because I had discovered that when I was not careful—or even when I was—my reading and writing often surprised me with its impurity. To prevent such impurity, I became very suspicious of my thoughts when I read or wrote. I was always asking myself why I was using this word, how I was using it, always afraid that I wasn't reading or writing correctly. What confused and frustrated me most was that I could not figure out why I was no longer able to read or write correctly without such painful deliberation.

I continued to read only because reading allowed me to keep my thoughts and confusion private. I hoped that somehow, if I watched myself carefully, I would figure out from the way I read whether I had really mastered the "languages." But writing became a dreadful chore. When I tried to keep a diary, I was so afraid that the voice of school might slip in that I could only list my daily activities. When I wrote for school, I worried that my Bourgeois sensibilities would betray me.

The more suspicious I became about the way I read and wrote, the more guilty I felt for losing the spontaneity with which I had learned to "use" these "languages." Writing the book report made me feel that my reading and writing in the "language" of either home or school could not be free of the interference of the other. But I was unable to acknowledge, grasp, or grapple with what I was experiencing, for both my parents and my teachers had suggested that, if I were a good student, such interference would and should not take place. I assumed that once I had "acquired" a discourse, I could simply switch it on and off every time I read and wrote as I would some electronic tool. Furthermore, I expected my readings and writings to come out in their correct forms whenever I switched the proper discourse on. I still regarded the discourse of home as natural and the discourse of school alien, but I never had doubted before that I could acquire both and switch them on and off according to the occasion.

When my experience in writing conflicted with what I thought should happen when I used each discourse, I rejected my experience because it contradicted what my parents and teachers had taught me. I shied away from writing to avoid what I assumed I should not experience. But trying to avoid what should not happen did not keep it from recurring whenever I had to write. Eventually my confusion and frustration over these recurring experiences compelled me to search for an explanation: how and why had I failed to learn what my parents and teachers had worked so hard to teach me?

I now think of the internal scene for my reading and writing about *The Revolutionary Family* as a heated discussion between myself, the voices of home, and those of school. The review on the back of the book, the sample student papers I came across in my composition classes, my philosophy teacher—these I heard as voices of one group. My parents and my home readings were the voices of an opposing group. But the conversation between these opposing voices in the internal scene of my writing was not as polite and respectful as the parlor scene Kenneth Burke has portrayed (see epigraph). Rather, these voices struggled to dominate the discussion, constantly incorporating, dismissing, or suppressing the arguments of each other, like the battles between the hegemonic and counter-hegemonic forces described in Raymond Williams' *Marxism and Literature* (108–14).

When I read *The Revolutionary Family* and wrote the first version of my report, I began with a quotation from the review. The voices of both home and school answered, clamoring to be heard. I tried to listen to one group and turn a deaf ear to the other. Both persisted. I negotiated my way through these conflicting voices, now agreeing with one, now agreeing with the other. I formed a reading out of my interaction with both. Yet I was afraid to have done so because both home and school had implied that I should speak in unison with only one of these groups and stand away from the discussion rather than participate in it.

My teachers and parents had persistently called my attention to the intensity of the discussion taking place on the external social scene. The story of my grandfather's failure and my father's success had from my early childhood made me aware of the conflict between Western and traditional Chinese cultures. My political education at school added another dimension to the conflict; the war of Marxist-Maoism against them both. Yet when my parents and teachers called my attention to the conflict, they stressed the anxiety of having to live through China's transformation from a semi-feudal, semi-capitalist, and semi-colonial society to a socialist one. Acquiring the discourse of the dominant group was, to them, a means of seeking alliance with that group and thus of surviving the whirlpool of cultural currents around them. As a result, they modeled their pedagogical practices on this utilitarian view of language. Being the eager student, I adopted this view of language as a tool for survival. It came to dominate my understanding of the discussion on the social and historical scene and to restrict my ability to participate in that discussion.

To begin with, the metaphor of language as a tool for survival led me to be passive in my use of discourse, to be a bystander in the discussion. In Burke's "parlor," everyone is involved in the discussion. As it goes on through history, what we call "communal discourses"— arguments specific to particular political, social, economic, ethnic, sexual, and family groups—form, re-form and transform. To use a discourse in such a scene is to participate in the argument and to contribute to the formation of the discourse. But when I was growing up, I could not take on the burden of such an active role in the discussion. For both home and school presented the existent conventions of the discourse each taught me as absolute laws for my action. They turned verbal action into a tool, a set of conventions produced and shaped prior to and outside of my own verbal acts. Because I saw language as a tool, I separated the process of producing the tool from the process of using it. The tool was made by someone else and was then acquired and used by me. How the others made it before I acquired it determined and guaranteed what it produced when I used it. I imagined that the more experienced and powerful members of the community were the ones responsible for making the tool. They were the ones who participated in the discussion and fought with opponents. When I used what they made, their labor and accomplishments would ensure the quality of my reading and writing. By using it, I could survive the heated discussion. When my immediate experience in writing the book report suggested that knowing the conventions of school did not guarantee the form and content of my report, when it suggested that I had to write the report with the work and responsibility I had assigned to those who wrote book reviews in the Publishing bureau, I thought I had lost the tool I had earlier acquired.

Another reason I could not take up an active role in the argument was that my parents and teachers contrived to provide a scene free of conflict for practicing my various languages. It was as if their experience had made them aware of the conflict between their discourse and other discourses and of the struggle involved in reproducing the conventions of any discourse on a scene where more than one discourse exists. They seemed convinced that such conflict and struggle would overwhelm someone still learning the discourse. Home and school each contrived a purified space where only one discourse was spoken and heard. In their choice of textbooks, in the way they spoke, and in the way they required me to speak, each jealously silenced any voice that threatened to break the unison of the scene. The homogeneity of home and of school implied that only one discourse could and should be relevant in each place. It led me to believe I should leave behind, turn a deaf ear to, or forget the discourse of the other when I crossed the boundary dividing them. I expected myself to set down one discourse whenever I took up another just as I would take off or put on a particular set of clothes for school or home.

Despite my parents' and teachers' attempts to keep home and school discrete, the internal conflict between the two discourses continued whenever I read or wrote. Although I tried to suppress the voice of one discourse in the name of the other, having to speak aloud in the voice I had just silenced each time I crossed the boundary kept both voices active in my mind. Every "I think . . ." from the voice of home or school brought forth a "However . . ." or a "But . . ." from the voice of the opponents. To identify with the voice of home or school, I had to negotiate through the conflicting voices of both by re-stating, taking back, qualifying my thoughts. I was unconsciously doing so when I did my book report. But I could not use the interaction comfortably and constructively. Both my parents and my teachers had implied that my job was to prevent that interaction from happening. My sense of having failed to accomplish what they had taught silenced me.

To use the interaction between the discourses of home and school constructively, I would have to have seen reading or writing as a process in which I worked my way towards a stance through a dialectical process of identification and division. To identify with an ally, I would have to have grasped the distance between where he or she stood and where I was positioning myself. In taking a stance against an opponent, I would have to have grasped where my stance identified with the stance of my allies. Teetering along the "wavering line of pressure and counter-pressure" from both allies and opponents, I might have worked my way towards a stance of my own (Burke, *A Rhetoric of Motives,* 23). Moreover, I would have to have understood that the voices in my mind, like the participants in the parlor scene, were in constant flux. As I came into contact with new and different groups of people or read different books, voices entered and left. Each time I read or wrote, the stance I negotiated out of these voices would always be at some distance from the stances I worked out in my previous and my later readings or writings.

I could not conceive such a form of action for myself because I saw reading and writing as an expression of an established stance. In delineating the conventions of a discourse, my parents and teachers had synthesized the stance they saw as typical for a representative member of the community. Burke calls this the stance of a "god" or the "prototype"; Williams calls it the "official" or "possible" stance of the community. Through the metaphor of the survival tool, my parents and teachers had led me to assume I could automatically reproduce the official stance of the discourse I used. Therefore, when I did my book report on *The Revolutionary Family,* I expected my knowledge of the official stance set by the book review to ensure the actual stance of my report. As it happened, I began by trying to take the official stance of the review. Other voices interrupted. I answered back. In the process, I worked out a stance approximate but not identical to the official stance I began with. Yet the experience of having to labor to realize my knowledge of the official stance or to prevent myself from wandering away from it frustrated and confused me. For even though I had been actually reading and writing in a Burkean scene, I was afraid to participate actively in the discussion. I assumed it was my role to survive by staying out of it.

Not long ago, my daughter told me that it bothered her to hear her friend "talk wrong." Having come to the United States from China with little English, my daughter has become sensitive to the way English, as spoken by her teachers, operates. As a result, she has amazed her teachers with her success in picking up the language and in adapting to life at school. Her concern to speak the English taught in the classroom "correctly" makes her uncomfortable when she hears people using "ain't" or double negatives, which her teacher considers "improper." I see in her the me that had eagerly learned and used the discourse of the Working class at school. Yet while I was torn between the two conflicting worlds of school and home, she moves with seeming ease from the conversations she hears over the dinner table to her teacher's words in the classroom. My husband and I are proud of the good work she does at school. We are glad she is spared the kinds of conflict between home and school I experienced at her age. Yet as we watch her becoming more and more fluent in the language of the classroom, we wonder if, by enabling her to "survive" school, her very fluency will silence her when the scene of her reading and writing expands beyond that of the composition classroom.

For when I listen to my daughter, to students, and to some composition teachers talking about the teaching and learning of writing, I am often alarmed by the degree to which the metaphor of a survival tool dominates their understanding of language as it once dominated my own. I am especially concerned with the way some composition classes focus on turning the classroom into a monological scene for the students' reading and writing. Most of our students live in a world similar to my daughter's, somewhere between the purified world of the classroom and the complex world of my adolescence. When composition classes encourage these students to ignore those voices that seem irrelevant to the purified world of the classroom, most students are often able to do so without much struggle. Some of them are so adept at doing it that the whole process has for them become automatic.

However, beyond the classroom and beyond the limited range of these students' immediate lives lies a much more complex and dynamic social and historical scene. To help these students become actors in such a scene, perhaps we need to call their attention to voices that may seem irrelevant to the discourse we teach rather than encourage them to shut them out. For example, we might intentionally complicate the classroom scene by bringing into it discourses that stand at varying distances from the one we teach. We might encourage students to explore ways of practicing the conventions of the discourse they are learning by negotiating through these conflicting voices. We could also encourage them to see themselves as responsible for forming or transforming as well as preserving the discourse they are learning.

As I think about what we might do to complicate the external and internal scenes of our students' writing, I hear my parents and teachers saying: "Not now. Keep them from the wrangle of the marketplace until they have acquired the discourse and are skilled at using it." And I answer: "Don't teach them to 'survive' the whirlpool of crosscurrents by avoiding it. Use the classroom to moderate the currents. Moderate the currents, but teach them from the beginning to struggle." When I think of the ways in which the teaching of reading and writing as classroom activities can frustrate the development of students, I am almost grateful for the overwhelming complexity of the circumstances in which I grew up. For it was this complexity that kept me from losing sight of the effort and choice involved in reading or writing with and through a discourse.

References

Burke, Kenneth. *The Philosophy of Literary Form: Studies in Symbolic Action.* 2nd ed. Baton Rouge: Louisiana State UP, 1967.
———. *A Rhetoric of Motives.* Berkeley: U of California P, 1969.
Freire, Paulo. *Pedagogy of the Oppressed.* Trans. M. B. Ramos. New York: Continuum, 1970.
Williams, Raymond. *Marxism and Literature.* New York: Oxford UP, 1977.

Only Daughter

Sandra Cisneros

Once, several years ago, when I was just starting out my writing career, I was asked to write my own contributor's note for an anthology[1] I was part of. I wrote: "I am the only daughter in a family of six sons. *That* explains everything."

Well, I've thought about that ever since, and yes, it explains a lot to me, but for the reader's sake I should have written: "I am the only daughter in a *Mexican* family of six sons." Or even: "I am the only daughter of a Mexican father and a Mexican-American mother." Or: "I am the only daughter of a working-class family of nine." All of these had everything to do with who I am today.

I was/am the only daughter and *only* a daughter. Being an only daughter in a family of six sons forced me by circumstance to spend a lot of time by myself because my brothers felt it beneath them to play with a *girl* in public. But that aloneness, that loneliness, was good for a would-be writer—it allowed me time to think and think, to imagine, to read and prepare myself.

Being only a daughter for my father meant my destiny would lead me to become someone's wife. That's what he believed. But when I was in the fifth grade and shared my plans for college with him, I was sure he understood. I remember my father saying, "*Que bueno, mi'ha,* that's good." That meant a lot to me, especially since my brothers thought the idea hilarious. What I didn't realize was that my father thought college was good for girls—good for finding a husband. After four years in college and two more in graduate school, and still no husband, my father shakes his head even now and says I wasted all that education.

In retrospect,[2] I'm lucky my father believed daughters were meant for husbands. It meant it didn't matter if I majored in something silly like English. After all, I'd find a nice professional eventually, right? This

---

[1]**anthology:** collection of stories and other literature in a book
[2]**retrospect:** thinking about things in the past

Reprinted from *Latina: Women's Voices from the Borderlands,* edited by Lillion Castillo-Speed (1995), by permission of the author.

allowed me the liberty to putter about embroidering[3] my little poems and stories without my father interrupting with so much as a "What's that you're writing?"

But the truth is, I wanted him to interrupt. I wanted my father to understand what it was I was scribbling, to introduce me as "My only daughter, the writer." Not as "This is only my daughter. She teaches." *Es maestra*—teacher. Not even *profesora*.

In a sense, everything I have ever written has been for him, to win his approval even though I know my father can't read English words, even though my father's only reading includes the brown-ink *Esto* sports magazines from Mexico City and the bloody *¡Alarma!* magazines that feature yet another sighting of *La Virgen de Guadalupe* on a tortilla or a wife's revenge on her philandering husband by bashing his skull in with a *molcajete* (a kitchen mortar[4] made of volcanic rock). Or the *fotonovelas*, the little picture paperbacks with tragedy and trauma erupting from the characters' mouths in bubbles.

My father represents, then, the public majority. A public who is disinterested in reading, and yet one whom I am writing about and for, and privately trying to woo.[5]

When we were growing up in Chicago, we moved a lot because of my father. He suffered bouts of nostalgia.[6] Then we'd have to let go of our flat,[7] store the furniture with mother's relatives, load the station wagon with baggage and bologna sandwiches and head south. To Mexico City.

We came back, of course. To yet another Chicago flat, another Chicago neighborhood, another Catholic school. Each time, my father would seek out the parish priest in order to get a tuition break,[8] and complain or boast: "I have seven sons."

He meant *siete hijos*, seven children, but he translated it as "sons." "I have seven sons." To anyone who would listen. The Sears Roebuck employee who sold us the washing machine. The short-order cook where my father ate his ham-and-eggs breakfasts. "I have seven sons." As if he deserved a medal from the state.

---

[3]**embroidering:** adding details to
[4]**mortar:** a very hard bowl in which things are ground into a fine powder
[5]**woo:** attract, interest
[6]**bouts of nostalgia:** short periods of time with homesickness
[7]**flat:** apartment
[8]**tuition break:** a decrease in the cost of going to a private school

My papa. He didn't mean anything by that mistranslation, I'm sure. But somehow I could feel myself being erased. I'd tug my father's sleeve and whisper: "Not seven sons. Six! and *one daughter.*"

When my oldest brother graduated from medical school, he fulfilled my father's dream that we study hard and use this—our heads, instead of this—our hands. Even now my father's hands are thick and yellow, stubbed by a history of hammer and nails and twine and coils[9] and springs. "Use this," my father said, tapping his head, "and not this," showing us those hands. He always looked tired when he said it.

Wasn't college an investment? And hadn't I spent all those years in college? And if I didn't marry, what was it all for? Why would anyone go to college and then choose to be poor? Especially someone who had always been poor.

Last year, after ten years of writing professionally, the financial rewards[10] started to trickle in. My second National Endowment for the Arts Fellowship. A guest professorship at the University of California, Berkeley. My book, which sold to a major New York publishing house.

At Christmas, I flew home to Chicago. The house was throbbing,[11] same as always: hot tamales and sweet tamales hissing in my mother's pressure cooker, and everybody—my mother, six brothers, wives, babies, aunts, cousins—talking too loud and at the same time. Like in a Fellini[12] film, because that's just how we are.

I went upstairs to my father's room. One of my stories had just been translated into Spanish and published in an anthology of Chicano[13] writing and I wanted to show it to him. Ever since he recovered from a stroke two years ago, my father likes to spend his leisure hours horizontally.[14] And that's how I found him, watching a Pedro Infante movie on Galavisión and eating rice pudding.

There was a glass filled with milk on the bedside table. There were several vials of pills and balled Kleenex. And on the floor, one black sock and a plastic urinal that I didn't want to look at but looked at anyway. Pedro Infante was about to burst into song, and my father was laughing.

---

[9]**twines and coils:** strings and loops
[10]**financial rewards:** money
[11]**throbbing:** beating
[12]**Fellini:** an Italian movie director
[13]**Chicano:** Mexican-American
[14]**horizontally:** lying down

I'm not sure if it was because my story was translated into Spanish, or because it was published in Mexico, or perhaps because the story dealt with Tepeyac, the *colonia* my father was raised in and the house he grew up in, but at any rate, my father punched the mute button on his remote control and read my story.

I sat on the bed next to my father and waited. He read it very slowly. As if he were reading each line over and over. He laughed at all the right places and read lines he liked out loud. He pointed and asked questions: "Is this So-and-so?" "Yes," I said. He kept reading.

When he was finally finished, after what seemed like hours, my father looked up and asked: "Where can we get more copies of this for the relatives?"

Of all the wonderful things that happened to me last year, that was the most wonderful.

African American Women Talkin' that Talk[1]

Denise Troutman

1. Background

The linguistic behavior of my foremothers and sisters and present-day mothers and sisters, African American women, is the topic of this chapter. To date, linguistic research has focused primarily on men (European and African American) and European American women. Smitherman (p.c.), the internationally-known African American woman scholar on African American English (AAE) and author of the widely read and cited book *Talkin and Testifyin: The Language of Black America* (1977), acknowledges that even her book reflects data gathered primarily from male speakers, just as the preponderance of data collected by sociolinguists (and dialectologists) stemmed from male speakers.

Over two decades ago, Thorne/Henley (1975) noted that "whole areas of study . . . have been virtually untouched, for example, the communication patterns of all-female groups, and of populations other than the white, middle class" (30). This same absence still exists. West/Lazar/Kramarae (1997) reiterate the omission of other voices in women's language research similar to the observation in Thorne/Henley (1975):

> much of what we 'know' about gender and discourse is really about white, middle-class, heterosexual women and men using English in Western societies. Studies like Etter-Lewis's (1991), Goodwin's (1990) . . . and Nichols's (1983) [all of whose works target African American females] are the exceptions, rather than the rule (137).

Because of the dearth in research on the language of African American women, this chapter, as well as my research in general, focuses on African American women's language (AAWL) and documents discourse

---

Reprinted from *Sociocultural and Historical Contexts of African American English* (2001), by permission of John Benjamins Publishing Company.

features of AAWL from a positive, insider's frame of reference. I have found features of AAWL similar to European American women's language. For example, African American women collaborate in conversations, acknowledging and building on other comments in conversations; they use empty adjectives (those expressing emotional rather than intellectual evaluation, such as *cute, precious, sweet, adorable*); and they use hedges (those words claimed to make utterances more tentative, less assertive (e.g., *you know, kinda, well*). Despite these similarities, differences remain. For example, the minimal responses in the discussions of the African American women differed in the type used (e.g., *Ow-w-w-w-w-w, nah-h-h, girl-l-l-l, girl please, girl stop, girlfriend,* and others).

At present, AAWL is still largely misunderstood and misrepresented in White mainstream society. An example of the extent of the myopic view of AAWL can be seen in some analyses of the 1991 Anita Hill-Clarence Thomas Senate Hearings. For example, Mendoza-Denton (1995) writes that the linguistic strategies available to Clarence Thomas—testifying, sermonizing, signifying—were "utterly unavailable to Hill" (64). She further states: " . . . if acting like a Black woman and capitalizing on Black speech style is seen as masculine and verbally (and implicitly sexually) aggressive, then the only recourse is to speak like a white woman" (Mendoza-Denton 1995: 62). This assessment bemoans "monolithic womanism" (Troutman-Robinson 1995) in our society and the current state of research in AAWL.

Given the dominant paradigm in research in women's language in which White women are privileged and Black women are silenced, one might assume there is a place for African American women in research on AAE. However, there is little research in AAE that corrects or redresses the absence of the discourse of African American women since research in AAE privileges African American men. Consequently, Black speech style is not viewed as available to or indicative of African American women. Furthermore, perceptions of African American speech are synonymous with African American men (just as it is seen as synonymous with White women's language in the literature on women's language) and leaves little or no room for actual voices of African American women. Until such time as scholars research AAWL and learn to describe it and portray it accurately, the following assertions will continue to surface:

> Black speech is male speech;
> Black speech is verbally aggressive;
> Black speech is, implicitly, sexually aggressive speech;

Black speech allows Black women to speak only like men, in verbally and sexually aggressive ways.

Black women have only one linguistic choice (to avoid being verbally and sexually aggressive)

Women's speech is White women's speech, therefore Black women's speech is White women's speech

Taking the premise that AAWL is different from White women's language and African American men's language in aspects not sufficiently explored, I focus on African American women's rich linguistic capabilities. In order to represent this speech community with greater accuracy and depth, and especially to aid in accurate social constructions of AAWL, I first report on several features of AAWL as presented in the research literature by and on African American women. Second, I elaborate on one characteristic of AAWL as used by Anita Hill in my analysis of her interaction with Arlen Specter, the lead Republican questioner during the Hill-Thomas Hearings. Finally, in my analysis of scenes from *The Women of Brewster Place and Jungle Fever*, I examine a feature of AAWL that is referred to within the African American community as "talking that talk."

2. Characteristics of African American Women's Language: What Do the Sistahs Have to Say?

In this section, I highlight the work on AAWL as identified by my sistahs in the struggle to represent a "refuse-to-be-silenced" speech community. African American women researchers have identified features of AAWL encountered in their work and experiences with African American women. Some of these features include reported speech, cooperative or collaborative speech, and "little" usage (Etter-Lewis 1993, 1991); reading dialect, which is one form of signifying (Morgan 1996); culturally-toned diminutives (Troutman 1996); performance (Foster 1995); assertiveness (Houston Stanback 1985; Troutman 1996); and "smart talk" (Houston Stanback 1985). I will elaborate on each of those features below.

2.1 Reported Speech

Etter-Lewis in *My Soul Is My Own* (1993) records and analyzes oral narratives of nine professional African American women between the ages of 60 to 95. She uses lengthy interviews as a means of revealing the women's experiences through the power of their own words. Racist and sexist experiences evolve from the content of the women's narratives. As well, Etter-Lewis (1993) notes several linguistic features of the narratives, such as the use of reported speech, especially the words of fathers or authority figures, with a shift from past tense to present tense: "My father said, 'Now you're ready to go to school' " (83). Etter-Lewis explains this occurrence of reported speech as a result of highly regarded mentor relationships established between the women narrators and their fathers. Also, reported speech of men, according to Etter-Lewis (1993), occurred as a result of women being socialized to "talk like a lady" (84) and "to listen to men" (84), thus giving deference to men's words.

2.2 Cooperative, Collaborative Speech

Etter-Lewis (1993) found that both the interviewees and the interviewer (i.e., Etter-Lewis) engaged in cooperative and collaborative speech interchanges willingly in order to work together. For example, Etter-Lewis (1993) allowed interviewees to "shape the interaction as they saw fit . . . [introducing] . . . topics into their stories as they felt necessary" (140):

(1) Q: And the grandparents on your fathers side?
     A: My grandfather was a coachman for a very wealthy family in the north. My grandmother did not work. And there is a very interesting story about them too. You want me to relate that?
     Q: Yes.
     A: Well, the story as my paternal aunt told me . . .
     Q: That was a wonderful story.
     A: I thought I would like to write about it someday.
     Q: Yes, please do. What was her maiden name?

In (1), collaboration occurs when Speaker A asks for permission to share a story about her grandparents and Speaker Q (Etter-Lewis) gives permission for the sharing of the story. Etter-Lewis cooperates with the interviewee's request, although it is not part of the prepared interviewer questions. The interviewee, according to Etter-Lewis, cooperates by offering to tell a story since she is aware of Etter-Lewis' aim. As a result of Etter-Lewis' collaborative action, person A shares a rich story, embellishing Etter-Lewis' data collection on oral narratives.

Collaborative, cooperative speech continues even after the telling of the story. One speaker's comments feed directly into the other's comments, allowing the speakers to work together. Etter-Lewis responds to the story by evaluating it as wonderful. Speaker A accepts this evaluative comment, feeding off of it by stating that she would like to record the story in writing. Lastly, Etter-Lewis feeds into Speaker A's comment by encouraging her to put the story in writing. Thus, the conversational pattern follows an idealized categorization of conversational turn-taking (Sacks/Schegloff/Jefferson 1974) where the pattern ABAB occurs (i.e., Speaker A and Speaker B take "rightful" turns at speaking). This pattern of speaking shows that the speakers are working together cooperatively.

Thirdly, non-verbal cues induced cooperation. When interviewees used long pauses or made particular facial expressions, Etter-Lewis encouraged the women to express their pensiveness, in many instances allowing interviewees to uncover information that may have gone undisclosed:

> (2) A: But I remember my aunt saying to me when I got ready to go to college. She persuaded me to go into teaching . . . and so I believed her and I did it and she was right you know, cause that was the size of what you [a Black woman] could do in those days.
>
>   Q: You're thinking of something.
>
>   A: I got tickled as I thought about Mary McCleod Bethune, you may know this story . . . (142).

Again, Etter-Lewis works with interviewees during pensive moments, which benefits her data collection. In this instance, after the sharing of the Mary McCleod Bethune story, the interviewee was able to discuss "connections between the various elements of her past" (Etter-Lewis 1993: 142), an important element in Etter-Lewis' analysis of oral narratives and the women's lives.

Lastly, in addition to other features denoting cooperation, Etter-Lewis (1993: 144) notes that group membership aided cooperative narrator-interviewer interactions.

> Many of the women acknowledged that they were interacting with a member of their own social group by marking their language overtly: '. . . as a black woman, I think that you might have . . .' Although there is no way to account for covert cues of such rapport, most of the women felt very comfortable talking to someone who shared their same background and experiences.

2.3 "Little" Usage

The African American women interviewed by Etter-Lewis used the word *little* to mean the opposite of its denotative meaning. Instead of meanings associated with diminution (smallness, brevity), "little" actually meant "very important" or "enormous." The women used the term to downplay very important roles or functions that they served or as understatement for important events in their lives:

> And that *little* case was written up in the newspapers and I got a *little* publicity and I was really very happy over that one . . . It may have been the early part of '34. Yes, I liked that case. I've kept a *little* scrapbook and that's one of my favorites (200).

The interviewee in this instance received a big boost in her career as a result of this "little" case. Etter-Lewis notes the regularity of this usage with all the "narrators produc[ing] at least one instance . . . In general, it was the most frequently occurring adjective in all of the narratives" (200).

2.4 Reading Dialect

Borrowing one portion of her phrase from the broader African American speech community, Morgan (1996) describes another feature of Black women's talk called **reading dialect**. To *read someone* means to denigrate them verbally because of some inappropriate action or words or, according to Smitherman (1994: 192), "to tell someone off in no uncertain terms and in a verbally elaborate manner." According to Morgan (1996), *reading dialect* is a means of contrasting two language varieties, specifically AAE and General American English (GAE), through the use of words, sentences, or discourse structures in order to signify on that person. Since AAE and GAE have words, grammar rules, sentences, and discourse features that are similar, speakers select one dialect or the other due to a distinct feature that it possesses in order to communicate an unambiguous point and, most importantly, to *read* a conversational partner.

For example, Speaker B, in a particular situation where Speaker A has extended a greeting using GAE, has a number of choices to select from in response to the greeting. Two possible choices are: "How are you doing" (GAE) or "Whazzup" (AAE). In order to convey a point (perhaps of dissatisfaction or power), Speaker B, in this exchange, consciously selects the second choice, greeting Speaker A with "Whazzup." In this instance, Speaker B "reads dialect."

Among African American women, a common way of reading dialect is through use of the expression, "Miss Thang." During a conversation, one speaker may want to "read" another person due to the latter's inappropriate behavior. In order to communicate dissatisfaction, then, the first person may refer to the targeted receiver as "Miss Thang": "We were doing alright until Miss Thang decided she didn't want to go along with the program." In this instance, the first person "reads dialect" using AAE, communicating a negative point about the targeted receiver. The expression "Miss Thang" within African American women's speech community is a direct put down of a targeted receiver. The broader African American speech community, as well as the African American women's speech community, interprets *thang* negatively since a thing is an object, lacking an identity and other human qualities (Smitherman in an interview with Troutman in 1998).

2.5 Culturally-Toned Diminutives

A major conversational feature resonant in the African American women's speech community is one that I refer to as **culturally-toned diminutives** (Troutman 1996), such as *girl*. A diminutive may refer to suffixes in English (e.g., *-let, -ling, -ette*), words used with suffixes (e.g., *piglet, dinette*), or words which express familiarity (e.g., *Gracie, Tommy*). Within the African American women's speech community, culturally-toned diminutives express solidarity. Besides *girl*, other diminutives are used within the African American women's speech community, including *sistah, sistah friend, honey, honey child, child, baby, baby girl, precious, muh'dear*.

For generations, African American women have used culturally-toned diminutives. The diminutive *girl*, for example, is a highly visible and popular word used by many African American females to show solidarity in all spheres of their existence, public and private, and in all age groups. If they view themselves as peers, one African American female can and will call another African American female *girl*. Thus, an African American five-year-old girl may say to her eight-year-old sister, "Girl, you beda stop dat" or "Girl, you crazy." These same sentences can be used by older African American females of any age. The females involved do not have to be blood relatives in order for this diminutive to be used appropriately, although they may be. The females could be cousins, neighbors, classmates, playmates, co-church members, or colleagues.

European American feminists, historically, have rejected the referent *girl* as a result of inequitable and demeaning treatment within the patriarchically dominant U.S. social system. Thus, European American feminists consciously avoid referring to other women as *girl*. The African American women's speech community permits and encourages the use of *girl* unobtrusively; this usage, in fact, is devoid of belittling or degrading denotations or connotations. African American women obviously do not see themselves diminished in any form through the use of this term, especially since it continues to be passed on to succeeding generations of women. Within my grandmother's generation, my mother's generation, and my own generation, *girl* usage is prominent. And now, the baton has been passed on to my daughter. Clearly, different lexicons exist for the two speech communities. For the speech community of African American women, a highly positive, unifying denotation and connotation are part of the lexicon. Due to cultural, communicative, and experiential differences, the lexicon diverges for African and European American women's speech communities with *girl* usage.[2]

2.6 Performance

Foster (1995: 333) defines **performance** as "a special kind of communicative event in which there is a particular relationship among stylized material, performer, and audience." Based on her collected data in a community-college classroom, Foster essentially found instances of teacher and student interactions that actively communicated the teaching point. Performances, in Foster's analysis, served as a different instructional vehicle. Instead of lecturing to convey salient points, the African American female teacher under study "performed" the teaching point, with students assisting in the construction of the performance as in (3) from Foster.[3] In (3), the teacher (T) of the course in which Foster collected data wanted to make sure that her students (S) understood, realistically, what a budget is. Performance occurred as follows (335):

(3) T: You have a master plan to beat this economic system?
       S: No, not yet. (laughs)
       T: Well, that's what a budget is.
       S: I was referring to budgeting money to for payin' the bills, runnin' my my house . . .
       T: Unhuh, that's a budget . . . Somebody else who wanna share their ideas about budget? I want to make sure everybody understands what a budget is before we go on. Yes, Miss Goins . . .

Both the teacher and the students construct a performance of the teaching point in the example. Instead of giving a "liturgical" definition of the word "budget," the instructor opts for a more concrete method of defining budget; thus, she engages her students in a co-constructed performance of the word. They perform (or enact) the meaning of budget. According to Foster (1995: 334), "a teacher was most likely to 'break into performance' when attempting to clarify a concept that students had encountered in a text or a lecture." Performing, essentially, enabled the instructor to make concepts concrete.

2.7 Assertiveness

Houston Stanback (1985, 1982) claims that African American women communicate in an assertive, outspoken way, just as African American men, due to African American women's work in public spheres. African American women, however, must curtail their outspokenness as a result of community standards, which only allow assertiveness to a certain point for women.

2.7.1 *Latching*

In an analysis of the discourse style of Anita Hill during the Hill-Thomas Senate Judiciary Hearing October 1991, I (Troutman-Robinson 1995) found that Hill used an assertive style when under fire from Senator Arlen Specter. Out of a total of four conversational interchanges, with each interchange consisting of at least 30 minutes of questions from the Democratic and Republican principal questioners (and up to 5 minutes of questions from other Senators), I focused on the first two conversational interchanges. The analysis showed that Hill (H) interrupted Specter (Sp) more often than the reverse (exercising more control during interchanges), used syllogistic reasoning more skillfully than Specter (thus, winning more verbal bouts), and used *latching* more (i.e., a turn-taking mechanism which occurs at the end of a conversational partner's speaking turn, avoiding an interruption or overlapping of a conversational partner's speech). Latching in the Hill-Specter analysis conveyed readiness on Hill's part of "setting the record straight." The two examples below demonstrate Hill's assertive style: (4) shows latching while (5) shows Hill's skill in quick reasoning (*capping*):

(4) Sp: His words are that you said quote the most laudatory com-
           ments unquote. ⌐
       H: └ I have no response to that because
           I don't know exactly what he is saying.

(5) Sp: Well (.) I'll repeat the question again. Was there any sub-
           stance in Ms. Berry's *flat* statement that (.) quote (.) Ms.
           Hill was disappointed and frustrated that Mr. Thomas did
           not show any sexual interest in her?
       H: No (.) there is not. There is no substance to that. He did
           show interest and I've explained to you how he did show
           that interest. (.) Now (.) she was not aware of that. If you're
           asking me (.) Could she have made that statement. (.) She
           could have made the statement if she wasn't aware of it. (.)
           But she wasn't aware of everything that happened.

In (4), Hill does not hesitate, pause, or back-channel in taking her
speaking turn nor does she interrupt Specter. She responds without
missing a beat in the ABAB conversational pattern, suggesting attentive, alert, perspicuous thinking. Her latch exudes assertiveness; she
takes her turn readily (essentially, she asserts her turn). Specter's statement does not surprise, stump, or throw Hill off guard. She demonstrates assertiveness by her readiness and confidence in beginning a
turn and does so by allowing little or no gap at the end of the current
speaker's utterance.

Of significance, also, is the fact that Hill's response is not a prepared one. The fourteen senators (some of whom profess expertise in
examining witnesses) have carefully considered and generated their
key questions in advance. Hill, of course, has anticipated some questions prior to presenting her testimony, yet she cannot anticipate
many of them. Thus, the fact that she does not have to ponder
Specter's accusation, but speaks instantaneously during a "rightful"
speaking turn, demonstrates the assertiveness of Hill's latch.

Furthermore, assertiveness arises in (4) with Hill's wording. She
is not mesmerized by a claim that she gave Thomas "the most laudatory comments." Hill responds aptly, unobstrusively, unaffectedly,
having critically analyzed the poignancy of Specter's probe within a
matter of seconds. Not only does she respond without hesitation,
but she also deflates Specter's line of examination. Hill does not
attempt to speculate or babble over the comment, which appears to
be taken out of context. She is not stupefied, but deflates the crux of

the argument ("I have no response to that because I don't know exactly what he is saying").

Conceivably, Hill could have attempted to account for giving "the most laudatory comments" to Thomas. Doing so would have produced at least two possible outcomes: Hill would have had to ramble mentally and orally to account for such a statement and its context, thereby presenting a less credible face, or Hill would have partially discredited and deflated her testimony against Clarence Thomas by accounting for laudatory comments given to him. Instead, Hill immediately analyzes Specter's line of approach and essentially asserts, "Brick wall. I am not going there because I don't know what he is talking about." With her response, Specter can no longer pursue the issue of "the most laudatory comments" but must move on to another line of questioning. *Touché!* is very appropriate for Hill in this instance. Her wording is assertive in view of an African American woman's perspective.

2.7.2 *Capping*

In (5), Hill uses an assertive tone as one piece of weaponry in the ensuing duel. At various points, she uses increased emphasis as a verbal weapon. Intellectually, she *caps* this conversational interchange. As a result of the context of the hearings (national television and other media coverage, Senate Judiciary Committee chambers, a broad array of on-lookers, etc.), Hill uses a formal manner of speaking. The potency of her response, her capping strategy may become more obvious if translated. Based on an informal pilot test, I asked other African American women scholars to convert Hill's wording(s) from the context of the hearings to an informal context using AAWL. Their translations (Tr) show directly the capping of the exchange:

Tr 1: No, there ain't no substance to none of that. Didn't I just explain to you the filthy things that that man did to show interest in me? What's wrong with you? Are you ignorant or something? Now look; Ms. Berry don't know everything. What you really want to ask me is could Ms. Berry have said that. Yes, she certainly *could* have said that, but she don't know everything. Saying that something is true and knowing that something is true is two different things. Do you get my drift?

Tr 2: NO, she doesn't know what she's talking about. Oh, he showed interest. Any fool who don't know the real deal could have made that statement. I didn't put all my business in the street to Ms. Berry, so she ain't know everything that happened.

Tr 3: No(.) That's not true. He was interested in me. I told you that, already (.) Now (.) She didn't know that. If you ask me (.) Could she have said that (.) She could have if she knew about it. (.) but she ain't know. (In other words, Ms. Berry might have known that Thomas didn't show interest in Anita Hill as a professional and she probably thought that that meant that Anita didn't lift her dress up to get a promotion or to get the respect she deserved. Berry is probably one of dem brainwashed sistas that think the only way a sista can get respect is to do the nasty—which is not really brainwashed but the way of the old world which sistas like Anita is trying to get rid of that kinda world.)

Tr 4: There ain't no basis to that. I told you he come on to me and I done told you how he come on to me. Now Gurlfriend didnt know bout him trying to get his groove on with me. So what she gon say but what she know.

2.7.3 *Smart talk*

Houston Stanback (1982) discusses assertiveness, as manifested in *smart talk,* in a positive manner, unlike the outsider perspective given by Abrahams (1975). According to Houston Stanback (1982), *sweet talk* reflects one sphere of African American women's existence—that of nurturer. It is used with children, female friends, and relatives to affirm and support (Houston Stanback 1982: 12). *Smart talk,* on the other hand, is reserved for all other communicants as a put-down, reflecting a combative style of language (Houston Stanback 1982: 12). Abrahams (1975), however, claims that *talking smart* is used by African American women to defend their respectability. Further, he conveys that *sweet talk* and *smart talk* represent the whole range of African American women's language, especially related to creating and negotiating respect. Thus, he projects the limited view that African American women are so critically concerned about respectability that *talking smart* results and is one of only two linguistic styles accessible to defend and negotiate respect. In fact, African American women have a larger repertoire of styles available to them and for varying purposes, as the present paper demonstrates.

Smart talk is one form of assertive language, according to Houston Stanback (1982). She aims to re-frame communication research which has glossed over the unique and individual communicative style of African American women, a style assumed to be synonymous with European American women or with African American men. Houston Stanback (1982) identifies three factors that influence AAWL:

1. the definition of African American womanhood (particularly the African American community's traditional definition);
2. relative verbal equity (between African American men and women); and
3. ambivalent interpretations of AAWL (within the African American community).

Signifying is one form of *smart talk*. Within the African American speech community, signifying is a game of verbal wit. Smitherman (1977) defines *signifying* as an indirect form of ritualized insult in which "a speaker puts down, talks about, needles—signifies on—the listener" (118). For example, (6) recounts an incident cited in Mitchell-Kernan (1972: 323) where she (MK) engages in signifying with a young man in his early twenties (YM) while two other young men of the same age (TM) are present:

(6) YM: Mama, you sho is fine.
     MK: That ain't no way to talk to your mother.
     TM: (Laughter)
     YM: You married?
     MK: Um hm.
     YM: Is your husband married?
     TM: (Laughter)

Within the African American speech community, permissibility rules allow speech community members who know the rules of the game to signify, regardless of gender. Furthermore, this game of verbal wit is marked positively by speech community members.

The research literature in this section indicates that AAWL encompasses a repertoire of features stemming from the broader African American speech community (signifying, "reading" someone) as well as the narrower African American women's speech community (diminutives, performance, assertiveness, "smart talk," and "sweet talk"). Positive evaluations are given to speakers who can use these features adeptly, perhaps due to the worldview of many African Americans that consummate verbal skills reflect mental acuity.

3. African American women "talking that talk!"

"Talking that talk" appears to be an overarching rubric under which *smart talk* and other verbal strategies fit and which is available to the African American speech community at-large, females and males, as exemplified in (7).

(7) A: Baby, you a real scholar. I can tell you want to learn. Now if you'll just cooperate a li'l bit, I'll show you what a good teacher I am. But first we got to get into my area of expertise.

B: I may be wrong but seems to me we already in your area of expertise.

A: You ain' so bad yourself, girl. I ain't heard you stutter yet. You a li'l fixated on your subject though. I want to help a sweet thang like you all I can. I figure all that book learning you got must mean you been neglecting other areas of your education.

C: Talk that talk! (Mitchell-Kernan 1972: 324)

Within the African American speech community, "talking that talk" is a referential phrase meaning that a particular speaker knows how to use language extremely well. Such a speaker knows how to cap or win conversational exchanges through the use of signifying (Smitherman 1977; Mitchell-Kernan 1972); loud talking, marking (Mitchell-Kernan 1972); rhyming, joking, reading dialect (Morgan 1996); and a variety of other verbal strategies ranging from the prosodic to the discursive. "Talking that talk" requires quick-wittedness, ingenuity, spontaneity, and sound thinking ability (a good mind). When engaged in word or speech games, which are a reflection of mental acuity, a speaker who can "talk that talk" plays superbly, easily constructing spontaneous, apt, humorous, and wise responses. "Talking that talk" serves as a vehicle whereby African Americans can play with language, display their mental adeptness, defeat a verbal opponent, and have fun simultaneously.

Major (1994: 466) defines "talking that talk" as "commendation for having great and 'hip' verbal skills; for being in style verbally; encouragement to be one's self." According to Smitherman (p.c.), "talking that talk" refers to "tapping into the linguistic culture, the linguistic wellspring of our history; hitting the registers that we know are Black, lively talk, real talk, colorful talk, full of flavor." Considering these insider perspectives, then, "talking that talk" appears to be a larger framework under which a number of other features within AAWL fit, both those features listed above and those yet unidentified.

When African American women friends gather together, conversations may focus on serious matters, yet lighter-toned conversations revolve around kidding and joking, which invoke and involve "talking that talk." Obviously, all African American women do not fall into this category, but there is a subset of African American women who enthrall us in spiritual, social, educational, and political gatherings with their intellectual prowess, good humor, and adeptness in "talking that talk." I have observed this language usage first-hand through women, such as my sisters, Cheryl and Dr. G.; my grandmothers, Mama Lloyd and Mama Willie; my auntie, Aunt Lilla; my friend, Tootsie; and second-hand through creators of literature and film, such as Maya Angelou (even though she appears miseducated about her linguistic heritage), Gloria Naylor, Terry McMillan, and Spike Lee.

My analysis of "talking that talk" stems from two primary sources: Gloria Naylor's novel *The Women of Brewster Place* (1982) and Spike Lee's film *Jungle Fever* (1991).

3.1 Talking that talk in *The Women of Brewster Place*

Oprah Winfrey produced and starred in the television mini-series based upon Naylor's *The Women of Brewster Place* in 1989. Its production added visibility to the novelist, the novel, the actresses/actors, and issues within the African American community, especially African American women's issues. Although this data is not based on real conversations, its authenticity establishes its legitimacy for analysis. Naylor has created characters whose voices and personalities are real. Many African Americans can attest to the credibility of Mattie Michael and Mrs. Eva, among other characters. There are many Mattie Michaels and Mrs. Evas throughout the African Diaspora. Their language and actions hold a commonplace in the memories and experiences of the African American speech community.

Before readers delve deeply into the text, the voices of the African American women become clearly established, first through the main character Mattie Michael, in (8).

(8) 'I heard you the first time, Butch Fuller, but I got a name, you know,' she said, without looking in his direction. 'Here's your water.' She almost threw it at him. 'I couldn't even deny a dog a drink on a day like today, but when you done drunk it, you better be gettin' on to wherever you was gettin' before you stopped' (Naylor 1982: 8–9).

In (8), from the opening scene of the novel, Naylor constructs Mattie's voice through word choice and tone. Mattie does not code her thoughts with polite indirectness, yet caustically and directly interacts with Butch. Naylor gives Mattie strong, bold language. Mattie ignores Butch when he first addresses her, succumbing only after a third bid for attention with the retort, "I got a name, you know" (Naylor 1982: 8). Naylor conveys a principle applied within the African American community of calling individuals by name, established perhaps in response to the residual effects of enslavement where people were identified as objects, not human beings. For example, "I got a name" (Naylor 1982: 8) is a common response to "hey you." She boldly lets Butch know that she heard him calling her "the first time" (Naylor 1982: 8), yet there are certain rules to abide by in order to merit receiving a person's attention.

Reacting to Butch's inappropriate attention-getter and in order to mask her affection for Butch, Mattie "comes on strong." She avoids looking at Butch (or even in his direction) and almost throws the water at him. Her final words in this speaking turn are abrasive—"I couldn't even deny a dog a drink on a day like today, but when you done drunk it, you better be gettin' on to wherever you was gettin' before you stopped" (Naylor 1982: 9). Without the contextual clues from Naylor (or without being privy to contextual rules within the African American community), readers would initially believe that Mattie truly hates Butch due to her strong wording. Orally, Butch is placed on the level of a dog and is instructed to be "lickety split" about moving on. Mattie's words are considered sharp: "done drunk" and "gettin' on to wherever you was gettin'" have been given potency within the African American speech community. Compounded here, the words build extra weight. There is urgency and completion conveyed in these words. The perfective tense of AAE occurs in the structure "done drunk," which emphasizes the completion of an action through the use of *done*. Essentially, Mattie tells Butch, "When you have finished, keep on trucking." Mattie imbues urgency in her words, "gettin' on to wherever you was gettin'" (Naylor 1982: 9). In other words, do not sit down; do not engage in small talk; do not pause, but go forward.

The repetition of "gettin'" also adds to the force of Mattie's words ("gettin' on to wherever you was gettin'"). Repetition holds positive power within the African American community. It provides greater emphasis and intensifies the meaning of particular points. Sermons from African American pastors convey the positive value of repetition as well as the words and works of African American orators, poets and writers, scholars, and philosophers due to its common occurrence in texts. For example, Malcolm X uses alliteration in the following, repeating [p] for emphasis, "Pimps, prostitutes, Ph.D.s—you all still in slavery." Martin Luther King, Jr. empowered many individuals through the repetition of the phrase, "I have a dream, today," in his most famous speech of all. As one result of the repetitive force of these words, African Americans and others outside the speech community began to place greater stock in dreams.

Butch is not offended by Mattie's caustic tone. In an underlying conversational dynamic, Mattie's abrasiveness is permissible since she and Butch both realize their self-worth and deep affection for one another. They also realize that Mattie has the "right" to be abrasive because Butch Fuller has established himself within certain parts of the community as an untrustworthy "lady killer." Other members of the community, including Mattie and Butch himself, recognize Butch as innovative, intelligent, witty, and strong, yet Mattie has to abide by the dictates of her father who does not want Butch on his property. Thus, Mattie respectfully upholds her father's attitude of dislike and distrust through her language, although she really cares for Butch.

In response to Butch's question, "You know how to eat sugar cane?" (Naylor 1982: 18), Mattie replies in (9):

(9)   You a crazy nigger, Butch Fuller. First you ask me 'bout my name and then come up with some out-the-way question like that. I been eating sugar cane all my life, fool! (Naylor 1982: 18).

In (9), Mattie speaks forthrightly and directly, letting Butch know the ludicrousness of his question by addressing him boldly as "nigger" and "fool." Mattie is not obligated to politeness (direct or indirect) as one result of the community standards and her father's rules regarding Butch. A person that speaks ridiculously or asks a simple question may legitimately be called a fool, particularly as used by older African Americans (thus, this usage may show age grading).

Permissibility rules within the African American speech community operate with use of the word "nigger" also. As Naylor (1998) has described in "'Nigger': The meaning of a word," two different contexts (at least) have been established for "nigger" for African Americans. A negative meaning has been applied by the broader European American community to African Americans generally. However, African Americans have exerted power in language usage by reappropriating and resemanticizing the term. In this sense, "nigger" may be used positively among African Americans, devoid of its capitalistic and racist origins within the U.S.

One point of interest in the dialogue in (10) between Mattie and Butch is the metalinguistic message that Naylor (1982: 9) allows to be conveyed through the voice of Butch:

(10) Lord, you Michael women got the sharpest tongues in the county, but I guess a man could die in a lot worst ways than being cut to death by such a beautiful mouth.

Naylor demonstrates some familiarity here with AAWL and has consciously injected it into her work, giving added visibility to the notion that African American women use language in a particular way. Mattie's language is cutting. Naylor has imbued this character with a linguistic style that is not fanciful, but which has social reality and which Naylor has witnessed, undoubtedly, firsthand. Naylor (1998) writes not only about language, but also about her family in Harlem: maternal grandparents who owned the apartment building in which they lived; aunts, uncles, friends, tenants who "let down their hair" (333) in the grandparents' ground floor apartment; children, simultaneous conversations, and games of checkers, especially a grandmother who "cheated shamelessly" (333). With such a multiplicitous, dynamic environment, Naylor knows of that which she writes.

In Butch's line above, Naylor writes specifically about the Michael women, yet other African American female characters in the novel show the same or greater sharpness of the tongue—so much so that their tongues become swords. Further, Naylor views this way of speaking positively since Butch replies, "I guess a man could die in a lot worst ways than being cut to death by such a beautiful mouth" (Naylor 1982: 9). Thus, the tongue is sharp, yet beautiful, for African American women who speak in this manner.

The language displayed here is one that many African American women endorse proudly, as evidenced by Naylor's use of it and by the longevity this linguistic system has sustained. Within the African American community, there appears to be resistance to eliminating Africanized linguistic elements, as seen in AAWL.

3.2 Talking that talk in *Jungle Fever*

In my study of the social construction of AAWL and the analysis of films, I have observed aspects of "talking that talk" and examined it, specifically in one segment of Spike Lee's film *Jungle Fever*. I present one example of the language, along with its context, then a discussion of "talking that talk."

The conversational exchange in (11) from *Jungle Fever* takes place in a "soul food" restaurant. The lead character, Flipper (Wesley Snipes), has had an affair with an Italian American woman, Angie

(Annabella Sciorra), his temporary secretary at an advertising firm. Flipper pursues the relationship with Angie, taking her out to dinner. In this scene, the restaurant is filled with African American customers and serviced by African American employees. The waitress (W), played by Queen Latifah, for Flipper (F) and Angie's (A) table has not waited on the couple, although thirty minutes have passed and customers around them have received service. Flipper, finally, hails the approaching waitress (see the Appendix for transcription notations):

(11) F: ((Low volume)) Dammit (.) ((Increased volume)) Excuse me Miss (.) Miss (.) may we order please.

W: ((Walks over to table calmly; avoids eye contact; uses a low, calm tone of voice)) Yes (.) may I take your order.

F: Is this your station?

W: Yes ((establishes eye contact with Flipper)) this is my station (.) unfortunately ((looks down to write on ticketing pad; bats eyes))

F: Look (.) you can take my order (.) matter of fact ((pointing finger)) you could've taken my order thirty minutes ago when I sat my Black ass ⌈ in this chair.

W: ((Looks at Angie)) ⌊ Can I take your order?

A: ((Surprised and speechless; stares back at waitress))

F: ((Jumps in)) Excuse me (1.0) uhm do you have a problem?

W: ((Establishes direct eye contact with Flipper)) Yes (.) I do have a problem to be honest with you (1.0) Fake (.) tired brothers like you coming in heah. Dass so typical. I can't even believe you brought huh stringy hair ass up heah to eat.

F: Ahh ahh let me tell you something (.) first of all Miss Al Sharpton (.) ⌈you don't have (.)

W: ⌊Why don't you parade (0.1)

F: It's not your business (0.1) ⌈who I bring in here

W: Why don't you parade (0.1) ⌊yo White friend somewhere else okay?]

F: Iss not yo business (.) you are a waitress (.) your job is to wait.

W: (0.3) ((Resumes soft, calm tone; goes into a routine recitation. Looks up, rolls eyes, looks down at pad)) Today's specials are the Maryland crab cakes (.) Creole shrimp (.) gumbo and blackened catfish (.) ((Speaks to Flipper, directly)) I suggest you have the blackened catfish.

F: Well I suggest you find the manager.

W: Oh you want my manager.

F: I want your manager.

W: Oh iss like dat right

F: ((Mumbles)) I want the [manager]

W: All right fine fine [fine (.) you git my] — I'll git my manager! ((Walks away from table to get manager))

F: ((Loudly)) You're fired!

W: ((Loudly)) You're tired!

The discussion here focuses primarily on the language used by the African American waitress. In the backdrop of the scene, the waitress, played by Queen Latifah, has obviously summed up the situation with Flipper and Angie. As a result, she makes a conscious decision not to give them service. Spike Lee captures the avoidance behavior of the waitress before any conversational exchange occurs. The waitress is shown graciously and contentedly giving information to and taking orders from two elderly women at the table immediately adjacent to Flipper and Angie's table. At this point, Angie has turned around in her chair, looking at the waitress expectantly. After collecting the menus from the two women, however, the waitress just walks on by, continuing her denial of service. Angie conveys exasperation non-verbally as the waitress walks away from their seated area to take care of other food orders, yet Angie does not voice her exasperation, partially because of the territory that she is in; she displays obligatory politeness. Flipper is aware that the waitress passes by, yet he is not affected by her lack of service at this point. He hunches his shoulders upward, communicating non-verbally and calmly to Angie, "Oh well" or "I don't know what the deal is with the waitress." He is caught up in his predicament and continues with small talk. Shortly thereafter, however, the waitress passes their area and he gets her attention ("Excuse me Miss (.) may we order please.")

In this antagonistic interaction in (11), the waitress demonstrates adeptness in "talking that talk," as gauged by African American standards. Quick-wittedness, humor, spontaneous and apt retorts (optionally accompanied by non-verbal movements) are marks of superior verbal acuity within the African American speech community. The waitress measures up to these standards superbly. Additionally, she uses lively, bold, direct talk (although in two instances she temporarily compels herself to perform obligatory duties in a modest, polite, acquiescent manner). The waitress uses smart talk, "reads" Flipper, reads dialect, and caps the conversational interchange—all elements of "talking that talk."

Once the waitress is called upon in her official capacity, she carries out her duties perfunctorily. She performs, hiding her true feelings and speaking in a very calm and controlled tone of voice, initially: "Yes (.) may I take your order." The waitress, in fact, gives the impression that she is ready to "take care of business." She is compelled to perform because this IS her station, this IS her job, and she does have an obligation to serve customers in her area. Although she does not like the idea of a "brothah" bringing a European American woman into African American territory, the waitress performs as though no problem exists (lines 3–4) in order to fulfill her obligations. Her tone suggests humility, yet that suggestion is short-lived. Flipper's next question, "Is this your station?" (line 5), brings out an element of "smart talk" (lines 6–7).

It is only at this time that the waitress establishes eye contact with Flipper. In this respect, she uses an avoidance strategy, which may translate into wording to the effect of "See no evil; speak no evil." Alternatively, the waitress may avoid direct eye contact to convey displeasure to the couple ("I do not have to look at things that I do not like."). An interplay of these dynamics seems operative here. She only establishes direct eye contact to show that she is prepared to defend "her station" or because she is asked a direct question.

Once the waitress establishes eye contact and answers Flipper's question, she moves boldly onward, remarking that it is unfortunate that her station is the one where the interracial couple is seated. The "batting" of her eyes intensifies the communication of displeasure and highlights her demeanor of frankness or preference for frankness. This non-verbal communicative behavior conveys a complexity of meanings within the African American speech community which depend on the context. Here, the waitress intensifies her displeasure through a non-verbal gesture and establishes the factuality of that displeasure. Essentially, the batting of her eyes communicates, "Now there, it's a fact; I've said it and you can deal with it or not." The mask is unveiled and obligatory politeness seeks compliance elsewhere.

The word "unfortunately," included as part of the answer, demonstrates an instance of "smart talk." The waitress gives an answer that does not suit her position (i.e., she is accountable to the customers that she serves and is expected to watch her behavior, including her linguistic behavior). Within the African American community, children and youth typically are warned about using "smart talk." Grandmothers, mothers, and aunts (among others) train the young folk in this mode of discourse: those instances when particular speech behavior amounts to "smart talk," when speech treads too closely to being "smart talk," when young folks should avoid "smart talk," even when "smart talk" may be used appropriately. The waitress knows these rules of the speech community and violates the usage in order to communicate her feelings.

This first instance of smart talk sets off the antagonistic interaction that transpires from this point on. The waitress has now ignited Flipper's wrath. He is cognizant of the discourse rules and speech acts within the African American speech community and he retaliates (lines 9–10). Flipper fights back through language and kinesics. The pointing of his finger strengthens his words and acts as an admonishment for inappropriate behavior. Adults typically point their fingers at children, particularly during teaching/lecturing/chastising moments. He peers at the waitress through the top of his eyeglasses, another non-verbal, demeaning strategy as the pointing of his finger. Flipper heightens his response orally by his tone of voice and the addition of an expletive. The waitress deploys the strength of his retaliation with an innovative game strategy. She fires back, not at Flipper, but at Angie (lines 12)—a fair tactic in verbal battle. The waitress' strategy is effective. She demonstrates that she is one step ahead of Flipper by using a contrapuntal response that Flipper does not anticipate. The norm within African American repartee places one speaker in an adversarial position against another, with the objective of capping (or beating) the opponent's final comment. Instead of the standard format, the waitress decides that more than two can play at this game. She responds by attacking in an area that she has deciphered as weak. She turns to Angie, lodging a new offense. All parties present are aware of the speech act here and its perlocutionary intent. The waitress is not sincerely interested in Angie's food order. Her sentence communicates a request for information directly, yet indirectly conveys a command in question form, "What do you have to say?" (or a bald command, "Put in your two cents.") The waitress' offensive plan has worked. She wins the antagonistic exchange, momentarily. (She leads, not follows.)

In the next segment of the interchange in (11), the verbal battle intensifies between waitress and customer. Flipper asks a question, "Do you have a problem?" (line 14), which opens the door to direct, bold language on the waitress' part (lines 15–18). Counter to the polite language tendencies described for "women's language" (Lakoff 1975), the waitress speaks her mind instead of hiding behind politeness strategies. Honest, direct communication characterizes her linguistic behavior here, regardless of her status or obligatory duties. Boldness in language and demeanor mark her response. She unhesitatingly calls Flipper fake, tired, and audacious. According to African American English and its community standards, the waitress is "in his face." Although her comments are brief (lines 15–18), the waitress shares her beliefs, "reading" Flipper adeptly. Flipper is a phony African American male, not a real one, because he has taken a European American woman on a date to an African American establishment. Not only is he fake, but he is also tired. In his slang dictionary, Major (1994) defines *tired* as "stupid, boring, lame" (477).

The waitress not only reads Flipper, but reads him metalinguistically as well. She code-switches from GAE to AAE. She only stops at Flipper and Angie's table because she is called upon. This action pulls her into an obligatory performance of her duties, which she performs (although perfunctorily) using GAE. When asked if she has a problem, the waitress "reads" Flipper his "rights," according to her law and language (lines 15–18). Here, the waitress "reads dialect" by signifying on Flipper and by using phonological and lexical AAE features. Indirectly, she puts Flipper down; she does not say directly, "You are fake and tired." Instead, she signifies by associating him with other brothers that are fake and tired. "Reading dialect" occurs phonologically with *that* pronounced as "dass" (line 16), *her* pronounced as "huh" (line 17), and *here* pronounced as "heah" (line 17). Also, the waitress uses lexical items specific to the African American speech community: *fake* (line 15), *tired* (line 15), and *brothers* (line 15).

While "reading" Flipper, the waitress brings Angie into the picture, insulting her: "I cain't even believe you brought huh stringy hair ass up heah to eat" (lines 17–18). The camera shows all three participants in this shot, with Angie raking her fingers through her hair upon hearing this comment. At this point, the battle ensues. It is "on"! Flipper takes offense and draws upon his community knowledge and weaponry. He signifies on the waitress: "ahh ahh let me tell you something (.) first of all Miss Al Sharpton" (lines 19–20). The context of the movie makes it clear that Flipper does not know the waitress, nor her name. He calls her "Miss Al Sharpton" as an indirect slur. Within some communities, Al Sharpton has been established as uncreditable and empty-mouthed. Through indirection, Flipper labels the waitress similarly. He does not directly call her pumped up or full of hot air, yet, by associating her with Al Sharpton, he retaliates in the game of verbal warfare. His strategy is effective but short-lived as the waitress disallows Flipper a full speaking turn, overlapping his talk with her input (lines 21, 23, 25). In this interchange, the waitress deploys the strength of the signification and the lecturing mode of Flipper by speaking simultaneously. She denies him full control of the floor and has the last word in the simultaneous speech segment.

After a brief (0.1 second) pause, Flipper continues lecturing the waitress, who allows his speaking turn: "Iss not yo business (.) you are a waitress (.) your job is to wait" (line 26). The waitress appears to "settle down" and listen to the customer's comments. She temporarily resumes her duties of waitressing, aloofly: "((Resumes soft, calm tone; goes into a routine recitation. Looks up, rolls eyes, looks down at pad)) Today's specials are the Maryland crab cakes (.) Creole shrimp (.) gumbo and blackened catfish" (lines 27–31). Performance occurs here: the waitress puts on an act, performing as a gentle, acquiescent server, indicated by her tone, volume, and other metalinguistic behavior. She assumes a calm tone, routinely reciting the day's specials, even though she must force herself to do so as indicated by kinesics. She puts on an act that things are okay and business can proceed. The waitress does not bite her tongue for long, though. Before this speaking turn is over, "smart talk" occurs a second time: "I suggest you have the blackened catfish" (lines 30–31).

Fear of repercussions does not appear to stop the waitress from responding "smartly." Although in both instances of "smart talk" she initially holds her peace, shortly thereafter she asserts her position directly and boldly, regardless of jeopardizing her job (lines 27–31). At the point of the second use of "smart talk," the waitress appears not to be concerned about fulfilling her tasks. She has conveyed her disapproval of Flipper's actions prior to this exchange and does not "cease and desist." She, again, boldly communicates her feelings: "I suggest you have the blackened catfish" (lines 30–31). The emphasis on the word "blackened" seems to suggest that Flipper is only superficially African American. Perhaps eating the "blackened" catfish will help him become a "real brothah."

Even though (11) occurred in a film produced, directed, and written by a male, the language represented in it for African American women has social reality, especially as legitimated by the research on AAWL. The waitress performs, reads dialect, and uses "smart talk," as described by African American women researchers. She "rap[s] in a powerful, convincing manner" (Smitherman 1994: 221), "talking that talk."

4. Conclusion

The literature on AAWL and the data analyzed here show that verbal strategies exist within the African American women's speech community that establish a distinct way of talking for African American women that is neither wholly like White women's language or African American men's language. There are other linguistic options available for African American women than may have been previously acknowledged in the literature. African American women may choose to signify, read dialect, perform, and/or speak assertively without feeling stereotypically masculine or aggressive, especially based upon an in-group perspective and construction.

Further, the literature and data suggest that some gendered parity exists in use of the strategies among speech community members and in the availability of the linguistic strategies to speech community members. Many African American women are highly skilled in verbal dueling as the waitress demonstrates in (11) and as Naylor has constructed for Mattie Michael (8 and 9) in *The Women of Brewster Place*. Mattie exerts linguistic power and control without challenge from Butch. Anita Hill displays skill in assertive linguistic behavior (4 and 5). Even though she codeswitches (as one would expect), she nonetheless maintains a linguistic style representative of AAWL. Smitherman (p.c.) reports on her own personal adeptness in "playing the dozens" and other verbal games as learned from a cousin. Smitherman was also known for her dexterity in "talking that talk" (Smitherman p.c.). These women (fictional and non-fictional) appear not to be afraid of cultural stereotypes of their speech, yet view their linguistic options (within AAWL) pridefully and positively. Within both the African American speech community and African American women's speech community, the features discussed in this paper are socially constructed as valuable and desirable. Speech community members, in general, admire speakers, both male and female, who can "talk that talk."

Notes

1. I dedicate this paper to Dr. Geneva Smitherman, a true revolutionary, a "woman warrior," who has given of her research, teaching, and lectures to the true, accurate, and positive depiction of language used by American Africans in the U.S. Dr. Smitherman served as one primary source for the interviews and tape-recordings during my collection of data. She very obviously is a speaker, writer, and defender of African American English. Dr. G,

the student-bestowed pseudonym for my colleague, has a long-standing tradition of mentoring and helping others, especially her people. The research included here serves, in part, as a tribute to her mentoring, assistance, and service given to me and the many thousands gone—spreading their wings, yet still held accountable to the lessons she has modeled.

2. As would be expected from the research of Turner (1949) and Herskovits (1958), a cultural continuum is evidenced with this diminutive. In discussions with women from Barbados, I have observed the same use of *girl* as described here for African women in the U.S.

3. Note that Foster does not consciously focus on this feature as one characteristic of AAWL. Such a designation is mine, based upon my reading of Foster (1995) as discussed here.

Appendix: Transcription Notations

(1) Numbers in parentheses preceding the transcribed text indicate examples.

\-- Dashes indicate that speech was interrupted.

(1.2) Numbers in parentheses within the transcribed text indicate silences in seconds and tenths of seconds.

(.) A period enclosed in parentheses marks silences that were too short to time precisely.

Z A large z-shaped symbol shows that latching occurs; little or no gap occurs between the end of current speaker's turn and the beginning of next speaker's turn.

[A left bracket indicates overlapped speech; next speaker begins a turn prior to the end of current speaker's turn.

= An equal sign shows that there was no silence or pause discernible within one speaker's utterances.

. A period indicates falling intonation, not grammar.

? A question mark indicates rising intonation, not grammar.

bold Boldfaced letters show emphasis, conveyed either by increased volume or pitch changes.

< The less-than symbol indicates a decrease in volume.

::: Colons mark the lengthening of the sound they follow.

(( )) Double parentheses relay transcriber comments, not transcribed text. ((???)), for example, indicates undecipherable language for the transcriber.

→ Marks a key example of the feature under discussion.

References

Abrahams, Roger D. 1975. "Negotiating respect: Patterns of presentation among Black women."*Journal of American Folklore* 88: 58–80.

Etter-Lewis, Gwendolyn. 1991. "Black women's life stories: Reclaiming self in narrative texts." In Sherna Berger Gluck & Daphne Patai, eds. *Women's Words: The Feminist Practice of Oral History*. New York: Routledge, 43–62.

———1993. *My Soul is My Own: Oral Narratives of African American Women in the Professions.* New York: Routledge.

Foster, Michele. 1995. "'Are you with me'?: Power and solidarity in the discourse of African American women." In Kira Hall & Mary Bucholtz, eds. 1995, 329–50.

Goodwin, Marjorie Harness. 1990. *He-Said-She-Said: Talk as Social Organization Among Black Children.* Bloomington: Indiana University Press.

Hall, Kira & Mary Bucholtz, eds. 1995. *Gender Articulated: Language and the Socially Constructed Self.* New York: Routledge.

Herskovits, Melville. 1958. *The Myth of the Negro Past.* Boston: Beacon Press.

Houston Stanback, Marsha. 1982. "Language and Black woman's place: Toward a description of Black women's communication." Paper presented to the Speech Communication Association.

Houston Stanback, Marsha. 1985. "Language and Black woman's place: Evidence from the Black middle class." In Paula A. Treichler, Cheris Kramarae, & Beth Stafford, eds. *For Alma Mater: Theory and Practice in Feminist Scholarship.* Urbana: University of Illinois Press, 177–93.

Lakoff, Robin. 1975. *Language and Woman's Place.* New York: Octagon Books.

Lee, Spike, dir. and prod. 1991. *Jungle Fever.*

Major, Clarence. 1994. *Juba to Jive: A Dictionary of African-American Slang.* New York: Viking.

Mendoza-Denton, Norma. 1995. "Pregnant pauses: Silence and authority in the Anita Hill-Clarence Thomas hearings." In Kira Hall & Mary Bucholtz, eds. 1995: 51–66.

Mitchell-Kernan, Claudia. 1972. "Signifying, loud-talking and marking." In Thomas Kochman, ed. *Rappin' and Stylin' Out.* Urbana: University of Illinois Press, 315–35.

Morgan, Marcyliena. 1996. "Conversational signifying: Grammar and indirectness among African American women." In Elinor Ochs, Emmanuel Schegloff, & Sandra Thompson, eds. *Interaction and Grammar.* Cambridge: Cambridge University Press, 405–34.

Naylor, Gloria. 1982. *The Women of Brewster Place.* New York: Viking.

———1998. "'Nigger': The meaning of a word." In Gary Goshgarian, ed. *Exploring Language.* 8th ed. New York: Longman, 332–4. (Originally published in *New York Times Magazine,* February 20, 1986.)

Nichols, Patricia C. 1983. "Linguistic options and choices for Black women in the rural South." In Barrie Thorne, Cheris Kramarae, & Nancy Henley, eds. *Language, Gender & Society.* Rowley, MA: Newbury House, 54–68.

Sacks, Harvey, Emmanuel Schegloff, & Gail Jefferson. 1974. "A simplest systematics for the organization of turn-taking for conversation." *Language* 50: 696–735.

Smitherman, Geneva. 1977. *Talkin and Testifyin: The Language of Black America.* Boston: Houghton Mifflin.

———1994. *Black Talk: Words and Phrases form the Hood to the Amen Corner.* New York: Houghton Mifflin.

———& Denise Troutman-Robinson. 1988. "Black women's language." In Wilma Mankiller, Gwendolyn Mink, Marysa Navarro, Barbara Smith and

Gloria Steinem (eds.), *The Reader's Companion to U.S. Women's History.* Boston: Houghton Mifflin Company.

Thorne, Barrie & Nancy Henley. 1975. "Difference and dominance: An overview of language, gender, and society." In Barrie Thorne & Nancy Henley, eds. 1975: *Language and Sex: Difference and Dominance.* Rowley, MA: Newbury House Publishers, 5–42.

Troutman, Denise. 1996. "Culturally-toned diminutives within the speech community of African American women." *Journal of Commonwealth and Postcolonial Studies* 4(1): 55–64.

Troutman-Robinson, Denise. 1995. "Tongue and sword: Which is to be master"? In Geneva Smitherman, ed. *African American Women Speak Out on Anita Hill-Clarence Thomas.* Detroit: Wayne State University Press, 208–23.

Turner, Lorenzo Dow. 1949. *Africanisms in the Gullah Dialect.* Chicago: University of Chicago Press.

West, Candace, Michelle Lazar, & Cheris Kramarae. 1997. "Gender in discourse." In Teun A. van Dijk, ed. *Discourse as Social Interaction.* London: Sage Publications, 119–43.

Lived Literacy Resources from T.E.D.com

On Creativity by Amy Tan
Gaming Can Make the World a Better Place by Jone
McGonigal

Wesch, A Vision of Students Today - http://www.youtube.com/
watch?v=dGCJ46vyR9o

Cultural Literacies

Cultural Literacies: Introduction

The readings in this section present some cultural practices that we think of people being more or less literate about: sports, school, music, gender stereotypes, etc. As you read, continue to think about the invention strategies these writers use to create their texts. For example, some writers in this section connect particular practices—like the leisurely pace of baseball—to larger cultural realities—such as the slower pace of life and prevalence of agricultural economies during the time that baseball becomes a national pastime.

These readings also give you an opportunity to think seriously about what new kinds of organizational plans you are introduced to while reading. In "Football Red and Baseball Green," for example, Murry Ross chooses to discuss one sport at length before moving to the next sport. This allows him to make what the concepts of time and the character of athletes imply about the larger topic of culture easier to integrate as particular to each sport he discusses. As you read, think about what other organizing strategies are at work in the essays. As you think about how you might define a subject and focus for your own cultural literacy paper, think about which organizing strategies might help you begin drafting your paper.

Reading as a writer means paying attention to the invention and arrangement strategies other writers use and adapting them for use in your own work.

School vs. Education

Russell Baker

*Russell Baker (1925–) was born in a rural town in Vir-
ginia and grew up in New Jersey and Maryland. He received his B.A. in English from Johns Hopkins University
in 1947 and worked as a reporter for the* Baltimore Sun
and then the New York Times. *In 1962 he began writing
his "Observer" column for the* Times, *which was syndicated in over 400 newspapers for more than two decades.
His topics range from the mundane everyday annoyances to
serious social problems, and his style is generally casual but
thoughtful. In 1979 he received the Pulitzer Prize for distinguished commentary; he received the Prize again for his
autobiography* Growing Up *(1982). His collections of
columns and essays include* All Things Considered
(1965), Poor Russell's Almanac *(1972),* So This is Depravity *(1980),* The Rescue of Miss Yaskell and Other
Pipe Dreams *(1983), and* There's a Country in My Cellar *(1990). The following piece, first published in his* New
York Times *column in 1975, intertwines serious commentary on American education and values with a spoof
on what our schools teach. As you read it, think about the
serious message Baker wants to communicate to us.*

By the age of six the average child will have completed the basic
American education and be ready to enter school. If the child
has been attentive in these preschool years, he or she will already have mastered many skills.

From television, the child will have learned how to pick a lock,
commit a fairly elaborate bank holdup, prevent wetness all day long,

Reprinted from *New York Times Magazine*, 1975, by permission of The New York
Times Company.

get the laundry twice as white, and kill people with a variety of sophisticated armaments.

From watching his parents, the child, in many cases, will already know how to smoke, how much soda to mix with whiskey, what kind of language to use when angry, and how to violate the speed laws without being caught.

At this point, the child is ready for the second stage of education, which occurs in school. There, a variety of lessons may be learned in the very first days.

The teacher may illustrate the economic importance of belonging to a strong union by closing down the school before the child arrives. Fathers and mothers may demonstrate to the child the social cohesion that can be built on shared hatred by demonstrating their dislike for children whose pigmentation displeases them. In the latter event, the child may receive visual instruction in techniques of stoning buses, cracking skulls with a nightstick, and subduing mobs with tear gas. Formal education has begun.

During formal education, the child learns that life is for testing. This stage lasts twelve years, a period during which the child learns that success comes from telling testers what they want to hear.

Early in this stage, the child learns that he is either dumb or smart. If the teacher puts intelligent demands upon the child, the child learns he is smart. If the teacher expects little of the child, the child learns he is dumb and soon quits bothering to tell the testers what they want to hear.

At this point, education becomes more subtle. The child taught by school that he is dumb observes that neither he, she, nor any of the many children who are even dumber, ever fails to be promoted to the next grade. From this, the child learns that while everybody talks a lot about the virtue of being smart, there is very little incentive to stop being dumb.

What is the point of school, besides attendance? the child wonders. As the end of the first formal stage of education approaches, school answers this question. The point is to equip the child to enter college.

Children who have been taught they are smart have no difficulty. They have been happily telling testers what they want to hear for twelve years. Being artists at telling testers what they want to hear, they are admitted to college joyously, where they promptly learn that they are the hope of America.

Children whose education has been limited to adjusting themselves to their schools' low estimates of them are admitted to less joyous colleges which, in some cases, may teach them to read.

At this stage of education, a fresh question arises for everyone. If the point of lower education was to get into college, what is the point of college? The answer is soon learned. The point of college is to prepare the student—no longer a child now—to get into graduate school. In college the student learns that it is no longer enough simply to tell the testers what they want to hear. Many are tested for graduate school; few are admitted.

Those excluded may be denied valuable certificates to prosper in medicine, at the bar, in the corporate boardroom. The student learns that the race is to the cunning and often, alas, to the unprincipled.

Thus, the student learns the importance of destroying competitors and emerges richly prepared to play his role in the great simmering melodrama of American life.

Afterward, the former student's destiny fulfilled, his life rich with Oriental carpets, rare porcelain, and full bank accounts, he may one day find himself with the leisure and the inclination to open a book with a curious mind, and start to become educated.

How We Listen to Music
Aaron Copland

Aaron Copland (1900–1990) was a well-known modern composer. Born in New York City, he studied music in New York and France. His early successes in his twenties led to a musical career that included many compositions, piano performances, teaching, and writing. His music is marked by adaptations of American folk stories, including his ballet Billy the Kid *(1939) and* John Henry *(1940). His most popular symphony is* El Salon Mexico *(1936); he also composed avant-garde compositions such as* Piano Variations *(1930). Among the several books he wrote about music is* What to Listen for in Music *(1939), from which the following essay is excerpted. Although many composers do not like to talk about what their music means or what it expresses, as Copland remarks in this essay, he believes we should try to understand music fully by paying attention to all its dimensions.*

We all listen to music according to our separate capacities. But, for the sake of analysis, the whole listening process may become clearer if we break it up into its component parts, so to speak. In a certain sense we all listen to music on three separate planes. For lack of a better terminology, one might name these: (1) the sensuous plane, (2) the expressive plane, (3) the sheerly musical plane. The only advantage to be gained from mechanically splitting up the listening process into these hypothetical planes is the clearer view to be had of the way in which we listen.

The simplest way of listening to music is to listen for the sheer pleasure of the musical sound itself. That is the sensuous plane. It is the plane on which we hear music without thinking, without considering

Reprinted from *What to Listen for in Music* (1988), by permission of the Aaron Copland Fund for Music, Inc.

it in any way. One turns on the radio while doing something else and absent-mindedly bathes in the sound. A kind of brainless but attractive state of mind is engendered by the mere sound appeal of the music.

You may be sitting in a room reading this book. Imagine one note struck on the piano. Immediately that one note is enough to change the atmosphere of the room—providing that the sound element in music is a powerful and mysterious agent, which it would be foolish to deride or belittle.

The surprising thing is that many people who consider themselves qualified music lovers abuse that plane in listening. They go to concerts in order to lose themselves. They use music as a consolation or an escape. They enter an ideal world where one doesn't have to think of the realities of everyday life. Of course they aren't thinking about the music either. Music allows them to leave it, and they go off to a place to dream, dreaming because of and apropos of the music yet never quite listening to it.

Yes, the sound appeal of music is a potent and primitive force, but you must not allow it to usurp a disproportionate share of your interest. The sensuous plane is an important one in music, a very important one, but it does not constitute the whole story.

There is no need to digress further on the sensuous plane. Its appeal to every normal human being is self-evident. There is, however, such a thing as becoming more sensitive to the different kinds of sound stuff as used by various composers. For all composers do not use that sound stuff in the same way. Don't get the idea that the value of music is commensurate with its sensuous appeal or that the loveliest sounding music is made by the greatest composer. If that were so, Ravel would be a greater creator than Beethoven. The point is that the sound element varies with each composer, that his usage of sound forms an integral part of his style and must be taken into account when listening. The reader can see, therefore, that a more conscious approach is valuable even on this primary plane of music listening.

The second plane on which music exists is what I have called the expressive one. Here, immediately, we tread on controversial ground. Composers have a way of shying away from any discussion of music's expressive side. Did not Stravinsky himself proclaim that his music was an "object," a "thing," with a life of its own, and with no other meaning than its own purely musical existence? This intransigent attitude of Stravinsky's may be due to the fact that so many people have tried to read different meanings into so many pieces. Heaven knows it is difficult enough to say precisely what it is that a piece of music means, to say it definitely, to say it finally so that everyone is satisfied with your explanation. But that should not lead one to the other extreme of denying to music the right to be "expressive."

My own belief is that all music has an expressive power, some more and some less, but that all music has a certain meaning behind the notes and that the meaning behind the notes constitutes, after all, what the piece is saying, what the piece is about. The whole problem can be stated quite simply by asking, "Is there a meaning to music?" My answer to that would be, "Yes." And "Can you state in so many words what the meaning is?" My answer to that would be, "No." Therein lies the difficulty.

Simple-minded souls will never be satisfied with the answer to the second of these questions. They always want music to have a meaning, and the more concrete it is the better they like it. The more the music reminds them of a train, a storm, a funeral, or any other familiar conception the more expressive it appears to be to them. This popular idea of music's meaning—stimulated and abetted by the usual run of musical commentator—should be discouraged wherever and whenever it is met. One timid lady once confessed to me that she suspected something seriously lacking in her appreciation of music because of her inability to connect it with anything definite. That is getting the whole thing backward, of course.

Still, the question remains, How close should the intelligent music lover wish to come to pinning a definite meaning to any particular work? No closer than a general concept, I should say. Music expresses, at different moments, serenity or exuberance, regrets or triumph, fury or delight. It expresses each of these moods, and many others, in a numberless variety of subtle shadings and differences. It may even express a state of meaning for which there exists no adequate word in any language. In that case, musicians often like to say that it has only a purely musical meaning. They sometimes go further and say that *all* music has only a purely musical meaning. What they really mean is that no appropriate word can be found to express the music's meaning and that, even if it could, they do not feel the need of finding it.

But whatever the professional musician may hold, most musical novices still search for specific words with which to pin down their musical reactions. That is why they always find Tschaikovsky easier to "understand" than Beethoven. In the first place, it is easier to pin a meaning-word on a Tschaikovsky piece than on a Beethoven one. Much easier. Moreover, with the Russian composer, every time you come back to a piece of his it almost always says the same thing to you, whereas with Beethoven it is often quite difficult to put your finger right on what he is saying. And any musician will tell you that that is why Beethoven is the greater composer. Because music which always says the same thing to you will necessarily soon become dull music, but music whose meaning is slightly different with each hearing has a greater chance of remaining alive.

Listen, if you can, to the forty-eight fugue themes of Bach's *Well Tempered Clavichord.* Listen to each theme, one after another. You will soon realize that each theme mirrors a different world of feeling. You will also soon realize that the more beautiful a theme seems to you the harder it is to find any word that will describe it to your complete satisfaction. Yes, you will certainly know whether it is a gay theme or a sad one. You will be able, in other words, in your own mind, to draw a frame of emotional feeling around your theme. Now study the sad one a little closer. Try to pin down the exact quality of its sadness. Is it pessimistically sad or resignedly sad; is it fatefully sad or smilingly sad?

Let us suppose that you are fortunate and can describe to your own satisfaction in so many words the exact meaning of your chosen theme. There is still no guarantee that anyone else will be satisfied. Nor need they be. The important thing is that each one feel for himself the specific expressive quality of a theme or, similarly, an entire piece of music. And if it is a great work of art, don't expect it to mean exactly the same thing to you each time you return to it.

Themes or pieces need not express only one emotion, of course. Take such a theme as the first main one of the *Ninth Symphony,* for example. It is clearly made up of different elements. It does not say only one thing. Yet anyone hearing it immediately gets a feeling of strength, a feeling of power. It isn't a power that comes simply because the theme is played loudly. It is a power inherent in the theme itself. The extraordinary strength and vigor of the theme results in the listener's receiving an impression that a forceful statement has been made. But one should never try to boil it down to "the fateful hammer of life," etc. That is where the trouble begins. The musician, in his exasperation, says it means nothing but the notes themselves, whereas the nonprofessional is only too anxious to hang on to any explanation that gives him the illusion of getting closer to the music's meaning.

Now, perhaps, the reader will know better what I mean when I say that music does have an expressive meaning but that we cannot say in so many words what that meaning is.

The third plane on which music exists is the sheerly musical plane. Besides the pleasurable sound of music and the expressive feeling that it gives off, music does exist in terms of the notes themselves and of their manipulation. Most listeners are not sufficiently conscious of this third plane. . . .

Professional musicians, on the other hand, are, if anything, too conscious of the mere notes themselves. They often fall into the error of becoming so engrossed with their arpeggios and staccatos that they forget the deeper aspects of the music they are performing. But from the layman's standpoint, it is not so much a matter of getting over bad habits on the sheerly musical plane as of increasing one's awareness of what is going on, in so far as the notes are concerned.

When the man in the street listens to the "notes themselves" with any degree of concentration, he is most likely to make some mention of the melody. Either he hears a pretty melody or he does not, and he generally lets it go at that. Rhythm is likely to gain his attention next, particularly if it seems exciting. But harmony and tone color are generally taken for granted, if they are thought of consciously at all. As for music's having a definite form of some kind, that idea seems never to have occurred to him.

It is very important for all of us to become more alive to music on its sheerly musical plane. After all, an actual musical material is being used. The intelligent listener must be prepared to increase his awareness of the musical material and what happens to it. He must hear the melodies, the rhythms, the harmonies, the tone colors in a more conscious fashion. But above all he must, in order to follow the line of the composer's thought, know something of the principles of musical form. Listening to all of these elements is listening on the sheerly musical plane.

Let me repeat that I have split up mechanically the three separate planes on which we listen merely for the sake of greater clarity. Actually, we never listen on one or the other of these planes. What we do is to correlate them—listening in all three ways at the same time. It takes no mental effort, for we do it instinctively.

Perhaps an analogy with what happens to us when we visit the theater will make this instinctive correlation clearer. In the theater, you are aware of the actors and actresses, costumes and sets, sounds and movements. All these give one the sense that the theater is a pleasant place to be in. They constitute the sensuous plane in our theatrical reactions.

The expressive plane in the theater would be derived from the feeling that you get from what is happening on the stage. You are moved to pity, excitement, or gayety. It is this general feeling, generated aside from the particular words being spoken, a certain emotional something which exists on the stage, that is analogous to the expressive quality in music.

The plot and plot development is equivalent to our sheerly musical plane. The playwright creates and develops a character in just the same way that a composer creates and develops a theme. According to the degree of your awareness of the way in which the artist in either field handles his material you will become a more intelligent listener.

It is easy enough to see that the theatergoer never is conscious of any of these elements separately. He is aware of them all at the same time. The same is true of music listening. We simultaneously and without thinking listen on all three planes.

In a sense, the ideal listener is both inside and outside the music at the same moment, judging it and enjoying it, wishing it would go one way and watching it go another—almost like the composer at the moment he composes it; because in order to write his music, the composer must also be inside and outside his music, carried away by it and yet coldly critical of it. A subjective and objective attitude is implied in both creating and listening to music.

What the reader should strive for, then, is a more *active* kind of listening. Whether you listen to Mozart or Duke Ellington, you can deepen your understanding of music only by being a more conscious and aware listener—not someone who is just listening, but someone who is listening *for* something.

The Myth of the Latin Woman: I Just Met a Girl Named María

Judith Ortiz Cofer

Judith Ortiz Cofer (1952–) was born in Hormigueros, Puerto Rico, and emigrated to the United States when she was four. Cofer attended Augusta College and Florida Atlantic University; she was also a Scholar of the English Speaking Union at Oxford University. She has worked as a bilingual teacher in the Florida public schools, and as a visiting writer at Vanderbilt University and the University of Michigan, Ann Arbor. Cofer is currently the Franklin Professor of English and Creative Writing at The University of Georgia. An award-winning poet, Cofer has received grants from the Witter Bynner Foundation and the National Endowment for the Arts. Her books include The Line of the Sun *(1989),* Silent Dancing *(1990),* The Latin Deli *(1993),* Reaching for the Mainland and Selected New Poems *(1995),* The Year of Our Revolution *(1998),* Woman In Front of the Sun: On Becoming a Writer *(2000),* A Love Story Beginning in Spanish: Poems *(2005), as well as a children's book,* Call Me Maria *(2004). Cofer, who has also written for* Glamour *and* The Kenyon Review, *often combines her love of language with her interest in the lives and traditions of Puerto Ricans. In this essay, from* The Latin Deli, *Cofer describes how her Latino ancestry attracts unpleasant stereotyping.*

On a bus trip to London from Oxford University where I was earning some graduate credits one summer, a young man, obviously fresh from a pub, spotted me and as if struck by

Reprinted from *The Latin Deli: Prose and Poetry*, by permission of the University of Georgia Press.

inspiration went down on his knees in the aisle. With both hands over his heart he broke into an Irish tenor's rendition of "Maria" from *West Side Story.* My politely amused fellow passengers gave his lovely voice the round of gentle applause it deserved. Though I was not quite as amused, I managed my version of an English smile: no show of teeth, no extreme contortions of the facial muscles—I was at this time of my life practicing reserve and cool. Oh, that British control, how I coveted it. But "Maria" had followed me to London, reminding me of a prime fact of my life: you can leave the island, master the English language, and travel as far as you can, but if you are a Latina, especially one like me who so obviously belongs to Rita Moreno's gene pool, the island travels with you.

This is sometimes a very good thing—it may win you that extra minute of someone's attention. But with some people, the same things can make *you* an island—not a tropical paradise but an Alcatraz, a place nobody wants to visit. As a Puerto Rican girl living in the United States and wanting like most children to "belong," I resented the stereotype that my Hispanic appearance called forth from many people I met.

Growing up in a large urban center in New Jersey during the 1960s, I suffered from what I think of as "cultural schizophrenia." Our life was designed by my parents as a microcosm of their *casas* on the island. We spoke in Spanish, ate Puerto Rican food bought at the *bodega,* and practiced strict Catholicism at a church that allotted us a one-hour slot each week for mass, performed in Spanish by a Chinese priest trained as a missionary for Latin America.

As a girl I was kept under strict surveillance by my parents, since my virtue and modesty were, by their cultural equation, the same as their honor. As a teenager I was lectured constantly on how to behave as a proper *senorita.* But it was a conflicting message I received, since the Puerto Rican mothers also encouraged their daughters to look and act like women and to dress in clothes our Anglo friends and their mothers found too "mature" and flashy. The difference was, and is, cultural; yet I often felt humiliated when I appeared at an American friend's party wearing a dress more suitable to a semi-formal than to a playroom birthday celebration. At Puerto Rican festivities, neither the music nor the colors we wore could be too loud.

I remember Career Day in our high school, when teachers told us to come dressed as if for a job interview. It quickly became obvious that to the Puerto Rican girls "dressing up" meant wearing their mother's ornate jewelry and clothing, more appropriate (by mainstream standards) for the company Christmas party than as daily office attire. That morning I had agonized in front of my closet, trying to figure out what a "career girl" would wear. I knew how to dress for school (at the Catholic school I attended, we all wore uniforms), I knew how to dress for Sunday mass, and I knew what dresses to wear for parties at my relatives' homes. Though I do not recall the precise details of my Career Day outfit, it must have been a composite of these choices. But I remember a comment my friend (an Italian American) made in later years that coalesced my impressions of that day. She said that at the business school she was attending, the Puerto Rican girls always stood out for wearing "everything at once." She meant, of course, too much jewelry, too many accessories. On that day at school we were simply made the negative models by the nuns, who were themselves not credible fashion experts to any of us. But it was painfully obvious to me that to the others, in their tailored skirts and silk blouses, we must have seemed "hopeless" and "vulgar." Though I now know that most adolescents feel out of step much of the time, I also know that for the Puerto Rican girls of my generation that sense was intensified. The way our teachers and classmates looked at us that day in school was just a taste of the cultural clash that awaited us in the real world, where prospective employers and men on the street would often misinterpret our tight skirts and jingling bracelets as a "come-on."

Mixed cultural signals have perpetuated certain stereotypes—for example, that of the Hispanic woman as the "hot tamale" or sexual firebrand. It is a one-dimensional view that the media have found easy to promote. In their special vocabulary, advertisers have designated "sizzling" and "smoldering" as the adjectives of choice for describing not only the foods but also the women of Latin America. From conversations in my house I recall hearing about the harassment that Puerto Rican women endured in factories where the "boss-men" talked to them as if sexual innuendo was all they understood, and worse, often gave them the choice of submitting to their advances or being fired.

It is custom, however, not chromosomes, that leads us to choose scarlet over pale pink. As young girls, it was our mothers who influenced our decisions about clothes and colors—mothers who had grown up on a tropical island where the natural environment was a riot of primary colors, where showing your skin was one way to keep cool as well as to look sexy. Most important of all, on the island, women perhaps felt freer to dress and move more provocatively since, in most cases, they were protected by the traditions, mores, and laws of a Spanish/Catholic system of morality and machismo whose main rule was: *You may look at my sister, but if you touch her I will kill you.* The extended family and church structure could provide a young woman with a circle of safety in her small pueblo on the island; if a man "wronged" a girl, everyone would close in to save her family honor.

My mother has told me about dressing in her best party clothes on Saturday nights and going to the town's plaza to promenade with her girl-friends in front of the boys they liked. The males were thus given an opportunity to admire the women and to express their admiration in the form of *piropos:* erotically charged street poems they composed on the spot. (I have myself been subjected to a few *piropos* while visiting the island, and they can be outrageous, although custom dictates that they must never cross into obscenity.) This ritual, as I understand it, also entails a show of studied indifference on the woman's part; if she is "decent," she must not acknowledge the man's impassioned words. So I do understand how things can be lost in translation. When a Puerto Rican girl dressed in her idea of what is attractive meets a man from the mainstream culture who has been trained to react to certain types of clothing as a sexual signal, a clash is likely to take place. I remember the boy who took me to my first formal dance leaning over to plant a sloppy, over-eager kiss painfully on my mouth; when I didn't respond with sufficient passion, he remarked resentfully: "I thought you Latin girls were supposed to mature early," as if I were expected to *ripen* like a fruit or vegetable, not just grow into womanhood like other girls.

It is surprising to my professional friends that even today some people, including those who should know better, still put others "in their place." It happened to me most recently during a stay at a classy metropolitan hotel favored by young professional couples for weddings. Late one evening after the theater, as I walked toward my room with a colleague (a woman with whom I was coordinating an arts program), a middle-aged man in a tuxedo, with a young girl in satin and lace on his arm, stepped directly into our path. With his champagne glass extended toward me, he exclaimed "Evita!"

Our way blocked, my companion and I listened as the man half-recited, half-bellowed "Don't Cry for Me, Argentina." When he finished, the young girl said: "How about a round of applause for my daddy?" We complied, hoping this would bring the silly spectacle to a close. I was becoming aware that our little group was attracting the attention of the other guests. "Daddy" must have perceived this too, and he once more barred the way as we tried to walk past him. He began to shout-sing a ditty to the tune of "La Bamba"—except the lyrics were about a girl named Maria whose exploits rhymed with her name and gonorrhea. The girl kept saying "Oh, Daddy" and looking at me with pleading eyes. She wanted me to laugh along with the others. My companion and I stood silently waiting for the man to end his offensive song. When he finished, I looked not at him but at his daughter. I advised her calmly never to ask her father what he had done in the army. Then I walked between them and to my room. My friend complimented me on my cool handling of the situation, but I confessed that I had really wanted to push the jerk into the swimming pool. This same man—probably a corporate executive, well-educated, even worldly by most standards—would not have been likely to regale an Anglo woman with a dirty song in public. He might have checked his impulse by assuming that she could be somebody's wife or mother, or at least *somebody* who might take offense. But, to him, I was just an Evita or a Maria: merely a character in his cartoon-populated universe.

Another facet of the myth of the Latin woman in the United States is the menial, the domestic—Maria the housemaid or counter-girl. It's true that work as domestics, as waitresses, and in factories is all that's available to women with little English and few skills. But the myth of the Hispanic menial—the funny maid, mispronouncing words and cooking up a spicy storm in a shiny California kitchen—has been perpetuated by the media in the same way that "Mammy" from *Gone with the Wind* became America's idea of the black woman for generations. Since I do not wear my diplomas around my neck for all to see, I have on occasion been sent to that "kitchen" where some think I obviously belong.

One incident has stayed with me, though I recognize it as a minor offense. My first public poetry reading took place in Miami, at a restaurant where a luncheon was being held before the event. I was nervous and excited as I walked in with notebook in hand. An older woman motioned me to her table, and thinking (foolish me) that she wanted me to autograph a copy of my newly published slender volume of verse, I went over. She ordered a cup of coffee from me, assuming that I was the waitress. (Easy enough to mistake my poems for menus, I suppose.) I know it wasn't an intentional act of cruelty. Yet of all the good things that happened later, I remember that scene most clearly, because it reminded me of what I had to overcome before anyone would take me seriously. In retrospect I understand that my anger gave my reading fire. In fact, I have almost always taken any doubt in my abilities as a challenge, the result most often being the satisfaction of winning a convert, of seeing the cold, appraising eyes warm to my words, the body language change, the smile that indicates I have opened some avenue for communication. So that day as I read, I looked directly at that woman. Her lowered eyes told me she was embarrassed at her faux pas, and when I willed her to look up at me, she graciously allowed me to punish her with my full attention. We shook hands at the end of the reading and I never saw her again. She has probably forgotten the entire incident, but maybe not.

Yet I am one of the lucky ones. There are thousands of Latinas without the privilege of an education or the entrees into society that I have. For them life is a constant struggle against the misconceptions perpetuated by the myth of the Latina. My goal is to try to replace the old stereotypes with a much more interesting set of realities. Every time I give a reading, I hope the stories I tell, the dreams and fears I examine in my work, can achieve some universal truth that will get my audience past the particulars of my skin color, my accent, or my clothes.

I once wrote a poem in which I called all Latinas "God's brown daughters." This poem is really a prayer of sorts, offered upward, but also, through the human-to-human channel of art, outward. It is a prayer for communication and for respect. In it, Latin women pray "in Spanish to an Anglo God/with a Jewish heritage," and they are "fervently hoping/that if not omnipotent,/at least He be bilingual."

The Merits of Meritocracy

David Brooks

David Brooks (1961–) is best known for his sharp and witty conservative commentary on public television's News Hour *with Jim Lehrer. Brooks graduated from the University of Chicago with a degree in history. He turned to writing political and social commentary and is now a leading commentator on PBS, CNN, and National Public Radio. He writes for* Newsweek *where he is a contributing editor, as well as for the* New York Times. *He is also a senior editor at the* Weekly Standard. *An anthology of his essays and commentaries is titled* Backward and Upward: The New Conservative Writing *(1996). His books include* Bobos in Paradise: The New Upper Class and How They Got There *(2000) and* On Paradise Drive: How We Live Now (and Always Have) *(2004).*

Children of the privileged must work very hard for what they have and for what they will get. Brooks uses the example of his daughter to show how busy she is and how she will have to compete to get into a great school and to find a greater job after school.

My daughter is a four-helmet kid. She has a regular helmet she wears bike riding, pogo sticking, and when she borrows her older brother's skateboard. She has a pink batting helmet, which she wears during her Little League baseball games. She has a helmet for horseback-riding lessons, on Sundays. And she has a helmet for ice hockey, which she plays on Friday afternoons. (For hockey she also has an equipment bag large enough to hold several corpses.) My

Reprinted from *The Atlantic Monthly,* May 2002, by permission of the author.

daughter's not even a jock (although she is something of a live wire). Her main interest is art, which she does in an after-school program on Tuesdays and at home on her own.

But it's her helmets that really got me thinking. They're generally scattered around the equipment racks in our garage, along with her brothers' helmet collections and all manner of sleds, mitts, scooters, bicycles, and balls, and they represent a certain sort of childhood—a childhood that has now become typical in middle-class America.

It's a busy childhood, filled with opportunities, activities, teams, coaches, and, inevitably, gear. It's a safety-conscious childhood, with ample adult supervision. And it is, I believe (at least I want to believe), a happy and fulfilling childhood that will prepare my daughter for a happy adult life.

This sort of childhood is different from the childhoods Americans have traditionally had. It's not an independent childhood, like Huck Finn's or the Bowery Boys'. Today's middle-class kids, by and large, don't live apart from adult society, free to explore and experiment and, through adventure and misadventure, teach themselves the important lessons of life. Nor is it a Horatio Alger childhood. Middle-class kids by definition haven't come from poverty and deprivation. Nor do they build self-discipline from having to work on a farm. If they hunger for success, it's not because they started at the bottom.

Today's mode of raising kids generates a lot of hand-wringing and anxiety, some of it on my part. We fear that kids are spoiled by the abundance and frenetic activity all around them. We fear that the world of suburban sprawl, Game Boys, Britney Spears CDs, and shopping malls will dull their moral senses. We fear that they are too deferential to authority, or that they are confronted with so many choices that they never have to make real commitments. Or we fear that they are skipping over childhood itself. The toy companies call this phenomenon "age compression": Kids who are ten no longer want toys that used to appeal to ten-year-olds. Now it is three- to five-year-olds who go for Barbie dolls. By the time a girl is seven she wants to be a mini-adult.

But I've come to believe that our fears are overblown. The problem is that the way kids (and, for that matter, the rest of us) live is estranged from the formulaic ideas we have about building character. We assume that character is forged through hardship—economic deprivation, war, and so on—and that we who have had it easy, who have grown up in this past half century of peace and prosperity, must necessarily have weak or suspect souls.

It's true that we live amid plenty; even in time of war we are told to keep shopping. But today's kids have a way of life that entails its own character-building process, its own ethical system. They live in a world of almost crystalline meritocracy. Starting at birth, middle-class Americans are called on to master skills, do well in school, practice sports, excel in extracurricular activities, get into college, build their résumés, change careers, be good in bed, set up retirement plans, and so on. This is a way of life that emphasizes individual achievement, self-propulsion, perpetual improvement, and permanent exertion.

The prime ethical imperative for the meritocrat is self-fulfillment. The phrase sounds New Agey; it calls to mind a Zen vegan sitting on the beach at dawn contemplating his narcissism. But over the past several years the philosophers Charles Taylor, of McGill University, and Alan Gewirth, of the University of Chicago, have argued that a serious moral force is contained in the idea of self-fulfillment. Meritocrats may not necessarily be able to articulate this morality, but they live by it nonetheless.

It starts with the notion that we have a lifelong mission to realize our capacities. "It is a bringing of oneself to flourishing completion, an unfolding of what is strongest or best in oneself, so that it represents the successful culmination of one's aspirations or potentialities," Gewirth wrote in *Self-Fulfillment* (1998). The way we realize our potential is through our activities. By ceaselessly striving to improve at the things we enjoy, we come to define, enlarge, and attain our best selves. These activities are the bricks of our identities; if we didn't write or play baseball or cook or litigate (or whatever it is we do well), we would cease to be who we are. This is what Karl Marx was describing when he wrote, "Milton produced *Paradise Lost* as a silkworm produces silk, as the activation of his own nature."

In this mode of living, character isn't something one forges as a youth and then retains thereafter. Morality doesn't come to one in a single revelation or a grand moment of epiphany. Instead, virtue and character are achieved gradually and must be maintained through a relentless struggle for self-improvement. We are in an ongoing dialogue with our inadequacies, and we are happiest when we are most deeply engaged in overcoming them.

This is not a solitary process. Once ensconced in an activity, we find ourselves surrounded by mentors, coaches, teachers, colleagues, teammates, consultants, readers, and audience members. Society helps us in two ways. First, it gives us opportunities to participate in the things that will allow us to realize our capacities: Parents earnestly cast about for activities their children will love, and then spend their weekends driving them from one to another. Good schools have extracurricular offerings. Good companies and organizations allow their employees and members to explore new skills, and great nations have open, fluid societies—so that individuals can find their best avenues and go as far as their merit allows.

Second, society surrounds the individual with a web of instruction, encouragement, and recognition. The hunger for recognition is a great motivator for the meritocrat. People define themselves in part by the extent to which others praise and appreciate them. In traditional societies recognition was determined by birth, breeding, and social station, but in a purified meritocracy people have to win it through performance. Each person responds to signals from those around him, working hard at activities that win praise and abandoning those that don't. (America no doubt leads the world in trophy production per capita.) An individual's growth, then, is a joint project of the self and society.

In this joint project individuals not only improve their capacities; they also come to realize that they cannot fully succeed unless they make a contribution to the society that helped to shape them. A scientist may be good at science, but she won't feel fulfilled unless she has made important discoveries or innovations that help those around her. Few meritocrats are content to master pointless tasks.

Social contributions—giving back—flow easily and naturally from the meritocrat's life mission. Baseball players enjoy clinics where they share tips with younger players. Parents devote many hours to coaching, or they become teachers, managers, and mentors. In the best relationships what follows is a sort of love affair. Mentor and pupil work hard to help each other and to honor each other's effort. Most find that they glimpse their best selves while working with others on an arduous undertaking, whether it is staging a play, competing for a championship, or arguing a case in court.

The great moral contest for the meritocrat is not between good and evil or virtue and vice. Most meritocrats are prudent, so they don't commit terrible crimes or self-destructive follies. The great temptation is triviality. Society recognizes the fulfillment of noble capacities, but it also rewards shallow achievements. A person can be famous simply for being rich or good-looking. Sometimes it's the emptiest but splashiest activities that win the most attention. It can be easy to fall into a comfortable pattern of self-approval. Society seems to be rewarding you for what you are doing. Your salary goes up. You get promoted. You win bonuses. But you haven't tapped your capacities to the fullest.

Meritocrats therefore face a continual struggle to choose worthy opportunities over trivial ones. Charles Taylor argues that each of us has an intuitive ability to make what he calls "strong evaluations" of which aspirations are noblest. We do this, he believes, by tapping into any of a variety of moral frameworks, which have been handed down through time and which have "significance independent of us or our desires." It is necessary, then, to dig deep into what it means to be a Christian or a Jew or an American or a doctor. By this way of thinking, society's rebels had it all wrong when they tried to find self-fulfillment by breaking loose from tradition. Their rebellions created selves without roots or moral reference points. Burrowing down into an inherited tradition allows the meritocrat to strive upward.

For decades social critics have sold Americans short. All those books about the Organization Man, the culture of narcissism, the last man, and the flat, commercial materialism of American life underestimated the struggles and opportunities to build character that are embedded in the meritocratic system. The critics applied bygone codes to today's way of life. Inevitably, they have found kids, and us, wanting, and not in the areas where we truly are wanting (chief among these being that we don't sufficiently educate our children in the substance of the moral traditions they are inheriting—the history of Christianity, the history of Judaism, the history of America).

Today's kids live amid peace and prosperity, true. But theirs is not an easy life. Has there ever been a generation compelled to accomplish so much—to establish an identity, succeed in school, cope with technological change, maneuver through the world of group dating and diverse sexual orientation, and make daily decisions about everything from cell-phone rate plans to brands of sugar substitute? The meritocrat's life is radically open, but its very openness creates a series of choices and challenges that are demanding and subtle because they are never-ending and because they are embedded in the pattern of every-day life—rather than being faced, say, at one crucial, life-determining moment on the battlefield.

There is virtue in trying to articulate the codes we live by, open and diverse and sprawling as those codes may be. Perhaps if we can reach a reasonably accurate understanding of the moral landscape of our lives, we will be better able to achieve our dreams and guide our ethical debates—though we will no doubt still have need of protective headgear.

Children, Wired: For Better and For Worse

Daphne Bavelier, C. Shawn Green, and Matthew W. G. Dye

Children encounter technology constantly at home and in school. Television, DVDs, video games, the Internet, and smart phones all play a formative role in children's development. The term "technology" subsumes a large variety of somewhat independent items, and it is no surprise that current research indicates causes for both optimism and concern depending upon the content of the technology, the context in which the technology immerses the user, and the user's developmental stage. Furthermore, because the field is still in its infancy, results can be surprising: video games designed to be reasonably mindless result in widespread enhancements of various abilities, acting, we will argue, as exemplary learning tools. Counterintuitive outcomes like these, besides being practically relevant, challenge and eventually lead to refinement of theories concerning fundamental principles of brain plasticity and learning.

Introduction

It is Monday morning at 7:58 A.M. when John enters the building. Immediately a dossier is uploaded to his iPad, complete with a schedule, maps to relevant locations, and background information for the various tasks he will need to complete. As

Reprinted from *Neuron*, September 9, 2010, by permission of Elsevier Inc.

he reads that his first assignment begins in 2 minutes in the physics lab two floors above, his walk becomes a light jog . . .

In this story John is not a spy, but is instead an average eighth grader sometime in the near future. In the physics lab, he will have to complete computer-administered problem sets on Newton's laws and work with a team to build a video game that incorporates the principles he has learned. While this scenario may seem far-fetched, pilot programs such as the School of One (2010) or the Quest to Learn (2010) program have already embarked on this journey, exploring how technology may be best harnessed for teaching.

Beyond these limited and controlled settings though, a far larger experiment of nature is unfolding before our eyes. While there are certainly innate or genetic limitations to our various capabilities, an enormous part of "who we are" is shaped by our experiences—experiences that today are defined by the pervasive influence of technology. This fact is particularly relevant in the case of children, both because children are at the forefront of the technological revolution (Rideout and Hamel, 2006) and because the developing brain is more malleable in response to experience than is the adult brain (Neville et al., 2009; Hensch, 2004). The central question for researchers is therefore not whether technology is affecting cognitive development—that is a given. The question is instead, *how* is technology affecting cognitive development? Are the changes for the better or for the worse? How can we harness technology to effect more changes for the better? How do we limit technology's ability to effect changes for the worse?

However, before we can begin, we must first admit that the overarching question "How is technology affecting cognitive development?" is poorly posed. "Technology" is not a single unique entity, and thus it is unlikely to have a single unique effect. One can no more ask, "How is *technology* affecting cognitive development"? than one can ask, "How is *food* affecting physical development?" As with food, the effects of technology will depend critically on what type of technology is consumed, how much of it is consumed, and for how long it is consumed.

Persistent, but Not Transient, Effects

Technology use is associated both with transient changes in arousal/mood and with long-term changes in behavior/brain function. Therefore, in the same way one cannot simply lump together the short-term effects of consuming a single caffeinated soda with the lasting effects of consuming multiple such sodas daily for years, we need to be sure to distinguish between the temporary and the long-term effects of technology consumption. Transient changes are likely to be shared across all experiences that similarly affect mood and arousal, rather than be specific for any one type of experience. One such example of this is what has been dubbed "the Mozart Effect," or the finding that listening to an up-tempo piece of music composed by Mozart temporarily enhances performance on some IQ tests (Rauscher et al., 1993). Subsequent research demonstrated that the Mozart Effect is not specific to pieces by Mozart, or even to classical music, but instead is observed after any experience that leads to a comparable temporary increase in arousal and mood (Thompson et al., 2001). Anyone who has played, or has even watched another individual playing, many of today's video games understands technology's ability to manipulate mood and arousal. Yet, as the Mozart Effect illustrates, any temporary effect of technology use, albeit important, is unlikely to be specific to technology per se. Furthermore, because changes in mood and arousal quickly diminish and eventually disappear following the cessation of the experience, so too do the changes in behavior. Because our interest is in sustained behavioral outcomes, the remainder of the review will therefore focus on the long-term effects of technology use, where changes induced by technology are visible for days, months, or even years afterwards.

Content Matters

In the same way that there is no single effect of "eating food," there is also no single effect of "watching television" or "playing video games." Different foods contain different chemical components and thus lead to different physiological effects; different kinds of media have different content, task requirements, and attentional demands and thus lead to different behavioral effects. Even products that seem on the surface to be extremely similar—for instance, the children's television shows "Dora the Explorer" and "Teletubbies"—can lead to markedly different effects (e.g., exposure to "Dora the Explorer" is associated with an increase in vocabulary and expressive language skills in two-year-olds, while exposure to "Teletubbies" is associated with a decrease in both measures; Linebarger and Walker, 2005). Furthermore, again as with food, the actual consequence of exposure to a given form of technology can confound "common sense" predictions. Technology specifically developed for the purpose of enhancing cognitive abilities, such as infant-directed media including the "Baby Einstein" collection or various "brain games" designed for adults, may lead to no effects or, worse, may lead to unanticipated negative effects (Owen et al., 2010; Zimmerman et al., 2007). Meanwhile, technological applications that on the surface seem rather mindless (such as action video games) can result in improvements in a number of basic attentional, motor, and visual skills (Green and Bavelier, 2008; Greenfield, 2009). Thus, although content clearly matters, the disconnect that can occur between the predicted and actual outcomes is a clarion call for more theoretically driven work in this new, emerging field.

Causes for Optimism and Concern

While a strictly dichotomous classification into "good" and "bad" makes for nice headlines (e.g., "Coffee: Science Says It's Good for You!"), such a scheme ignores the fact that human experience is intrinsically multidimensional; almost all experiences are "good" in some ways and "bad" in others. Not surprisingly, then, technology has been linked with both positive and negative effects (Johnson, 2005; Small and Vorgan, 2008). Here we consider the behavioral and cognitive effects of technology use separated by the intent of the technology. We will first examine the effects of "educational" technology, followed by the effects of "entertainment" technology. As we will see, some products designed to benefit cognitive development actually hinder it, while some products designed purely for entertainment purposes lead to long-lasting benefits.

Educational Media

Lessons from 60 Years of Television. Television first entered our households more than 60 years ago, and for nearly as long, individuals have sought to harness the form for the betterment of children. Because the introduction of television in the 1950s did not occur simultaneously throughout America, but was instead geographically localized, this allowed researchers to follow preschoolers who had access to television and compare them to preschoolers from matching demographics who happened to live in an area where television was introduced later. Preschoolers whose family owned a television set showed an overall positive, albeit small, effect years later on their adolescent test scores as compared with those that did not view television as preschoolers (Gentzkow and Shapiro, 2008). Although suggestive, this positive outcome could be due to the stimulating effect of introducing a new experience in the life of preschoolers rather than the specific technology per se. Of greater interest is the research that has compared and refined television programs intended specifically for young children. And indeed, although the literature is certainly mixed, exposure during the preschool years (2.5 years to 5 years) to certain educational media has been linked to many positive effects (Anderson et al., 2001). For instance, a number of shows over the years have been developed in an attempt to promote language literacy and early mathematical skills in children. "Sesame Street," which premiered in 1969, has been repeatedly associated with various positive outcomes including school readiness, vocabulary size, and numeracy skills (Zill et al., 1994; Fisch and Truglio, 2001; Schmidt and Anderson, 2007). Relatively newer programs including "Blue's Clues," "Dora the Explorer," and "Clifford the Big Red Dog" have also been correlated with positive outcomes such as greater vocabulary and higher expressive language skills (Linebarger and Walker, 2005). Whereas these studies are typically correlational in nature (i.e., cross-sectional or longitudinal designs), a recent randomized controlled trial in preschoolers, the Ready to Learn Initiative, compared a literacy curriculum that included television shows such as "Sesame Street" with a science curriculum with more science-based television shows (Penuel et al., 2009). After 10 weeks, the students in the literacy group showed increased literacy skills as compared with those in the science group, indicating a direct causal link between the media activities in the literacy curriculum and improvements in literacy.

However, it is not the case that all television/media intended for children have positive effects. For example, time spent watching the children's television show "Teletubbies" has been linked with a reduction in language skills (Linebarger and Walker, 2005). Such contrasts in outcome—between "Sesame Street," "Blue's Clues," "Clifford the Big Red Dog," and "Dora the Explorer" on one hand, and "Teletubbies" on the other—are theoretically important because they allow us to ask what characteristics lead to beneficial outcomes and what characteristics lead to negative outcomes. In the case of promoting early literacy, the use of child-directed speech, elicitation of responses, object labeling, and/or a coherent storybook-like framework throughout the show appears positively related to vocabulary acquisition and better language expression (Linebarger and Walker, 2005). Thus, to be effective, early intervention programs need not only engage the young viewer, but they

117

must also elicit direct participation from the child, provide a strong language model, avoid overloading the child with distracting stimulation, and include a well-articulated narrative structure. In addition, effective educational shows also exemplify how to resolve social conflicts and productively manage disagreements and frustration. This social teaching may be as important to child development as academic content, because antisocial behavior has been linked to poor academic outcomes (Caprara et al., 2000). The advances in our understanding of the content and structures that best foster learning in young children have only been possible by strong partnerships between content producers and scientific researchers that were first formed in the early days of public broadcasting. Unfortunately, the economics of television, and media at large, has shifted since those early days, creating an ever-widening gap between the entertainment industry and educational media, severely diminishing the ability of those seeking to create educational media to leverage the knowledge and infrastructure possessed by the entertainment industry (Mayo, 2009).

Formal and Informal Access to Media. A recurrent concern about television viewing is the passive mode it enforces upon the user. The best television shows (given the goal of enhancing cognitive development) foster active participation of the viewers, such as asking the child to repeat, point, or answer questions at the same time as the lead character. Given the importance of active participation, it is no surprise that personal computers and the interactive opportunities they afford have recently captured the attention of policy makers and educators as a tool for learning (Wellings and Levine, 2009). The data are still relatively scarce, but again a positive trend is emerging (Vogel et al., 2006; Greenfield, 2009). Computer access in informal settings outside of school improves school readiness and enhances academic achievement in young children as well as older ones (Li and Atkins, 2004; Fiorini, 2010; Beltran et al., 2008). In one such study conducted in the U.S., home computer ownership was associated with a 7% greater probability of graduating from high school, even after controlling for a number of confounding factors such as parental and home characteristics (Beltran et al., 2008). The impact of home computer use on social and emotional skills is more mixed. Whereas some studies report no effect, others document both positive and negative effects (Fiorini, 2010; Subrahmanyam et al., 2001; Kutner and Olson, 2008).

Current theories suggest that technology in informal settings may have positive effects because the activities it displaces are presumed to be of low educational value, such as hanging around with friends, playing sports, or watching entertainment television shows. This time displacement hypothesis contends that technology use has no intrinsic value per se, but instead has value only with respect to the activities it displaces (Vandewater et al., 2006; Mutz et al., 1993). Such a hypothesis leads to the prediction that technology in school settings, which displaces an already rich academic content, may not produce more learning than what human teachers are currently facilitating (and could even produce less; Angrist and Lavy, 2002). Consistent with this view, technology use in the K–12 school setting has led to mixed outcomes. An instructional computer program known as FastForWord designed to train language skills did not lead to widespread gain in either language acquisition or reading skills when introduced in U.S. grades 3–6 (Rouse and Krueger, 2004), and in one of the most comprehensive studies of its kind, conducted by the U.S. Department of Education, various types of reading software were not associated with enhanced literacy in first and fourth graders (Dynarski et al., 2007). The case for mathematics software seems more hopeful. Although some studies report no effect (Dynarski et al., 2007), many others indicate an increase in mathematics test scores (Banerjee et al., 2007; Barrow et al., 2009; Kebritchi et al., 2010).

All parties agree that more research on this topic is needed, but two caveats come to mind. First, it seems urgent to run randomized, controlled studies in which the control group does not just follow the standard math or literacy curriculum. Introduction of new media in a school curriculum may stimulate students just because of the novelty of the experience and the resulting "I am special" feeling it may engender in students. However, once the media becomes the norm, such an effect would vanish. Studies need to establish that it is the *content* of the media that triggers the increase in knowledge. Second, while a key goal of the educational system is certainly to teach the basics of literacy and mathematics, it also aims to prepare students for the workforce in a 21st century economy. Given this, introducing technology in schools becomes not just a passing fad, but an educational necessity. This seems all the more urgent because a child in a family with a low socioeconomic status is more likely to suffer from lack of technology access and thus is more likely to be "left behind" (Attewell, 2001; Wenglinsky, 1998; Siegler and Ramani, 2008; Mackey et al., 2010).

Finally, it is striking that most, if not all, of the studies that address the impact of technology on academic achievement do so using standardized tests developed in the 20th century. Whether these tests are valid tools to evaluate how well our educational system prepares children for the demands of the 21st century economy remains largely unaddressed. Indeed, this may prove to be a significant challenge, because digital literacy is likely to become a key determinant of productivity and creativity.

Entertainment Media

While exposure to educational media is increasingly prevalent in the early 21st century, the preponderance of exposure to technology comes from entertainment media. This content, rather than being driven by the goal of improving human development, is driven exclusively by what sells—and what sells may not be the things that are good for us! Current research indicates that children may be wired, but also as a result, they may also be more violent, addicted, and distracted.

Violence. Perhaps the number one concern regarding the influence of technology among the general public is the potential for media to increase behavioral aggression and violent conduct. Children are often exposed to violent media, whether it is through television or video games (60% of TV programs contained violence in 1997 and this number is unlikely to be lower now, and 94% of games that are rated as appropriate for teenagers contain some violence; Wilson et al., 1997; Roberts et al., 2005; Haninger and Thompson, 2004). Because young children develop beliefs about social norms and acceptable behavior based on the content of their experiences, any activity that promotes violence is likely to be a risk factor for violent behavior in adulthood and is worthy of careful scientific examination. Meta-analyses, combining data from hundreds of individual studies, confirm an association between exposure to violence in media and antisocial tendencies such as aggression (note that aggression in this literature does not exclusively refer to aggressive or violent actions, but also includes aggressive thoughts or violent feelings; Huesmann, 2009; Gentile et al., 2009; Paik and Comstock, 1994). Because long-term intervention studies are unethical, the best studies in this domain are arguably of the longitudinal variety, where a group of children is followed for several months or years, with researchers quantifying how their aggressive behavior evolves as a function of exposure to violent media. The effect size in these longitudinal studies, while again statistically significant, is small compared to other public health effects, accounting for less than 1% of the variance when confounding factors like gender are controlled for (whether these effects are large enough to be practically relevant is a matter of intense current debate; Gentile et al., 2009; Ferguson and Kilburn, 2009; 2010; Ferguson, 2007; Bushman et al., 2010). Thus, while exposure to violent media in childhood should be of concern, it should not overshadow addressing other known causes of aggressive behavior such as abusive home environments, substance abuse, and poor performance in school (Ferguson et al., 2008).

Addiction. A second growing concern is the potential for some forms of technology to be addictive. Anecdotal examples of technology addiction constantly hit the headlines—e.g., a 28-year-old collapsed on his game console in an Internet cafe after playing the game Starcraft for 50 hr in a row with only short pauses for basic needs (BBC News, 2005); a couple starved their 3-month-old baby girl to death as a result of becoming obsessed with caring for a virtual girl in the role-playing online game Prius (CNN News, 2010). While incidents of this severity are isolated, the general phenomena appear to be much more widespread. Recent surveys indicate that about 2% of youth can be described as having Internet addiction with 10%–20% engaging in at-risk Internet use (Johansson and Götestam, 2004; Cao and Su, 2007).

Actual scientific research on the topic has been somewhat hindered by the lack of firmly established standards (Byun et al., 2009). The American Medical Association does not currently recognize video game and Internet addiction as psychiatric disorders (see arguments for and against its recognition; Block, 2008; Pies, 2009). However, there does appear to be an emerging scientific consensus that Internet use and video game play has the potential to become pathological, with researchers adopting and/or adapting the criteria for pathological gambling (Tejeiro Salguero and Morán, 2002; Gentile, 2009; Griffiths and Hunt, 1998; Lam and Peng, 2010). It is important to note that "pathological" means more than simply spending a substantial amount of time playing video games or using the Internet—rather, it implies an actual reduction in the ability of the individual to function normally in society. Thus, while some individuals may be able to invest large amounts of their time in technology use without becoming a pathological user, others may exhibit pathological signs with relatively lighter use (Gentile, 2009; Han et al., 2007). Professional gamers, for example, may spend several hours a day training to perfect their skills without their behavior becoming pathological; such deliberate choice to practice a skill over engaging in other activities is a key determinant of expertise (Ericsson et al., 1993), be it in chess, music, or in this case, video game play.

A key issue for future research concerns the neural pathways involved in pathological use of technology. The fronto-striatal pathway, which has been strongly implicated in both drug addiction and behavioral disorders such as pathological gambling (Hyman et al., 2006; Miedl et al., 2010; Hewig et al., 2010), is also activated by interaction with certain types of media technology, video games in particular (Han et al., 2007; Hoeft et al., 2008; Koepp et al., 1998; Matsuda and Hiraki, 2006). Unfortunately, little is known about how these pathways mature or how their development is affected by technology use. Such research seems urgently needed given how disruptive technology use may be to some children's ability to function normally in society.

Distraction. We watch television while playing games on our laptops; we take part in meetings while checking email on our phones; we browse the web while instant messaging with friends—and frankly, some of us have probably done all of these things simultaneously. Technology allows an incredible amount of information and potential stimulation to be constantly, and concurrently, accessible. However, there may be a behavioral cost to such multitasking in the form of attentional difficulties. For instance, in a recent study, Ophir et al. (2009) asked more than 250 Stanford University students about their use of different media forms, from print media to video games to web surfing. Those who reported high concurrent usage of several types of media were less able to filter out distracting information in their environment, more likely to be distracted by irrelevant information in memory, and less efficient when they were required to quickly switch from one task to another. Other studies have also linked time spent using technology with negative effects such as teacher-reported problems, paying attention in class, and deficits in attention, visual memory, imagination, and sleep (Swing et al., 2010; Kumari and Ahuja, 2010; Dworak et al., 2007).

Is Technology to Blame? Although there are clearly a number of potentially negative effects associated with technology use, the interpretation of these studies is not as straightforward as it appears at first glance. For example, most of these studies tabulate only total hours spent using technology rather than classifying technology use as a function of content type. As content clearly matters, the results from such reports are inherently noisy and thus provide unreliable data. Second, the vast majority of the work is correlational in nature and as we know, correlation per se cannot be used to infer causation.

Technology use, in particular, is highly correlated with other factors that are strong predictors of poor behavioral outcomes, making it difficult to disentangle the true causes of the observations. For instance, children who watch the most television also tend to live in lower income homes and tend to have mothers with lower levels of education, both of which are strong predictors of a variety of diminished capabilities. In one large study of 800 infants, average daily television exposure was strongly correlated with lower language skills at 3 years of age when such factors were not considered, but when these (and many additional factors, some as detailed as the length of breast feeding) were controlled for, no relationship between television exposure and language development was observed (Schmidt et al., 2009). Furthermore, children who have attentional problems may very well be attracted to technology because of the constant variety of activities it permits. Accordingly, the strength of the relationship between technology use and attention disorders is significantly reduced after controlling for whether the child suffered from attentional problems at the start of the study (Swing et al., 2010). Although researchers nearly always attempt to statistically control for known confounding variables, the possibility of additional lurking variables always remains. Controlled intervention studies would avoid these potential pitfalls and demonstrate a clear causal relationship between technology use and behavioral outcomes.

Although there are clear ethical concerns in doing large-scale randomized interventions when the predicted result is a long-term negative behavioral effect, these are not beyond our reach and are, we would argue, critical to society. A possible route is to select parents who plan to introduce a new technology in their homes and ask half of them to delay the introduction of the new technology by a few months, allowing researchers to compare children with and without access to the technology. A recent study by Weis and Cerankosky (2010) followed a similar logic to test the hypothesis that video game console ownership negatively affects academic performance. A large group of parents who were planning on purchasing video game consoles for their children were promised a video game console in exchange for their children participating in the study. The children were then split into two groups; the researchers provided consoles for one group immediately, while the other group did not receive their consoles for 4 months. Over the course of those 4 months, those children that received consoles demonstrated significant reductions in reading and writing skills (more than one-half of a standard deviation in the case of writing) as compared with the control group of peers who did not receive consoles yet. Teachers also tended to rate those children who received their consoles immediately as having greater learning difficulties, although no attentional problems were observed. We would note for future studies that, given the distinctly negative hypothesized effect of the introduction of technology in this case, there are definite ethical concerns about researchers actually providing the technology of interest and failing to inform the parents as to the true hypothesis being tested, both of which were true of this study. A more ethical design may involve researchers encouraging a subset of parents who are planning to introduce technology that has a predicted negative effect to not do so, while not intervening in a corresponding group (in which case the intervention has a predicted positive effect).

Defying Common Sense: "Good" Things Can Be Bad and "Bad" Things Can Be Good

When Good Turns Out Bad. The past decade has seen an explosion in the popularity of "baby DVDs," or media designed to enhance the cognitive capabilities of infants and toddlers. Forty percent of parents believe that child-friendly programming may benefit their infant or toddler, and some estimates suggest that roughly one in three U.S. infants were exposed to baby DVDs. However, this boom now appears to be a case of marketing and parents' common sense beliefs outpacing actual science. At best, current research suggests that these DVDs produce no changes in cognitive development—for instance, babies exposed to DVDs designed to teach new words, such as *Baby-Wordsworth* (The Baby Einstein Company; Glendale, CA), show no evidence of specific word learning (Richert et al., 2010; Robb et al., 2009). More worrisome however is that some studies actually report negative effects (Zimmerman and Christakis, 2005). For example, in a recent cross-sectional study, Zimmerman et al. (2007) surveyed over 1,000 parents of 2- to 24-month old children. The parents were asked questions about general demographics and their child's television and DVD viewing habits, and were asked to complete a measure of language development. A large negative association between viewing baby DVDs (e.g., "Baby Einstein" or "Brainy Baby") and language development score was found for the youngest children (8–16 months), or in other words, each hour of daily viewing/listening in this group was associated with a significant decrement in the pace of language development. Furthermore, the size of the decrement was not minor—whereas daily reading with a parent is associated with a 7-point increase in language score, each hour of daily baby DVD viewing was associated with a 17-point decrease. What is the reason for this? Babies learn an enormous amount from real-world experience as they watch their parents or caregivers interact with the world or with them, yet when the same material is delivered through audiovisual media, much less is learned (Kuhl et al., 2003; Krcmar, 2010). Although videos are capable of attracting babies' attention (Barr et al., 2008), this alone is not necessarily sufficient to induce learning. A key determinant of whether learning occurs may be the ability of the infant to appreciate the symbolic nature of the video (DeLoache and Chiong, 2009). Very young children may not always be able to link objects, persons, and events in a video to reality. Therefore, young learners may not reach a maturational state at which they can truly learn from media until their preschool years. Research on technology and brain development may benefit from more systematically addressing the cognitive state of the learner, especially when it comes to the boundaries between video content, reality, and fantasy.

When Bad Turns Out Good. Although entertainment media is typically designed for entertainment purposes only, some forms of this technology have exhibited effects far beyond simple amusement. For instance, action video games, where avatars run about elaborate landscapes while eliminating enemies with well-placed shots, are often thought of as rather mindless by parents. However, a burgeoning literature indicates that playing action video games is associated with a number of enhancements in vision, attention, cognition, and motor control (for a review see Green and Bavelier, 2008). For instance, action video game experience heightens the ability to view small details in cluttered scenes and to perceive dim signals, such as would be present when driving in fog (Green and Bavelier, 2007; Li et al., 2009). Avid players display enhanced top-down control of attention and choose among different options more rapidly (Hubert-Wallander et al., 2010; Dye et al., 2009a). They also exhibit better visual short-term memory (Boot et al., 2008; Green and Bavelier, 2006), and can more flexibility switch from one task to another (Boot et al., 2008; Colzato et al., 2010; Karle et al., 2010).

Furthermore, these enhancements have been found to have real-world applications. On the medical front, action games have been harnessed for the rehabilitation of patients with amblyopia, a developmental deficit of vision (Li et al., 2010), and are being considered to treat attentional problems in children (NASA, 2003). Playing games, especially in a virtual reality environment, also appears to increase pain tolerance in both controls and patients (Mahrer and

Gold, 2009). On the job-training front, laparoscopic surgeons who are habitual video game players have been observed to be better surgeons than their more experienced peers, both in terms of their speed of execution and their reliability during surgery (Rosser et al., 2007; Lynch et al., 2010). Video game play also appears to be useful training for pilots (Gopher et al., 1994). Following this trend, in 2009, the Royal Air Force stopped requiring that only trained pilots control unmanned drone flight missions and opened its door to less experienced young gamers, after studies indicated that the best drone pilots were often young video game players (Daily Mail, 2009). This is not to say that all aspects of behavior may change for the better as a result of action video game play, but this abridged list already indicates much more benefit than one would have immediately suspected from watching an average 14-year-old blast monsters.

One of the strong points of the action video game literature is that, in contrast to much of the literature discussed earlier, a direct causal relationship has been established between the action game experience and the behavioral outcomes. The impact of action game play has been causally related to improved performance by having non-game players play action games for an extended period of time (e.g., 50 total hours spaced over 6 weeks) in a controlled laboratory environment. Furthermore, in addition to this experimental intervention group, these studies always also include a control group of subjects, drawn from the same participant pool as the experimental group, but who are required to play *non-action* games. These non-action games are also commercially available entertainment games, selected in part to be as equally enticing and stimulating as action games. All participants undergo visual, attentional, or cognitive tests before and after their respective video game training. Importantly, the post-tests take place at least 24 hr. after the final session of video game play to ensure that any effects cannot be attributed to temporary changes in mood or arousal. Clear enhancements are noted in those that underwent action game training as compared with control game training. Furthermore, these effects last much longer than a few days after the final training session—in fact, enhancements are still noted anywhere from 6 months to 2 or more years later (Feng et al., 2007; Li et al., 2009). While a strong causal link has been observed between action game experience and improvements in perceptual, attentional, and cognitive skills, it should be noted that these studies have been carried out exclusively in young adults (18–30 years old), as it is ethically questionable to train children on action games (which tend to contain significant amounts of violence). However, despite the lack of training studies in children, we know that children who report playing action games show significantly increased attentional skills as compared with those who do not (Dye et al., 2009b; Dye and Bavelier, 2010; Trick et al., 2005). On some measures of attention, such as the temporal dynamics of attention, 7- to 10-year-old action gamers function at adult levels, indicating significant deviations from age-related norms.

Action video game training is of substantial theoretical interest because the improvements in performance that occur as a result of such training also transfer to tasks beyond the training regimen itself. In other words, playing an action game results in behavioral changes in nongaming environments. This is in strict contrast with most other training regimens, wherein the learning is highly specific to the exact task, stimuli, and environment used during training (Fahle and Poggio, 2002; Fine and Jacobs, 2002; Owen et al., 2010). A possible mechanism for such wide transfer after action video game play may be that this activity teaches the player how to swiftly adapt to current task demands. Action game players may dynamically retune connectivity across and within different brain areas to augment information processing, and may thus be in a position to make more informed decisions. This was recently confirmed experimentally in the case of perceptually driven decisions (Green et al., 2010). According to this view, action video game experience would promote an essential feature of human cognition, "learning to learn." This proposal is appealing because it readily captures why the effects of action game play transfer so widely. It will be, however, for future work to assess whether this "learning to learn" benefit is also found when information has to be retrieved from internal representations rather than from the external environment, such as when one thinks or solves problems.

The contrast between the widespread benefits observed after playing action video games and the limited value of training on "mini brain games" suggests that we may need to drastically rethink how educational games should be structured. While action game developers intuitively value emotional content, arousing experiences, and richly structured scenarios, educational games have until now, for the most part, shied away from these attractive features that video games offer. Instead, educational games have mostly exploited the interactivity and the repetitive nature of practice-makes-perfect that computer-based games can afford—often reducing the experience to automated flashcards. It is only very recently that the richness that the video game medium has to offer has been considered as an integral part of the learning experience (Mayo, 2009; Gee, 2003). However, in such rich environments, only a fine line separates a stimulating and successful media from an overloading experience, making the development of such games challenging (Kalyuga and Plass, 2009). Dimension M (from Tabula Digita), an action-packed video game geared toward teaching linear algebra to seventh and eighth graders, represents one such first attempt, and early results appear promising. In a recent intervention study, its introduction into high school mathematics classes led to significant benefits on benchmark mathematics tests (Kebritchi et al., 2010). Yet a gap remains between the entertainment industry and such "Serious Game" initiatives (Mayo, 2009). Theoretical work suggests that when the concepts to be learned are experienced across multiple contexts and domains, learning is more likely to transfer to new tasks or situations beyond those experienced during training (Schmidt and Bjork, 1992; Kornell and Bjork, 2008). The highly complex architecture of action games, afforded by sophisticated game engines, ensures a variety of emotional, cognitive, and attentional states as the player progresses in the game, which should foster learning and its transfer to new situations. In an elegant evaluation of this claim, Gentile and Gentile (2008) have shown that this is indeed the case with the violent content action games typically contain. Action games, thanks to their rich structure, efficiently teach aggression. Replacing violent content with educational content is not out of reach, but it will require a degree of sophistication in game design and financial means that may call for a coherent, multidisciplinary "Big Science" approach rather than the proliferation of small, fragmented, and often uncoordinated endeavors.

Understanding Wired Brains

Much of what we know about technology and child development has been driven by advances in the fields of education and behavioral sciences. Yet, understanding how the brain is altered by technology use is essential to a furthering of this emerging field. Granted, no one will be surprised to learn that the visual cortex is activated when one watches a video, or that the motor cortex is challenged when playing an action game. Of greater interest is our understanding of how technology impacts regular brain functioning and changes brain organization over time. This calls for an array of studies, given the need to separately address different types of technology and content, as well as users. A recent seminal study by Brem et al. (2010) compared the impact of playing a grapheme-to-phoneme game versus a mathematics game in 6- to 7-year-olds on the maturation of the visual word form area (VWFA), a brain area important in mediating literacy. As assessed by functional magnetic resonance imaging, the group trained with the phoneme-to-grapheme game showed greater maturation of the VWFA than the control group, suggesting direct involvement of the VWFA in the acquisition of reading skills. In a similar vein, Rueda et al. (2005) compared the impact of playing simple games aimed at training attention versus watching popular children's videos in 4- and 6-year-olds. Event-related potentials revealed more adult-like markers of the executive attention network after attention-game training than after watching videos. A working hypothesis is that the attention-game training may have allowed the brain system mediating conflict resolution to become more efficient, as it would during typical development. It is worth noting that in both this study and the Brem study, experimental trainees demonstrated significant brain changes from pre- to post-test compared with the control group, but with no significant behavioral improvement differences. Thus, brain-imaging studies may provide a more sensitive assay of the effects of technology than do behavioral studies. Brain imaging can also be used to document whose brain may best benefit from technology. In a recent study, structural brain scans of young adults were acquired before they learned to play a first generation computer game, Space Fortress (University of Illinois; Erickson et al., 2010). Those individuals with an initially larger caudate nucleus and putamen, two basal ganglia nuclei involved in the control of movement, reinforcement learning, and reward, were most likely to learn efficiently. In contrast, the size of the hippocampus, a key structure in memory and learning for declarative knowledge, was not predictive of learning. Thus, a computer game like Space Fortress requires cognitive and motor control skills best predicted by structures that regulate habit formation and reward processing rather than content learning.

Another fruitful line of research will be the investigation of which events during technology use enhance learning and brain plasticity. It is only recently that we have acquired the means to follow brain activity in real time as participants interact with technology (Spiers and Maguire, 2007). Thanks to these developments, we are in a position to isolate from a continuous media stream key events hypothesized to foster learning and brain plasticity (such as rewarding or salient events). Then by injecting content along with these events, learning can be directly assessed. This approach builds on an ever-growing literature documenting the critical role of neuromodulators in the control of learning and brain plasticity. Events that are arousing, and thus likely to trigger a release of acetylcholine, are prime targets for such a manipulation (Kilgard and Merzenich, 1998). It is hypothesized that acetylcholine facilitates the retuning of existing connectivity in an experience-dependent manner, which allows for better behavioral inference from the learned experience (Yu and Dayan, 2005; Goard and Dan, 2009). Dopamine, a neuromodulator implicated in executive functions and the control of attention, also promotes brain plasticity. Its concurrent release during an auditory tone discrimination task increased the cortical area and the receptive field selectivity to learned tones in rats (Bao et al., 2001). This facilitatory effect was obtained by stimulating the origin of dopaminergic cell bodies, the ventral tegmental area, which is not only a key player in motivation and reward, but also in drug addiction. Unfortunately, only mixed reports exist about neuromodulator release and technology use (Koepp et al., 1998; Egerton et al., 2009). Future research should capitalize on all of the tools at our disposal, from traditional neuroscience techniques such as PET and fMRI (Egerton et al., 2009; Shapiro et al., 2010) to the wealth of new tools becoming available, including cameras that monitor facial emotions, smart controllers that record galvanic skin response and heart rate, and helmets fitted with electrodes that assess brain state, so as to adapt media experience in real time according to the user's current experience.

Finally, the possibility of developing an animal model of young, wired learners is not as far-fetched as it may seem. Using a new virtual reality system in which a mouse interacts with a virtual maze through a spherical treadmill, Harvey et al. (2009) have characterized the intracellular dynamics of hippocampal coding in awake, behaving animals. Adapting such virtual navigation systems to study decision making and learning in fast-paced, mice-enticing environments will certainly require new developments, but appears within reach.

Concluding Remarks

The past half-century has seen a dramatic increase in the amount of technology available to and used by children—a fact that has clearly shaped the way children learn, develop, and behave. Given the multifaceted nature of technology, it is perhaps unsurprising that the story of its impact on child development is extremely complex and multisided. Some forms of technology have no effect on the form of behavior they were designed to transform, while others have effects that reach far beyond their intended outcomes. All of this is indicative of a field that is still emerging. What we do know is that, in technology, we have a set of tools that has the capability to drastically modify human behavior. What remains, which is not trivial, is to determine how to purposefully direct this capability to produce desired outcomes. In this endeavor it will be key for the field, which to this point has been largely behavioral in nature, to partner with neuroscience (Meltzoff et al., 2009). For instance, given the goal of predicting behavioral outcomes, it would likely be of substantial benefit to describe forms of technology quantitatively in terms of the neural processing they demand, rather than describe them qualitatively based upon surface characteristics. Such collaboration would also benefit neuroscientific theories of learning, as it offers an opportunity to "reverse engineer" the learning problem—starting with a tool that strongly promotes learning and determining how and why it works, rather than starting with low-level principles of neural learning and building tools that may or may not produce the desired outcomes.

Acknowledgments

We are thankful to T. Jacques as well as L. Takeuchi and G. Cayton-Hodges from the Joan Ganz Cooney Center at Sesame Workshop for their help in literature searches. We also thank T. Jacques for invaluable help with manuscript preparation. This work was funded by EY016880, the James S. McDonnell Foundation, and the Office of Naval Research (MURI Program) to D.B.

References

Anderson, D.A., Huston, A.C., Schmitt, K.L., Linebarger, D.L., and Wright, J.C. (2001). Chapter V. Creativity. Monogr. Soc. Res. Child Dev. 66, 67–78.

Angrist, J., and Lavy, V. (2002). New evidence on classroom computers and pupil learning. Econ. J. 112, 735–765.

Attewell, P. (2001). The first and second digital divides. Sociol. Educ. 74, 252–259.

Banerjee, A.V., Cole, S., Duflo, E., and Linden, L. (2007). Remedying education: Evidence from two randomized experiments in India. Q. J. Econ. 122, 1235–1264.

Bao, S., Chan, V.T., and Merzenich, M.M. (2001). Cortical remodelling induced by activity of ventral tegmental dopamine neurons. Nature *412*, 79–83.

Barr, R., Zack, E., Garcia, A., and Muentener, P. (2008). Infants' attention and responsiveness to television increases with prior exposure and parental interaction. Infancy *13*, 30–56.

Barrow, L., Markman, L., and Rouse, C.E. (2009). Technology's edge: The educational benefits of computer-aided instruction. American Economic Journal: Economic Policy *1*, 52–74.

BBC News (2005). S Korean dies after games session. BBC news. Available from http://news.bbc.co.uk/2/hi/technology/4137782.stm.

Beltran, D.O., Das, K.K., and Fairlie, R.W. (2008). Are computers good for children? The effects of home computers on educational outcomes. Discussion Paper No. 576. The Australian National University Centre for Economic Policy Research.

Block, J.J. (2008). Issues for DSM-V: internet addiction. Am. J. Psychiatry *165*, 306–307.

Boot, W.R., Kramer, A.F., Simons, D.J., Fabiani, M., and Gratton, G. (2008). The effects of video game playing on attention, memory, and executive control. Acta Psychol. (Amst.) *129*, 387–398.

Brem, S., Bach, S., Kucian, K., Guttorm, T.K., Martin, E., Lyytinen, H., Brandeis, D., and Richardson, U. (2010). Brain sensitivity to print emerges when children learn letter-speech sound correspondences. Proc. Natl. Acad. Sci. USA *107*, 7939–7944.

Bushman, B.J., Rothstein, H.R., and Anderson, C.A. (2010). Much ado about something: Violent video game effects and a school of red herring: Reply to Ferguson and Kilburn (2010). Psychol. Bull. *136*, 182–187.

Byun, S., Ruffini, C., Mills, J.E., Douglas, A.C., Niang, M., Stepchenkova, S., Lee, S.K., Loutfi, J., Lee, J.-K., Atallah, M., and Blanton, M. (2009). Internet addiction: metasynthesis of 1996–2006 quantitative research. Cyberpsychol. Behav. *12*, 203–207.

Cao, F., and Su, L. (2007). Internet addiction among Chinese adolescents: prevalence and psychological features. Child Care Health Dev. *33*, 275–281.

Caprara, G.V., Barbaranelli, C., Pastorelli, C., Bandura, A., and Zimbardo, P.G. (2000). Prosocial foundations of children's academic achievement. Psychol. Sci. *11*, 302–306.

CNN News (2010). Report: South Korean couple starved child while raising "virtual baby." CNN news. Available from http://www.cnn.com/2010/WORLD/asiapcf/03/05/korea.baby.starved.

Colzato, L.S., van Leeuwen, P.J.A., van den Wildenberg, W.P.M., and Hommel, B. (2010). DOOM'd to switch: superior cognitive flexibility in players of first person shooter games. Frontiers in Psychology *1*, 1–5.

Daily Mail, 2009. RAF jettisons its top guns: Drones to fly sensitive missions over Afghanistan. Available from http://www.dailymail.co.uk/news/worldnews/article-1158084/RAF-jettisons-Top-Guns-Drones-fly-sensitive-missions-Afghanistan.html.

DeLoache, J.S., and Chiong, C. (2009). Babies and baby media. Am. Behav. Sci. *52*, 1115–1135.

Dworak, M., Schierl, T., Bruns, T., and Strüder, H.K. (2007). Impact of singular excessive computer game and television exposure on sleep patterns and memory performance of school-aged children. Pediatrics *120*, 978–985.

Dye, M.W.G., and Bavelier, D. (2010). Differential development of visual attention skills in school-age children. Vision Res. *50*, 452–459.

Dye, M.W., Green, C.S., and Bavelier, D. (2009a). Increasing Speed of Processing With Action Video Games. Curr. Dir. Psychol. Sci. *18*, 321–326.

Dye, M.W.G., Green, C.S., and Bavelier, D. (2009b). The development of attention skills in action video game players. Neuropsychologia *47*, 1780–1789.

Dynarski, M., Agodini, R., Heaviside, S., Novak, T., Carey, N., Campuzano, L., Means, B., Murphy, R., Penuel, W., Javitz, H., Emery, D., and Sussex, W. (2007). Effectiveness of reading and mathematics software products: Findings from the first student cohort. U.S. Department of Education Report. National Center for Educational Evaluation and Regional Assistance. http://hal.archives-ouvertes.fr/hal-00190019/.

Egerton, A., Mehta, M.A., Montgomery, A.J., Lappin, J.M., Howes, O.D., Reeves, S.J., Cunningham, V.J., and Grasby, P.M. (2009). The dopaminergic basis of human behaviors: A review of molecular imaging studies. Neurosci, Biobehav. Rev. *33*, 1109–1132.

Erickson, K.I., Boot, W.R., Basak, C., Neider, M.B., Prakash, R.S., Voss, M.W., Graybiel, A.M., Simons, D.J., Fabiana, M., Gratton, G., and Kramer, A.F. (2010). Striatal volume predicts level of video game skill acquisition. Cereb. Cortex, in press. Published online January 20, 2010. 10.1093/cercor/bhp293.

Ericsson, K.A., Krampe, R.T., and Tesch-Römer, C. (1993). The role of deliberate practice in the acquisition of expert performance. Psychol. Rev. *100*, 363–406.

Fahle M. and Poggio T., eds. (2002). Perceptual Learning (Cambridge, MA: The MIT Press).

Feng, J., Spence, I., and Pratt, J. (2007). Playing an action video game reduces gender differences in spatial cognition. Psychol. Sci. *18*, 850–855.

Ferguson, C.J. (2007). Evidence for publication bias in video game violence effects literature: A meta-analytic review. Aggress. Violent. Behav. *12*, 470–482.

Ferguson, C.J., and Kilburn, J. (2009). The public health risks of media violence: a meta-analytic review. J. Pediatr. *154*, 759–763.

Ferguson, C.J., and Kilburn, J. (2010). Much ado about nothing: the misestimation and overinterpretation of violent video game effects in eastern and western nations: comment on Anderson et al. (2010). Psychol. Bull. *136*, 174–178, discussion 182–187.

Ferguson, C.J., Rueda, S.M., Cruz, A.M., Ferguson, D.E., Fritz, S., and Smith, S.M. (2008). Violent video games and aggression: Causal relationship or byproduct of family violence and intrinsic violence motivation? Crim. Justice Behav. *35*, 311–332.

Fine, I., and Jacobs, R.A. (2002). Comparing perceptual learning tasks: a review. J. Vis. *2*, 190–203.

Fiorini, M. (2010). The effect of home computer use on children's cognitive and non-cognitive skills. Econ. Educ. Rev. *29*, 55–72.

Fisch, S. and Truglio, R., eds. (2001). "G" Is for "Growing": Thirty Years of Sesame Street Research (Mahwah, NJ: Lawrence Erlbaum).

Gee, J.P. (2003). What video games have to teach us about learning and literacy. Computers in Entertainment *1*, 1–4.

Gentile, D.A. (2009). Pathological video-game use among youth ages 8 to 18: a national study. Psychol. Sci. *20*, 594–602.

Gentile, D.A., and Gentile, J.R. (2008). Violent video games as exemplary teachers: A conceptual analysis. J. Youth Adolesc. *37*, 127–141.

Gentile, D.A., Anderson, C.A., Yukawa, S., Ihori, N., Saleem, M., Ming, L.K., Shibuya, A., Liau, A.K., Khoo, A., Bushman, B.J., et al. (2009). The effects of prosocial video games on prosocial behaviors: international evidence from correlational, longitudinal, and experimental studies. Pers. Soc. Psychol. Bull. *35*, 752–763.

Gentzkow, M., and Shapiro, J.M. (2008). Preschool television viewing and adolescent test scores: Historical evidence from the Coleman study. Q. J. Econ. *123*, 279–323.

Goard, M., and Dan, Y. (2009). Basal forebrain activation enhances cortical coding of natural scenes. Nat. Neurosci. *12*, 1444–1449.

Gopher, D., Weil, M., and Bareket, T. (1994). Transfer of skill from a computer game trainer to flight. Hum. Factors *36*, 387–405.

Green, C.S., and Bavelier, D. (2006). Enumeration versus multiple object tracking: the case of action video game players. Cognition *101*, 217–245.

Green, C.S., and Bavelier, D. (2007). Action-video-game experience alters the spatial resolution of vision. Psychol. Sci. *18*, 88–94.

Green, C.S., and Bavelier, D. (2008). Exercising your brain: a review of human brain plasticity and training-induced learning. Psychol. Aging *23*, 692–701.

Green, C.S., Pouget, A., and Bavelier, D. (2010). Improved probabilistic inference as a general learning mechanism with action video games. Curr. Biol., in press.

Greenfield, P.M. (2009). Technology and informal education: what is taught, what is learned. Science *323*, 69–71.

Griffiths, M.D., and Hunt, N. (1998). Dependence on computer games by adolescents. Psychol. Rep. *82*, 475–480.

Han, D.H., Lee, Y.S., Yang, K.C., Kim, E.Y., Lyoo, I.K., and Renshaw, P.F. (2007). Dopamine genes and reward dependence in adolescents with excessive internet video game play. J. Addict. Med. *1*, 133–138.

Haninger, K., and Thompson, K.M. (2004). Content and ratings of teen-rated video games. JAMA *291*, 856–865.

Harvey, C.D., Collman, F., Dombeck, D.A., and Tank, D.W. (2009). Intracellular dynamics of hippocampal place cells during virtual navigation. Nature *461*, 941–946.

Hensch, T.K. (2004). Critical period regulation. Annu. Rev. Neurosci. *27*, 549–579.

Hewig, J., Kretschmer, N., Trippe, R.H., Hecht, H., Coles, M.G.H., Holroyd, C.B., and Miltner, W.H.R. (2010). Hypersensitivity to reward in problem gamblers. Biol. Psychol. *67*, 781–783.

Hoeft, F., Watson, C.L., Kesler, S.R., Bettinger, K.E., and Reiss, A.L. (2008). Gender differences in the mesocorticolimbic system during computer gameplay. J. Psychiatr. Res. *42*, 253–258.

Hubert-Wallander, B.P., Green, C.S., and Bavelier, D. (2010). Stretching the limits of visual attention: The case of action video games. Wiley Interdisciplinary Reviews: Cognitive Science, in press.

Huesmann, L.R. (2009). The impact of electronic media violence: Scientific theory and research. J. Adolesc. Health *41*, S6–S13.

Hyman, S.E., Malenka, R.C., and Nestler, E.J. (2006). Neural mechanisms of addiction: the role of reward-related learning and memory. Annu. Rev. Neurosci. *29*, 565–598.

Johansson, A., and Götestam, K.G. (2004). Internet addiction: characteristics of a questionnaire and prevalence in Norwegian youth (12–18 years). Scand. J. Psychol. *45*, 223–229.

Johnson, S. (2005). Everything Bad Is Good for You: How Today's Popular Culture Is Actually Making us Smarter (New York: Riverhead Books).

Kalyuga, S., and Plass, J.L. (2009). Evaluating and managing cognitive load in games. In Handbook of Research of Effective Electronic Gaming in Education, R.E. Ferdig, ed. (Hershey, PA: Information Science Reference).

Karle, J.W., Watter, S., and Shedden, J.M. (2010). Task switching in video game players: Benefits of selective attention but not resistance to proactive interference. Acta Psychol. (Amst.) *134*, 70–78.

Kebritchi, M., Hirumi, A., and Bai, H. (2010). The effects of modern mathematics computer games on mathematics achievement and class motivation. Comput. Educ. *55*, 427–443.

Kilgard, M.P., and Merzenich, M.M. (1998). Cortical map reorganization enabled by nucleus basalis activity. Science *279*, 1714–1718.

Koepp, M.J., Gunn, R.N., Lawrence, A.D., Cunningham, V.J., Dagher, A., Jones, T., Brooks, D.J., Bench, C.J., and Grasby, P.M. (1998). Evidence for striatal dopamine release during a video game. Nature *393*, 266–268.

Kornell, N., and Bjork, R.A. (2008). Learning concepts and categories: is spacing the "enemy of induction"? Psychol. Sci. *19*, 585–592.

Krcmar, M. (2010). Assessing the research on media, cognitive development, and infants. Journal of Children and Media *4*, 119–134.

Kuhl, P.K., Tsao, F.M., and Liu, H.M. (2003). Foreign-language experience in infancy: effects of short-term exposure and social interaction on phonetic learning. Proc. Natl. Acad. Sci. USA *100*, 9096–9101.

Kumari, S., and Ahuja, S. (2010). Video viewing and cognitive development in preadolescents. Soc. Sci. Comput. Rev. *28*, 170–176.

Kutner, L., and Olson, C.K. (2008). Grand Theft Childhood: The Surprising Truth about Violent Video Games and What Parents Can Do (New York: Simon & Schuster).

Lam, L.T., and Peng, Z.W. (2010). Effect of pathological use of the internet on adolescent mental health: A prospective study. Arch. Pediatr. Adolesc. Med., in press. Published online August 2, 2010. 10.1001/archpediatrics.2010.159.

Li, X., and Atkins, M.S. (2004). Early childhood computer experience and cognitive and motor development. Pediatrics *113*, 1715–1722.

Li, R., Polat, U., Makous, W., and Bavelier, D. (2009). Enhancing the contrast sensitivity function through action video game training. Nat. Neurosci. *12,* 549–551.

Li, R., Ngo, C., Nguyen, J., and Levi, D.M. (2010). Video game play induces plasticity in the visual system of adults with amblyiopia. PLoS, in press.

Linebarger, D.L., and Walker, D. (2005). Infants' and toddlers' television viewing and language outcomes. Am. Behav. Sci. *48,* 624–645.

Lynch, J., Aughwane, P., and Hammond, T.M. (2010). Video games and surgical ability: a literature review. J. Surg. Educ. *67,* 184–189.

Mackey, A.P., Hill, S.S., Stone, S.I., and Bunge, S.A. (2010). Dissociable effects of reasoning and speed training in children. Dev. Sci., in press.

Mahrer, N.E., and Gold, J.I. (2009). The use of virtual reality for pain control: a review. Curr. Pain Headache Rep. *13,* 100–109.

Matsuda, G., and Hiraki, K. (2006). Sustained decrease in oxygenated hemoglobin during video games in the dorsal prefrontal cortex: a NIRS study of children. Neuroimage *29,* 706–711.

Mayo, M.J. (2009). Video games: a route to large-scale STEM education? Science *323,* 79–82.

Meltzoff, A.N., Kuhl, P.K., Movellan, J., and Sejnowski, T.J. (2009). Foundations for a new science of learning. Science *325,* 284–288.

Miedl, S.F., Fehr, T., Meyer, G., and Herrman, M. (2010). Neurobiological correlates of problem gambling in a quasi-realistic blackjack scenerio as revealed by fMRI. Psychiatry Res. Neuroimaging *181,* 165–173.

Mutz, D.C., Roberts, D.F., and van Vuuren, D.P. (1993). Reconsidering the displacement hypothesis: Television's influence on children's time use. Communic. Res. *20,* 51–75.

National Aeronautics and Space Administration (NASA), (2003). A real attention-getter. Spinoff 2003. U.S. Government Printing Office (pamphlet). http://www.sti.nasa.gov/tto/spinoff2003/hm_2.html.

Neville, H.J. (Executive Producer), Marquez, A. (Producer/Director), Taylor, P. (Producer), and Pakulak, E. (Producer). (2009). Changing brains: Effects of experience on human brain development [Motion picture]. United States: CPR.

Ophir, E., Nass, C., and Wagner, A.D. (2009). Cognitive control in media multitaskers. Proc. Natl. Acad. Sci. USA *106,* 15583–15587.

Owen, A.M., Hampshire, A., Grahn, J.A., Stenton, R., Dajani, S., Burns, A.S., Howard, R.J., and Ballard, C.G. (2010). Putting brain training to the test. Nature *465,* 775–778.

Paik, H., and Comstock, G. (1994). The effects of television violence on antisocial behavior: A meta-analysis. Communic. Res. *21,* 516–546.

Penuel, W.R., Pasnik, S., Bates, L., Townsend, E., Gallagher, L.P., Llorente, C., and Hupert, N. (2009). Summative evaluation of the Ready to Learn initiative. Menlo Park, CA: Education Development Center, Inc.; and Newton, MA: SRI International (pamphlet).

Pies, R. (2009). Should DSM-V designate "internet addiction" a mental disorder? Psychiatry (Edgmont) *6,* 31–37.

Quest to Learn (2010). Quest to Learn School. Available from http://q21.org/.

Rauscher, F.H., Shaw, G.L., and Ky, K.N. (1993). Music and spatial task performance. Nature *365*, 611.

Richert, R.A., Robb, M.B., Fender, J.G., and Wartella, E. (2010). Word learning from baby videos. Arch. Pediatr. Adolesc. Med. *164*, 432–437.

Rideout, V., and Hamel, E. (2006). The Media Family: Electronic Media in the Lives of Infants, Toddlers, Preschoolers and Their Parents (Menlo Park, CA: The Henry J. Kaiser Family Foundation).

Robb, M.B., Richert, R.A., and Wartella, E.A. (2009). Just a talking book? Word learning from watching baby videos. Br. J. Dev. Psychol. *27*, 27–45.

Roberts, D.F., Foehr, U.G., and Rideout, V. (2005). Generation M: Media in the Lives of 8–18 Year-Olds (Menlo Park, CA: The Henry J. Kaiser Family Foundation).

Rosser, J.C.J., Jr., Lynch, P.J., Cuddihy, L., Gentile, D.A., Klonsky, J., and Merrell, R. (2007). The impact of video games on training surgeons in the 21st century. Arch. Surg. *142*, 181–186, 186.

Rouse, C.E., and Krueger, A.B. (2004). Putting computerized instruction to the test: a randomized evaluation of a "scientifically based" reading program. Econ. Educ. Rev. *23*, 323–338.

Rueda, M.R., Rothbart, M.K., McCandliss, B.D., Saccomanno, L., and Posner, M.I. (2005). Training, maturation, and genetic influences on the development of executive attention. Proc. Natl. Acad. Sci. USA *102*, 14931–14936.

Schmidt, M.E., and Anderson, D.A. (2007). The impact of television on cognitive development and educational achievement. In Children and Television: Fifty Years of Research, N.O. Pecora, J.P. Murray, and E. Wartella, eds. (Mahwah, NJ: Lawrence Erlbaum Associates).

Schmidt, R.A., and Bjork, R.A. (1992). New conceptualizations of practice: Common principles in three paradigms suggest new concepts for training. Psychol. Sci. *3*, 207–217.

Schmidt, M.E., Rich, M., Rifas-Shiman, S.L., Oken, E., and Taveras, E.M. (2009). Television viewing in infancy and child cognition at 3 years of age in a U.S. cohort. Pediatrics *123*, e370–e375.

School of One (2010). School of One. Available from http://schools.nyc .gov/community/innovation/SchoolofI.S.One/default.htm.

Shapiro, M.G., Westmeyer, G.G., Romero, P.A., Szablowski, J.O., Küster, B., Shah, A., Otey, C.R., Langer, R., Arnold, F.H., and Jasanoff, A. (2010). Directed evolution of a magnetic resonance imaging contrast agent for noninvasive imaging of dopamine. Nat. Biotechnol. *28*, 264–270.

Siegler, R.S., and Ramani, G.B. (2008). Playing linear numerical board games promotes low-income children's numerical development. Dev. Sci. *11*, 655–661.

Small, G., and Vorgan, G. (2008). iBrain: Surviving the Technological Alteration of the Modern Mind (New York: Harper Collins).

Spiers, H.J., and Maguire, E.A. (2007). Decoding human brain activity during real-world experiences. Trends Cogn. Sci. *11*, 356–365.

Subrahmanyam, K., Greenfield, P.M., Kraut, R., and Gross, E. (2001). The impact of computer use on children's and adolescents' development. J. Appl. Dev. Psychol. *22*, 7–30.

Swing, E.L., Gentile, D.A., Anderson, C.A., and Walsh, D.A. (2010). Television and video game exposure and the development of attention problems. Pediatrics *126*, 214–221.

Tejeiro Salguero, R.A., and Morán, R.M.B. (2002). Measuring problem video game playing in adolescents. Addiction *97*, 1601–1606.

Thompson, W.F., Schellenberg, E.G., and Husain, G. (2001). Arousal, mood, and the Mozart effect. Psychol. Sci. *12*, 248–251.

Trick, L.M., Jaspers-Fayer, F., and Sethi, N. (2005). Multiple-object tracking in children: The "Catch the Spies" task. Cogn. Dev. *20*, 373–387.

Vandewater, E.A., Bickham, D.S., and Lee, J.H. (2006). Time well spent? Relating television use to children's free-time activities. Pediatrics *117*, e181–e191.

Vogel, J.J., Vogel, D.S., Cannon-Bowers, J., Bowers, C.A., Muse, K., and Wright, M. (2006). Computer gaming and interactive simulations for learning: A meta-analysis. J. Educ. Comput. Res. *34*, 229–243.

Weis, R., and Cerankosky, B.C. (2010). Effects of video-game ownership on young boys' academic and behavioral functioning: a randomized, controlled study. Psychol. Sci. *21*, 463–470.

Wellings, J., and Levine, M.H. 2009. The Digital Promise: Transforming Learning with Innovative Uses of Technology: A White Paper on Literacy and Learning in a New Media Age (New York: Apple Inc.)

Wenglinsky, H. (1998). Does It Compute? The Relationship between Educational Technology and Student Achievement in Mathematics (Princeton, NJ: Policy Information Center, Educational Testing Service).

Wilson, B.J., Kunkel, D., Linz, D., Potter, J., Donnerstein, E., Smith, S.L., Blumenthal, E., and Gray, T. (1997). In National Television Violence Study, M. Seawall, ed. (Thousand Oaks, CA: Sage Publications).

Yu, A.J., and Dayan, P. (2005). Uncertainty, neuromodulation, and attention. Neuron *46*, 681–692.

Zill, N., Davies, E., and Daly, M. (1994). Viewing of Sesame Street by preschool children in the United States and its relation to school readiness (Rockville, MD: Westat, Inc.).

Zimmerman, F.J., and Christakis, D.A. (2005). Children's television viewing and cognitive outcomes: a longitudinal analysis of national data. Arch. Pediatr. Adolesc. Med. *159*, 619–625.

Zimmerman, F.J., Christakis, D.A., and Meltzoff, A.N. (2007). Associations between media viewing and language development in children under age 2 years. J. Pediatr. *151*, 364–368.

Fighting for Our Lives

Deborah Tannen

This is not another book about civility. "Civility" suggests a superficial, pinky-in-the-air veneer of politeness spread thin over human relations like a layer of marmalade over toast. This book is about a pervasive warlike atmosphere that makes us approach public dialogue, and just about anything we need to accomplish, as if it were a fight. It is a tendency in Western culture in general, and in the United States in particular, that has a long history and a deep, thick, and far-ranging root system. It has served us well in many ways but in recent years has become so exaggerated that it is getting in the way of solving our problems. Our spirits are corroded by living in an atmosphere of unrelenting contention—an argument culture.

The argument culture urges us to approach the world—and the people in it—in an adversarial frame of mind. It rests on the assumption that opposition is the best way to get anything done: The best way to discuss an idea is to set up a debate; the best way to cover news is to find spokespeople who express the most extreme, polarized views and present them as "both sides"; the best way to settle disputes is litigation that pits one party against the other; the best way to begin an essay is to attack someone; and the best way to show you're really thinking is to criticize.

Our public interactions have become more and more like having an argument with a spouse. Conflict can't be avoided in our public lives any more than we can avoid conflict with people we love. One of the great strengths of our society is that we can express these conflicts openly. But just as spouses have to learn ways of settling their differences without inflicting real damage on each other, so we, as a society, have to find constructive ways of resolving disputes and differences. Public discourse requires *making* an argument for a point of view, not *having* an argument—as in having a fight.

Reprinted from *The Argument Culture: Stopping America's War of Words* (1998), by permission of Random House, Inc.

The war on drugs, the war on cancer, the battle of the sexes, politicians' turf battles—in the argument culture, war metaphors pervade our talk and shape our thinking. Nearly everything is framed as a battle or game in which winning or losing is the main concern. These all have their uses and their place, but they are not the only way—and often not the best way—to understand and approach our world. Conflict and opposition are as necessary as cooperation and agreement, but the scale is off balance, with conflict and opposition overweighted. In this book, I show how deeply entrenched the argument culture is, the forms it takes, and how it affects us every day—sometimes in useful ways, but often creating more problems than it solves, causing rather than avoiding damage. As a sociolinguist, a social scientist, I am trained to observe and explain language and its role in human relations, and that is my biggest job here. But I will also point toward other ways for us to talk to each other and get things done in our public lives.

The Battle of the Sexes

My interest in the topic of opposition in public discourse intensified in the years following the publication of *You Just Don't Understand,* my book about communication between women and men. In the first year I appeared on many television and radio shows and was interviewed for many print articles in newspapers and magazines. For the most part, that coverage was extremely fair, and I was—and remain—indebted to the many journalists who found my ideas interesting enough to make them known to viewers, listeners, and readers. But from time to time—more often than I expected—I encountered producers who insisted on setting up a television show as a fight (either between the host and me or between another guest and me) and print journalists who made multiple phone calls to my colleagues, trying to find someone who would criticize my work. This got me thinking about what kind of information comes across on shows and in articles that take this approach, compared to those that approach topics in other ways.

At the same time, my experience of the academic world that had long been my intellectual home began to change. For the most part, other scholars, like most journalists, were welcoming and respectful in their responses to my work, even if they disagreed on specific points or had alternative views to suggest. But about a year after *You Just Don't Understand* became a best-seller—the wheels of academia grind more slowly than those of the popular press—I began reading attacks on my work that completely misrepresented it. I had been in academia for over fifteen years by then, and had valued my interaction with other researchers as one of the greatest rewards of academic life. Why, I wondered, would someone represent me as having said things I had never said or as having failed to say things I had said?

The answer crystallized when I put the question to a writer who I felt had misrepresented my work: "Why do you need to make others wrong for you to be right?" Her response: "It's an argument!" Aha, I thought, that explains it. When you're having an argument with someone, your goal is not to listen and understand. Instead, you use every tactic you can think of—including distorting what your opponent just said—in order to win the argument.

Not only the level of attention *You Just Don't Understand* received but, even more, the subject of women and men, triggered the tendency to polarize. This tendency to stage a fight on television or in print was posited on the conviction that opposition leads to truth. Sometimes it does. But the trouble is, sometimes it doesn't. I was asked at the start of more than one talk show or print interview, "What is the most controversial thing about your book?" Opposition does not lead to truth when the most controversial thing is not the most important.

The conviction that opposition leads to truth can tempt not only members of the press but just about anyone seeking to attract an audience to frame discussions as a fight between irreconcilable opposites. Even the Smithsonian Institution, to celebrate its 150th anniversary, sponsored a series of talks billed as debates. They invited me to take part in one titled "The Battle of the Sexes." The organizer preempted my objection: "I know you won't be happy with this title, but we want to get people interested." This is one of many assumptions I question in this book: Is it necessary to frame an interchange as a battle to get people interested? And even if doing so succeeds in capturing attention, does it risk dampening interest in the long run, as audiences weary of the din and begin to hunger for more substance?

Thought-provoking or Just Provocative?

In the spring of 1995, Horizons Theatre in Arlington, Virginia, produced two one-act plays I had written about family relationships. The director, wanting to contribute to the reconciliation between Blacks and Jews, mounted my plays in repertory with two one-act plays by an African-American playwright, Caleen Sinnette Jennings. We had both written plays about three sisters that explored the ethnic identities of our families (Jewish for me, African-American for her) and the relationship between those identities and the American context in which we grew up. To stir interest in the plays and to explore the parallels between her work and mine, the theater planned a public dialogue between Jennings and me, to be held before the plays opened.

As production got under way, I attended the audition of actors for my plays. After the auditions ended, just before everyone headed home, the theater's public relations volunteer distributed copies of the flyer announcing the public dialogue that she had readied for distribution. I was horrified. The flyer announced that Caleen and I would discuss "how past traumas create understanding and conflict between Blacks and Jews today." The flyer was trying to grab by the throat the issue that we wished to address indirectly. Yes, we were concerned with conflicts between Blacks and Jews, but neither of us is an authority on that conflict, and we had no intention of expounding on it. We hoped to do our part to ameliorate the conflict by focusing on commonalities. Our plays had many resonances between them. We wanted to talk about our work and let the resonances speak for themselves.

Fortunately, we were able to stop the flyers before they were distributed and devise new ones that promised something we could deliver: "a discussion of heritage, identity, and complex family relationships in African-American and Jewish-American culture as represented in their plays." Jennings noticed that the original flyer said the evening would be "provocative" and changed it to "thought-provoking." What a world of difference is implied in that small change: how much better to make people think, rather than simply to "provoke" them—as often as not, to anger.

It is easy to understand why conflict is so often highlighted: Writers of headlines or promotional copy want to catch attention and attract an audience. They are usually under time pressure, which lures them to established, conventionalized ways of expressing ideas in the absence of leisure to think up entirely new ones. The promise of controversy seems an easy and natural way to rouse interest. But serious consequences are often unintended: Stirring up animosities to get a rise out of people, though easy and "provocative," can open old wounds or create new ones that are hard to heal. This is one of many dangers inherent in the argument culture.

For the Sake of Argument

In the argument culture, criticism, attack, or opposition are the predominant if not the only ways of responding to people or ideas. I use the phrase "culture of critique" to capture this aspect. "Critique" in this sense is not a general term for analysis or interpretation but rather a synonym for criticism.

It is the *automatic* nature of this response that I am calling attention to—and calling into question. Sometimes passionate opposition, strong verbal attack, are appropriate and called for. No one knows this better than those who have lived under repressive regimes that forbid public opposition. The Yugoslavian-born poet Charles Simic is one. "There are moments in life," he writes, "when true invective is called for, when it becomes an absolute necessity, out of a deep sense of justice, to denounce, mock, vituperate, lash out, in the strongest possible language." I applaud and endorse this view. There are times when it is necessary and right to fight—to defend your country or yourself, to argue for right against wrong or against offensive or dangerous ideas or actions.

What I question is the ubiquity, the knee-jerk nature, of approaching almost any issue, problem, or public person in an adversarial way. One of the dangers of the habitual use of adversarial rhetoric is a kind of verbal inflation—a rhetorical boy who cried wolf: The legitimate, necessary denunciation is muted, even lost, in the general cacophony of oppositional shouting. What I question is using opposition to accomplish *every* goal, even those that do not require fighting but might also (or better) be accomplished by other means, such as exploring, expanding, discussing, investigating, and the exchanging of ideas suggested by the word "dialogue." I am questioning the assumption that *everything* is a matter of polarized opposites, the proverbial "two sides to every question" that we think embodies open-mindedness and expansive thinking.

In a word, the type of opposition I am questioning is what I call "agonism." I use this term, which derives from the Greek word for "contest," *agonia,* to mean an automatic warlike stance—not the literal opposition of fighting against an attacker or the unavoidable opposition that arises organically in response to conflicting ideas or actions. An agonistic response, to me, is a kind of programmed contentiousness—a prepatterned, unthinking use of fighting to accomplish goals that do not necessarily require it.

How Useful are Fights?

Noticing that public discourse so often takes the form of heated arguments—of having a fight—made me ask how useful it is in our personal lives to settle differences by arguing. Given what I know about having arguments in private life, I had to conclude that it is, in many cases, not very useful.

In close relationships it is possible to find ways of arguing that result in better understanding and solving problems. But with most arguments, little is resolved, worked out, or achieved when two people get angrier and less rational by the minute. When you're having an argument with someone, you're usually not trying to understand what the other person is saying, or what in their experience leads them to say it. Instead, you're readying your response: listening for weaknesses in logic to leap on, points you can distort to make the other person look bad and yourself look good. Sometimes you know, on some back burner of your mind, that you're doing this—that there's a kernel of truth in what your adversary is saying and a bit of unfair twisting in what you're saying. Sometimes you do this because you're angry, but sometimes it's just the temptation to take aim at a point made along the way because it's an easy target.

Here's an example of how this happened in an argument between a couple who had been married for over fifty years. The husband wanted to join an HMO by signing over their Medicare benefits to save money. The wife objected because it would mean she could no longer see the doctor she knew and trusted. In arguing her point of view, she said, "I like Dr. B. He knows me, he's interested in me. He calls me by my first name." The husband parried the last point: "I don't like that. He's much younger than we are. He shouldn't be calling us by first name." But the form of address Dr. B. uses was irrelevant. The wife was trying to communicate that she felt comfortable with the doctor she knew, that she had a relationship with him. His calling her by first name was just one of a list of details she was marshaling to explain her comfort with him. Picking on this one detail did not change her view—and did not address her concern. It was just a way to win the argument.

We are all guilty, at times, of seizing on irrelevant details, distorting someone else's position the better to oppose it, when we're arguing with those we're closest to. But we are rarely dependent on these fights as sources of information. The same tactics are common when public discourse is carried out on the model of personal fights. And the results are dangerous when listeners are looking to these inter-changes to get needed information or practical results.

Fights have winners and losers. If you're fighting to win, the temptation is great to deny facts that support your opponent's views and to filter what you know, saying only what supports your side. In the extreme form, it encourages people to misrepresent or even to lie. We accept this risk because we believe we can tell when someone is lying. The problem is, we can't.

Paul Ekman, a psychologist at the University of California, San Francisco, studies lying. He set up experiments in which individuals were videotaped talking about their emotions, actions, or beliefs—some truthfully, some not. He has shown these videotapes to thou-sands of people, asking them to identify the liars and also to say how sure they were about their judgments. His findings are chilling: Most people performed not much better than chance, and those who did the worst had just as much confidence in their judgments as the few who were really able to detect lies. Intrigued by the implications of this research in various walks of life, Dr. Ekman repeated this experi-ment with groups of people whose jobs require them to sniff out lies: judges, lawyers, police, psychotherapists, and employees of the CIA, FBI, and ATF (Bureau of Alcohol, Tobacco, and Firearms). They were no better at detecting who was telling the truth than the rest of us. The only group that did significantly better were members of the U.S. Secret Service. This finding gives some comfort when it comes to the Secret Service but not much when it comes to every other facet of public life.

Two Sides to Every Question

Our determination to pursue truth by setting up a fight between two sides leads us to believe that every issue has two sides—no more, no less: If both sides are given a forum to confront each other, all the rele-vant information will emerge, and the best case will be made for each side. But opposition does not lead to truth when an issue is not com-posed of two opposing sides but is a crystal of many sides. Often the truth is in the complex middle, not the oversimplified extremes.

We love using the word "debate" as a way of representing issues: the abortion debate, the health care debate, the affirmative action debate—even "the great backpacking vs. car camping debate." The ubiquity of this word in itself shows our tendency to conceptualize issues in a way that predisposes public discussion to be polarized, framed as two opposing sides that give each other no ground. There are many problems with this approach. If you begin with the assumption that there *must* be an "other side," you may end up scouring the margins of science or the fringes of lunacy to find it. As a result, proven facts, such as what we know about how the earth and its inhabitants evolved, are set on a par with claims that are known to have no basis in fact, such as creationism.

The conviction that there are two sides to every story can prompt writers or producers to dig up an "other side," so kooks who state outright falsehoods are given a platform in public discourse. This accounts, in part, for the bizarre phenomenon of Holocaust denial. Deniers, as Emory University professor Deborah Lipstadt shows, have been successful in gaining television airtime and campus newspaper coverage by masquerading as "the other side" in a "debate."

Appearance in print or on television has a way of lending legitimacy, so baseless claims take on a mantle of possibility. Lipstadt shows how Holocaust deniers dispute established facts of history, and then reasonable spokespersons use their having been disputed as a basis for questioning known facts. The actor Robert Mitchum, for example, interviewed in *Esquire,* expressed doubt about the Holocaust. When the interviewer asked about the slaughter of six million Jews, Mitchum replied, "I don't know. People dispute that." Continual reference to "the other side" results in a pervasive conviction that everything has another side—with the result that people begin to doubt the existence of any facts at all.

The Expense of Time and Spirit

Lipstadt's book meticulously exposes the methods used by deniers to falsify the overwhelming historic evidence that the Holocaust occurred. That a scholar had to invest years of her professional life writing a book unraveling efforts to deny something that was about as well known and well documented as any historical fact has ever been—while those who personally experienced and witnessed it are still alive—is testament to another way that the argument culture limits our knowledge rather than expanding it. Talent and effort are wasted refuting outlandish claims that should never have been given a platform in the first place. Talent and effort are also wasted when individuals who have been unfairly attacked must spend years of their creative lives defending themselves rather than advancing their work. The entire society loses their creative efforts. This is what happened with scientist Robert Gallo.

Dr. Gallo is the American virologist who codiscovered the AIDS virus. He is also the one who developed the technique for studying T-cells, which made that discovery possible. And Gallo's work was seminal in developing the test to detect the AIDS virus in blood, the first and for a long time the only means known of stemming the tide of death from AIDS. But in 1989, Gallo became the object of a four-year investigation into allegations that he had stolen the AIDS virus from Luc Montagnier of the Pasteur Institute in Paris, who had independently identified the AIDS virus. Simultaneous investigations by the National Institutes of Health, the office of Michigan Congressman John Dingell, and the National Academy of Sciences barreled ahead long after Gallo and Montagnier settled the dispute to their mutual satisfaction. In 1993 the investigations concluded that Gallo had done nothing wrong. Nothing. But this exoneration cannot be considered a happy ending. Never mind the personal suffering of Gallo, who was reviled when he should have been heralded as a hero. Never mind that, in his words, "These were the most painful years and horrible years of my life." The dreadful, unconscionable result of the fruitless investigations is that Gallo had to spend four years fighting the accusations instead of fighting AIDS.

The investigations, according to journalist Nicholas Wade, were sparked by an article about Gallo written in the currently popular spirit of demonography: not to praise the person it features but to bury him—to show his weaknesses, his villainous side. The implication that Gallo had stolen the AIDS virus was created to fill a requirement of the discourse: In demonography, writers must find negative sides of their subjects to display for readers who enjoy seeing heroes transformed into villains. The suspicion led to investigations, and the investigations became a juggernaut that acquired a life of its own, fed by the enthusiasm for attack on public figures that is the culture of critique.

Metaphors: We are What We Speak

Perhaps one reason suspicions of Robert Gallo were so zealously investigated is that the scenario of an ambitious scientist ready to do anything to defeat a rival appeals to our sense of story; it is the kind of narrative we are ready to believe. Culture, in a sense, is an environment of narratives that we hear repeatedly until they seem to make self-evident sense in explaining human behavior. Thinking of human interactions as battles is a metaphorical frame through which we learn to regard the world and the people in it.

All language uses metaphors to express ideas; some metaphoric words and expressions are novel, made up for the occasion, but more are calcified in the language. They are simply the way we think it is natural to express ideas. We don't think of them as metaphors. Someone who says, "Be careful: You aren't a cat; you don't have nine lives," is explicitly comparing you to a cat, because the cat is named in words. But what if someone says, "Don't pussyfoot around; get to the point"? There is no explicit comparison to a cat, but the comparison is there nonetheless, implied in the word "pussyfoot." This expression probably developed as a reference to the movements of a cat cautiously circling a suspicious object. I doubt that individuals using the word "pussyfoot" think consciously of cats. More often than not, we use expressions without thinking about their metaphoric implications. But that doesn't mean those implications are not influencing us.

At a meeting, a general discussion became so animated that a participant who wanted to comment prefaced his remark by saying, "I'd like to leap into the fray." Another participant called out, "Or share your thoughts." Everyone laughed. By suggesting a different phrasing, she called attention to what would probably have otherwise gone unnoticed: "Leap into the fray" characterized the lively discussion as a metaphorical battle.

Americans talk about almost everything as if it were a war. A book about the history of linguistics is called *The Linguistics Wars*. A magazine article about claims that science is not completely objective is titled "The Science Wars." One about breast cancer detection is "The Mammogram War"; about competition among caterers, "Party Wars"—and on and on in a potentially endless list. Politics, of course, is a prime candidate. One of innumerable possible examples, the headline of a story reporting that the Democratic National Convention nominated Bill Clinton to run for a second term declares, "DEMOCRATS SEND CLINTON INTO BATTLE FOR A 2D TERM." But medicine is as frequent a candidate, as we talk about battling and conquering disease.

Headlines are intentionally devised to attract attention, but we all use military or attack imagery in everyday expressions without thinking about it: "Take a shot at it," "I don't want to be shot down," "He went off half cocked," "That's half the battle." Why does it matter that our public discourse is filled with military metaphors? Aren't they just words? Why not talk about something that matters—like actions?

Because words matter. When we think we are using language, language is using us. As linguist Dwight Bolinger put it (employing a military metaphor), language is like a loaded gun: It can be fired intentionally, but it can wound or kill just as surely when fired accidentally. The terms in which we talk about something shape the way we think about it—and even what we see.

The power of words to shape perception has been proven by researchers in controlled experiments. Psychologists Elizabeth Loftus and John Palmer, for example, found that the terms in which people are asked to recall something affect what they recall. The researchers showed subjects a film of two cars colliding, then asked how fast the cars were going; one week later, they asked whether there had been any broken glass. Some subjects were asked, "About how fast were the cars going when they bumped into each other?" Others were asked, "About how fast were the cars going when they smashed into each other?" Those who read the question with the verb "smashed" estimated that the cars were going faster. They were also more likely to "remember" having seen broken glass. (There wasn't any.)

This is how language works. It invisibly molds our way of thinking about people, actions, and the world around us. Military metaphors train us to think about—and see—everything in terms of fighting, conflict, and war. This perspective then limits our imaginations when we consider what we can do about situations we would like to understand or change.

Even in science, common metaphors that are taken for granted influence how researchers think about natural phenomena. Evelyn Fox Keller describes a case in which acceptance of a metaphor led scientists to see something that was not there. A mathematical biologist, Keller outlines the fascinating behavior of cellular slime mold. This unique mold can take two completely different forms: It can exist as single-cell organisms, or the separate cells can come together to form multicellular aggregates. The puzzle facing scientists was: What triggers aggregation? In other words, what makes the single cells join together? Scientists focused their investigations by asking what entity issued the order to start aggregating. They first called this bosslike entity a "founder cell," and later a "pacemaker cell," even though no one had seen any evidence for the existence of such a cell. Proceeding nonetheless from the assumption that such a cell must exist, they ignored evidence to the contrary:

For example, when the center of the aggregate is removed, other centers form.

Scientists studying slime mold did not examine the interrelationship between the cells and their environment, nor the interrelationship between the functional systems within each cell, because they were busy looking for the pacemaker cell, which, as eventually became evident, did not exist. Instead, under conditions of nutritional deprivation, each individual cell begins to feel the urge to merge with others to form the conglomerate. It is a reaction of the cells to their environment, not to the orders of a boss. Keller recounts this tale to illustrate her insight that we tend to view nature through our understanding of human relations as hierarchical. In her words, "We risk imposing on nature the very stories we like to hear." In other words, the conceptual metaphor of hierarchical governance made scientists "see" something—a pacemaker cell—that wasn't there.

Among the stories many Americans most like to hear are war stories. According to historian Michael Sherry, the American war movie developed during World War II and has been with us ever since. He shows that movies not explicitly about war were also war movies at heart, such as westerns with their good guy–bad guy battles settled with guns. *High Noon,* for example, which became a model for later westerns, was an allegory of the Second World War: The happy ending hinges on the pacifist taking up arms. We can also see this story line in contemporary adventure films: Think of *Star Wars,* with its stirring finale in which Han Solo, having professed no interest in or taste for battle, returns at the last moment to destroy the enemy and save the day. And precisely the same theme is found in a contemporary low-budget independent film, *Sling Blade,* in which a peace-loving retarded man becomes a hero at the end by murdering the man who has been tormenting the family he has come to love.

Put up Your Dukes

If war provides the metaphors through which we view the world and each other, we come to view others—and ourselves—as warriors in battle. Almost any human encounter can be framed as a fight between two opponents. Looking at it this way brings particular aspects of the event into focus and obscures others.

Framing interactions as fights affects not only the participants but also the viewers. At a performance, the audience, as well as the performers, can be transformed. This effect was noted by a reviewer in *The New York Times,* commenting on a musical event:

> **Showdown at Lincoln Center.** Jazz's ideological war of the last several years led to a pitched battle in August between John Lincoln Collier, the writer, and Wynton Marsalis, the trumpeter, in a debate at Lincoln Center. Mr. Marsalis demolished Mr. Collier, point after point after point, but what made the debate unpleasant was the crowd's blood lust; humiliation, not elucidation, was the desired end.

Military imagery pervades this account: the difference of opinions between Collier and Marsalis was an "ideological war," and the "debate" was a "pitched battle" in which Marsalis "demolished" Collier (not his arguments, but him). What the commentator regrets, however, is that the audience got swept up in the mood instigated by the way the debate was carried out: "the crowd's blood lust" for Collier's defeat.

This is one of the most dangerous aspects of regarding intellectual interchange as a fight. It contributes to an atmosphere of animosity that spreads like a fever. In a society that includes people who express their anger by shooting, the result of demonizing those with whom we disagree can be truly tragic.

But do audiences necessarily harbor within themselves a "blood lust," or is it stirred in them by the performances they are offered? Another arts event was set up as a debate between a playwright and a theater director. In this case, the metaphor through which the debate was viewed was not war but boxing—a sport that is in itself, like a debate, a metaphorical battle that pitches one side against the other in an all-out effort to win. A headline describing the event set the frame: "AND IN THIS CORNER . . . ," followed by the subhead "A Black Playwright and White Critic Duke It Out." The story then reports:

> the face-off between August Wilson, the most successful black playwright in the American theater, and Robert Brustein, longtime drama critic for The New Republic and artistic director of the American Repertory Theatre in Cambridge, Mass. These two heavyweights had been battling in print since last June. . . .
> Entering from opposite sides of the stage, the two men shook hands and came out fighting—or at least sparring.

Wilson, the article explains, had given a speech in which he opposed Black performers taking "white" roles in color-blind casting; Brustein

151

had written a column disagreeing; and both followed up with further responses to each other.

According to the article, "The drama of the Wilson-Brustein confrontation lies in their mutual intransigence." No one would question that audiences crave drama. But is intransigence the most appealing source of drama? I happened to hear this debate broadcast on the radio. The line that triggered the loudest cheers from the audience was the final question put to the two men by the moderator, Anna Deavere Smith: "What did you each learn from the other in this debate?" The loud applause was evidence that the audience did not crave intransigence. They wanted to see another kind of drama: the drama of change—change that comes from genuinely listening to someone with a different point of view, not the transitory drama of two intransigent positions in stalemate.

To encourage the staging of more dramas of change and fewer of intransigence, we need new metaphors to supplement and complement the pervasive war and boxing match metaphors through which we take it for granted issues and events are best talked about and viewed.

Mud Splatters

Our fondness for the fight scenario leads us to frame many complex human interactions as a battle between two sides. This then shapes the way we understand what happened and how we regard the participants. One unfortunate result is that fights make a mess in which everyone is muddied. The person attacked is often deemed just as guilty as the attacker.

The injustice of this is clear if you think back to childhood. Many of us still harbor anger as we recall a time (or many times) a sibling or playmate started a fight—but both of us got blamed. Actions occur in a stream, each a response to what came before. Where you punctuate them can change their meaning just as you can change the meaning of a sentence by punctuating it in one place or another.

Like a parent despairing of trying to sort out which child started a fight, people often respond to those involved in a public dispute as if both were equally guilty. When champion figure skater Nancy Kerrigan was struck on the knee shortly before the 1994 Olympics in Norway and the then-husband of another champion skater, Tonya Harding, implicated his wife in planning the attack, the event was characterized as a fight between two skaters that obscured their differing roles. As both skaters headed for the Olympic competition, their potential meeting was described as a "long-anticipated figure-skating shootout." Two years later, the event was referred to not as "the attack on Nancy Kerrigan" but as "the rivalry surrounding Tonya Harding and Nancy Kerrigan."

By a similar process, the Senate Judiciary Committee hearings to consider the nomination of Clarence Thomas for Supreme Court justice at which Anita Hill was called to testify are regularly referred to as the "Hill-Thomas hearings," obscuring the very different roles played by Hill and Thomas. Although testimony by Anita Hill was the occasion for reopening the hearings, they were still the Clarence Thomas confirmation hearings: Their purpose was to evaluate Thomas's candidacy. Framing these hearings as a two-sides dispute between Hill and Thomas allowed the senators to focus their investigation on cross-examining Hill rather than seeking other sorts of evidence, for example by consulting experts on sexual harassment to ascertain whether Hill's account seemed plausible.

Slash-and-Burn Thinking

Approaching situations like warriors in battle leads to the assumption that intellectual inquiry, too, is a game of attack, counterattack, and self-defense. In this spirit, critical thinking is synonymous with criticizing. In many classrooms, students are encouraged to read someone's life work, then rip it to shreds. Though criticism is one form of critical thinking— and an essential one—so are integrating ideas from disparate fields and examining the context out of which ideas grew. Opposition does not lead to the whole truth when we ask only "What's wrong with this?" and never "What can we use from this in building a new theory, a new understanding?"

There are many ways that unrelenting criticism is destructive in itself. In innumerable small dramas mirroring what happened to Robert Gallo (but on a much more modest scale), our most creative thinkers can waste time and effort responding to critics motivated less by a genuine concern about weaknesses in their work than by a desire to find something to attack. All of society loses when creative people are discouraged from their pursuits by unfair criticism. (This is particularly likely to happen since, as Kay Redfield Jamison shows in her book *Touched with Fire,* many of those who are unusually creative are also unusually sensitive; their sensitivity often drives their creativity.)

If the criticism is unwarranted, many will say, you are free to argue against it, to defend yourself. But there are problems with this, too. Not only does self-defense take time and draw off energy that would better be spent on new creative work, but any move to defend yourself makes you appear, well, defensive. For example, when an author wrote a letter to the editor protesting a review he considered unfair, the reviewer (who is typically given the last word) turned the very fact that the author defended himself into a weapon with which to attack again. The reviewer's response began, "I haven't much time to waste on the kind of writer who squanders his talent drafting angry letters to reviewers."

The argument culture limits the information we get rather than broadening it in another way. When a certain kind of interaction is the norm, those who feel comfortable with that type of interaction are drawn to participate, and those who do not feel comfortable with it recoil and go elsewhere. If public discourse included a broad range of types, we would be making room for individuals with different temperaments to take part and contribute their perspectives and insights. But when debate, opposition, and fights overwhelmingly predominate, those who enjoy verbal sparring are likely to take part—by calling in to talk shows, writing letters to the editor or articles, becoming journalists—and those who cannot comfortably take part in oppositional discourse, or do not wish to, are likely to opt out.

This winnowing process is easy to see in apprenticeship programs such as acting school, law school, and graduate school. A woman who was identified in her university drama program as showing exceptional promise was encouraged to go to New York to study acting. Full of enthusiasm, she was accepted by a famous acting school where the teaching method entailed the teacher screaming at students, goading and insulting them as a way to bring out the best in them. This worked well with many of the students but not with her. Rather than rising to the occasion when attacked, she cringed, becoming less able to draw on her talent, not more. After a year, she dropped out. It could be that she simply didn't have what it took—but this will never be known, because the adversarial style of teaching did not allow her to show what talent she had.

Polarizing Complexity: Nature or Nurture?

Few issues come with two neat, and neatly opposed, sides. Again, I have seen this in the domain of gender. One common polarization is an opposition between two sources of differences between women and men: "culture," or "nurture," on one hand and "biology," or "nature," on the other.

154

Shortly after the publication of *You Just Don't Understand,* I was asked by a journalist what question I most often encountered about women's and men's conversational styles. I told her, "Whether the differences I describe are biological or cultural." The journalist laughed. Puzzled, I asked why this made her laugh. She explained that she had always been so certain that any significant differences are cultural rather than biological in origin that the question struck her as absurd. So I should not have been surprised when I read, in the article she wrote, that the two questions I am most frequently asked are "Why do women nag?" and "Why won't men ask for directions?" Her ideological certainty that the question I am most frequently asked was absurd led her to ignore my answer and get a fact wrong in her report of my experience.

Some people are convinced that any significant differences between men and women are entirely or overwhelmingly due to cultural influences—the way we treat girls and boys, and men's dominance of women in society. Others are convinced that any significant differences are entirely or overwhelmingly due to biology: the physical facts of female and male bodies, hormones, and reproductive functions. Many problems are caused by framing the question as a dichotomy: Are behaviors that pattern by sex biological or cultural? This polarization encourages those on one side to demonize those who take the other view, which leads in turn to misrepresenting the work of those who are assigned to the opposing camp. Finally, and most devastatingly, it prevents us from exploring the interaction of biological and cultural factors—factors that must, and can only, be understood together. By posing the question as either/or, we reinforce a false assumption that biological and cultural factors are separable and preclude the investigations that would help us understand their interrelationship. When a problem is posed in a way that polarizes, the solution is often obscured before the search is under way.

Who's up? Who's down?

Related to polarization is another aspect of the argument culture: our obsession with ratings and rankings. Magazines offer the 10, 50, or 100 best of everything: restaurants, mutual funds, hospitals, even judges. Newsmagazines tell us Who's up, Who's down, as in *Newsweek*'s "Conventional Wisdom Watch" and *Time*'s "Winners and Losers." Rankings and ratings pit restaurants, products, schools, and people against each other on a single scale, obscuring the myriad differences among them.

Maybe a small Thai restaurant in one neighborhood can't really be compared to a pricey French one in another, any more than judges with a vast range of abilities and beliefs can be compared on a single scale. And timing can skew results: Ohio State University protested to *Time* magazine when its football team was ranked at the bottom of a scale because only 29 percent of the team graduated. The year before it would have ranked among the top six with 72 percent.

After a political debate, analysts comment not on what the candidates said but on the question "Who won?" After the president delivers an important speech, such as the State of the Union Address, expert commentators are asked to give it a grade. Like ranking, grading establishes a competition. The biggest problem with asking what grade the president's speech deserves, or who won and who lost a campaign debate, is what is not asked and is therefore not answered: What was said, and what is the significance of this for the country?

An Ethic of Aggression

In an argument culture aggressive tactics are valued for their own sake. For example, a woman called in to a talk show on which I was a guest to say, "When I'm in a place where a man is smoking, and there's a no-smoking sign, instead of saying to him 'You aren't allowed to smoke in here. Put that out,' I say, 'I'm awfully sorry, but I have asthma, so your smoking makes it hard for me to breathe. Would you mind terribly not smoking?' Whenever I say this, the man is extremely polite and solicitous, and he puts his cigarette out, and I say, 'Oh, thank you, thank you!' as if he's done a wonderful thing for me. Why do I do that?"

I think this woman expected me to say that she needs assertiveness training to learn to confront smokers in a more aggressive manner. Instead, I told her that there was nothing wrong with her style of getting the man to stop smoking. She gave him a face-saving way of doing what she asked, one that allowed him to feel chivalrous rather than chastised. This is kind to him, but it is also kind to herself, since it is more likely to lead to the result she desires. If she tried to alter his behavior by reminding him of the rules, he might well rebel: "Who made you the enforcer? Mind your own business!" Indeed, who gives any of us the authority to set others straight when we think they're breaking rules?

Another caller disagreed with me, saying the first caller's style was "self-abasing" and there was no reason for her to use it. But I persisted: There is nothing necessarily destructive about conventional self-effacement. Human relations depend on the agreement to use such verbal conventions. I believe the mistake this caller was making—a mistake many of us make—was to confuse *ritual* self-effacement with the literal kind. All human relations require us to find ways to get what we want from others without seeming to dominate them. Allowing others to feel they are doing what you want for a reason less humiliating to them fulfills this need.

Thinking of yourself as the wronged party who is victimized by a lawbreaking boor makes it harder to see the value of this method. But suppose you are the person addicted to smoking who lights up (knowingly or not) in a no-smoking zone. Would you like strangers to yell at you to stop smoking, or would you rather be allowed to save face by being asked politely to stop in order to help them out? Or imagine yourself having broken a rule inadvertently (which is not to imply rules are broken only by mistake; it is only to say that sometimes they are). Would you like some stranger to swoop down on you and begin berating you, or would you rather be asked politely to comply?

As this example shows, conflicts can sometimes be resolved without confrontational tactics, but current conventional wisdom often devalues less confrontational tactics even if they work well, favoring more aggressive strategies even if they get less favorable results. It's as if we value a fight for its own sake, not for its effectiveness in resolving disputes.

This ethic shows up in many contexts. In a review of a contentious book, for example, a reviewer wrote, "Always provocative, sometimes infuriating, this collection reminds us that the purpose of art is not to confirm and coddle but to provoke and confront." This false dichotomy encapsulates the belief that if you are not provoking and confronting, then you are confirming and coddling—as if there weren't myriad other ways to question and learn. What about exploring, exposing, delving, analyzing, understanding, moving, connecting, integrating, illuminating . . . or any of innumerable verbs that capture other aspects of what art can do?

The Broader Picture

The increasingly adversarial spirit of our contemporary lives is fundamentally related to a phenomenon that has been much remarked upon in recent years: the breakdown of a sense of community. In this spirit, distinguished journalist and author Orville Schell points out that in his day journalists routinely based their writing on a sense of connection to their subjects—and that this sense of connection is missing from much that is written by journalists today. Quite the contrary, a spirit of demonography often prevails that has just the opposite effect: Far from encouraging us to feel connected to the subjects, it encourages us to feel critical, superior—and, as a result, distanced. The cumulative effect is that citizens feel more and more cut off from the people in public life they read about.

The argument culture dovetails with a general disconnection and breakdown of community in another way as well. Community norms and pressures exercise a restraint on the expression of hostility and destruction. Many cultures have rituals to channel and contain aggressive impulses, especially those of adolescent males. In just this spirit, at the 1996 Republican National Convention, both Colin Powell and Bob Dole talked about growing up in small communities where everyone knew who they were. This meant that many people would look out for them, but also that if they did something wrong, it would get back to their parents. Many Americans grew up in ethnic neighborhoods that worked the same way. If a young man stole something, committed vandalism, or broke a rule or law, it would be reported to his relatives, who would punish him or tell him how his actions were shaming the family. American culture today often lacks these brakes.

Community is a blend of connections and authority, and we are losing both. As Robert Bly shows in his book by that title, we now have a *Sibling Society:* Citizens are like squabbling siblings with no authority figures who can command enough respect to contain and channel their aggressive impulses. It is as if every day is a day with a substitute teacher who cannot control the class and maintain order.

The argument culture is both a product of and a contributor to this alienation, separating people, disconnecting them from each other and from those who are or might have been their leaders.

What Other Way Is There?

Philosopher John Dewey said, on his ninetieth birthday, "Democracy begins in conversation." I fear that it gets derailed in polarized debate.

In conversation we form the interpersonal ties that bind individuals together in personal relationships; in public discourse, we form similar ties on a larger scale, binding individuals into a community. In conversation, we exchange the many types of information we need to live our lives as members of a community. In public discourse, we exchange the information that citizens in a democracy need in order to decide how to vote. If public discourse provides entertainment first and foremost—and if entertainment is first and foremost watching fights—then citizens do not get the information they need to make meaningful use of their right to vote.

Of course it is the responsibility of intellectuals to explore potential weaknesses in others' arguments, and of journalists to represent serious opposition when it exists. But when opposition becomes the overwhelming avenue of inquiry—a formula that *requires* another side to be found or a criticism to be voiced; when the lust for opposition privileges extreme views and obscures complexity; when our eagerness to find weaknesses blinds us to strengths; when the atmosphere of animosity precludes respect and poisons our relations with one another; then the argument culture is doing more damage than good.

I offer this book not as a frontal assault on the argument culture. That would be in the spirit of attack that I am questioning. It is an attempt to examine the argument culture—our use of attack, opposition, and debate in public discourse—to ask, What are its limits as well as its strengths? How has it served us well, but also how has it failed us? How is it related to culture and gender? What other options do we have?

I do not believe we should put aside the argument model of public discourse entirely, but we need to rethink whether this is the *only* way, or *always* the best way, to carry out our affairs. A step toward broadening our repertoires would be to pioneer reform by experimenting with metaphors other than sports and war, and with formats other than debate for framing the exchange of ideas. The change might be as simple as introducing a plural form. Instead of asking "What's the other side?" we might ask instead, "What are the other sides?" Instead of insisting on hearing "both sides," we might insist on hearing "all sides."

Another option is to expand our notion of "debate" to include more dialogue. This does not mean there can be no negativity, criticism, or disagreement. It simply means we can be more creative in our ways of managing all of these, which are inevitable and useful. In dialogue, each statement that one person makes is qualified by a statement made by someone else, until the series of statements and qualifications moves everyone closer to a fuller truth. Dialogue does not preclude negativity. Even saying "I agree" makes sense only against the background assumption that you might disagree. In dialogue, there is opposition, yes, but no head-on collision. Smashing heads does not open minds.

There are times when we need to disagree, criticize, oppose, and attack—to hold debates and view issues as polarized battles. Even cooperation, after all, is not the absence of conflict but a means of managing conflict. My goal is not a make-nice false veneer of agreement or a dangerous ignoring of true opposition. I'm questioning the *automatic* use of adversarial formats—the assumption that it's *always* best to address problems and issues by fighting over them. I'm hoping for a broader repertoire of ways to talk to each other and address issues vital to us.

The Rhetoric of Celebrity Cookbooks

Christine M. Mitchell

Christine M. Mitchell is an associate professor at South-eastern Louisiana University. She teaches classes in American literature, educational methods, and composition and rhetoric. Currently, she is completing an article on the effect of the Twilight *series on the town in which the novels are set.*

Cooking is big business in America. We need only look at statistics from the Food Network to see how big. The Network has grown steadily since its inception in 1993; it is currently available by subscription to eighty-seven million households in the United States and over sixty countries internationally ("Food Network Fact Sheet"). It has varied its programming from strictly cooking shows, such as *Emeril Live* and *30-Minute Meals* to include general food and lifestyle shows such as *Unwrapped* (the secrets of classic American treats like M&M's) and *Behind the Bash* (behind the scenes with event planners and chefs) (Downey). Its audience is large and diverse: "its key demographic, adults 25–54, . . . was up 9 percent" from fourth quarter 2003 to 2004 (Downey). The Network is also trying to attract both younger and male viewers with programming focused on kids' cooking (especially during the holidays) and shows like *Iron Chef America*.

In addition, cookbooks, particularly those associated with celebrity chefs from the Food Network, are big sellers. Simba Information, a media industry forecaster, predicted in April 2005 that

> the momentum in cookbook sales that gathered in 2004 will continue and revenues from the subject category will grow 5.1% in 2005 from 2004 to reach $493.9 million. The market will continue to be dominated by recognized authors and series. . . .
>
> ("Simba Projects" 4)

Reprinted from the *Journal of Popular Culture* 43, no. 3 (2010), by permission of John Wiley & Sons, Inc.

Current statistics show that these "recognized authors and series" account for ten of the top twenty-five general cookbooks sold at Amazon ("Top Sellers List," October 10, 2005). Moreover, figures from Barnes and Noble and a *Los Angeles Times* poll confirm that the same authors remain among the top sellers. And who are these top-selling authors? Rachael Ray, Emeril Lagasse, and Bobby Flay—all Food Network stars—continue to top the charts (Barnes and Noble.com; *St. Petersburg Times Online*). Add to this the fact that Julia Child's cookbooks "have generated consistent sales over the past ten years," with her death in August 2004 prompting a surge in demand (Simba Information, "Death" 5), and it is clear to see that celebrities are big news in cooking and publishing.

With some sixty shows about food and cooking, the Food Network cannot (and does not) legitimately call all of the personalities "chefs." Indeed, a close look at their credentials reveals that only about one-third of the shows' hosts have had professional training. As might be expected, Emeril Lagasse, Bobby Flay, and Sara Moulton are among those who do, and their cookbooks are quite successful and popular. Yet the best-selling cookbooks come from professional and self-taught cooks alike. So an initial question arises: Are there differences between books written by professional chefs and those written by cooking "celebrities?" A brief look at the backgrounds of some "celebrity chefs" serves as an introduction for a later examination of the cookbooks they have written.

Julia Child

Any discussion of cooking, cookbooks, and television in America must begin with Julia Child, the grande dame of television cooking shows. While at the American Embassy in Paris with her husband post-World War II, Child took classes at Le Cordon Bleu Cooking School, where she met her future collaborators, Simone Beck and Louisette Bertholle. Subsequently, the three women opened a cooking school and published their first book, *Mastering the Art of French Cooking*, in 1961. On February 11, 1963, *The French Chef* first appeared on WGBH-Boston. Child went on to host several other shows, both alone and with fellow chefs, and to write more than fifteen influential cookbooks ("Julia Child"; "Chef Julia Child's Biography").

Emeril Lagasse

According to the Food Network ("Bio: Emeril Lagasse"), Emeril Lagasse began his cooking career at a neighborhood bakery in Massachusetts. After earning a degree from the prestigious Johnson and Wales culinary arts program, Lagasse studied in France. He returned to the United States and, after nearly eight years as executive chef at Commander's Palace in New Orleans, has since made his name with a number of successful restaurants and eleven cookbooks. Lagasse has also become a national television personality as host of two highly rated Food Network programs, *The Essence of Emeril* and *Emeril Live,* and as food correspondent for ABC's *Good Morning America* ("Chef Emeril Lagasse's Biography").

Sara Moulton is another celebrity chef deserving of that title. Moulton graduated from the Culinary Institute of America with highest honors in 1977 and went on to work and study in Boston, New York, and Chartres, France. In addition to being a master chef, she has taught at the Institute of Culinary Education in New York and worked on numerous cooking shows. She serves as the executive chef at *Gourmet* magazine and is the author of three cookbooks ("Sara Moulton: Biography").

Bobby Flay began his culinary career rather inauspiciously, working as a busboy in one of his father's restaurants (Miller and Greissinger). He went on to train at the French Culinary Institute in Manhattan, from which he was awarded the school's first Outstanding Graduate Award in 1993. He worked at several top-tier restaurants in New York until he opened the Mesa Grill in 1991. In spite of the fact that Flay had never visited the Southwest, the restaurant quickly "drew a cult following" (Miller and Greissinger) for Flay's adaptations of Southwestern cuisine. Flay has authored several popular cookbooks and opened two more restaurants, Bolo and Mesa Grill Las Vegas. He "works tirelessly to amaze diners and influence the way Americans view and taste food—making it bold, vibrant and always fun" ("Bobby Flay's Biography").

Rachael Ray, who has entered "the pantheon of America's highest-paid cookbook authors," is described as a "food television phenomenon" by *Los Angeles Times* food critic Corie Brown (F1). Ray has "no professional credentials" (Brown F1), yet she is currently the top-selling cookbook author, with six books in the top thirty cookbook sales at Amazon and two in the top ten at Barnes and Noble. Ray's experience comes from watching her parents and grandfather cook and from working in the family restaurant. Additionally, she gained experience managing gourmet shops and eventually teaching classes for people who wanted to learn to cook quick-and-easy meals. Her appeal to budding cooks is not her culinary background, but the fact that she is "charismatic, accessible, [and] upbeat" (Brown F2). Home cooks are not intimidated by Ray, for, as Brown says, "[t]here's no attempt at culinary excellence," a detail that is unsettling to "the food world's intelligentsia" (F2).

In reviewing the books written by these cooking personalities, four professionally trained chefs and one self-taught "foodie," I set out to answer two questions:

1. Is there anything significant about cookbooks written by people who are celebrities in the world of culinary arts, those who are not simply best-selling cookbook authors, but "stars" of television cooking shows, past and present?
2. Are the cookbooks they write at all helpful in teaching us to cook, or are the books simply vehicles to promote the stars who write them?

The five cookbooks examined in this article—Julia Child's *The Way to Cook, Sara Moulton Cooks at Home,* Emeril Lagasse's *Louisiana: Real and Rustic, Bobby Flay's Boy Meets Grill,* and Rachel Ray's *30-Minute Meals*—reveal some contradictory answers to those questions. The significance lies in the fact that those books written by the women concentrate on teaching readers about cooking as a practice that they can develop and continue. The women do not see themselves as stars, but as cooks and teachers. In contrast, the men's cookbooks are much more about the authors themselves—their likes, dislikes, and restaurants. Men's books do indeed promote them as celebrities. An examination of these books reveals interesting differences in purpose and in the rhetoric used to achieve that purpose.

The dust cover of *The Way to Cook* proclaims: "[Child] takes you into her kitchen and tells you—and shows you—everything she knows about the essentials of good cooking *today.*" Child was a well-respected icon in the culinary world. When a reader contemplates learning "everything [Child] knows," that reader is confronted with a vast store of knowledge about all manner of food preparation. In addition, Child's own words reveal her purpose in writing the cookbook:

> While attitudes about food have changed [since the 1960s], fortunately the principles of good cooking have not. The more one knows about it, the less mystery there is, the faster cooking becomes, and the easier it is to be creative and to embrace new trends and ideas. . . . I am aiming this, my seventh book, at the new generation of cooks who have not grown up in the old tradition, yet who need a basic knowledge of good food. (ix)

Child clearly sees her role as a teacher—someone to give her readers information on which they can build to become successful cooks. Her focus is on her readers, on showing them how to read the cookbook, encouraging them as they learn and experiment, and providing them with useful photographs "to complete the text" (x). Her encouragement is clear:

> You are becoming a cook. After doing the chicken another time or two, it's part of your repertoire, you know it by instinct, and you can start playing around with the variations. . . . You gradually build up your knowledge and confidence as well as your store of techniques, and you begin feeling that you really are on the way to becoming a cook. (x)

Child rarely focuses on herself, instead choosing to focus her attention on the reader and emerging home cook.

Sara Moulton also writes with the reader in mind. She does begin the introduction to her book by talking about herself, but it is clearly with an eye to providing readers with insight to the recipes:

> When it came time to write the headnote to each recipe, my mind seemed naturally to flash back to the first time I'd ever tried the dish in question. How old was I then? Where was I living? Who was the cook? And, then, why have I continued to love it? . . .
>
> This is a great time to be cooking in America. When I was a kid, TV dinners and Hamburger Helper were big. The cardboard tomato was king. Lettuce was Iceberg. . . .
>
> But then Julia Child started appearing on television with a message of pure empowerment: You—yes, *you*—can cook well at home . . .
>
> I also think it's important to cook and eat at home. Indeed this is a home cookbook. . . . I have tried to make this an accessible cookbook. . . . I've also tried to provide you with as many shortcuts and tips as I know. Cooking well is cooking with intelligence. (x–xii)

Like Child, Moulton tries to encourage and empower her readers, to make them believe that by following her instructions and learning the basics of the culinary arts, they, too, can prepare healthful and tasty meals for their friends and families. Dale Curry, food editor of the New Orleans *Times-Picayune,* writes that Moulton's central desire is "to teach technique so that cooks can learn not only a recipe but tips for cooking in general; and to help people overcome the fear of failure in the kitchen" (F-4).

These women chefs, although proficient and knowledgeable, use a rhetoric that is intended to inspire confidence in their readers, to expose them to techniques and ingredients through which the readers, too, can become poised and successful cooks, if only in their own home kitchens. Even when the authors use unusual ingredients or suggest specialized equipment, the idea is always that if the home cook follows the recipe and practices making the dish, he or she can have the same results as, for example, Julia Child, a woman who put America at ease with her professional yet relaxed attitudes about cooking.

The cookbook by the acknowledged king of the Food Network— perhaps of contemporary dining in America—is quite different in focus. In the introduction to *Louisiana Real and Rustic,* Emeril Lagasse begins this way: "When I moved to New Orleans to take over the reins as executive chef at Commander's Palace, I knew very little about the rest of Louisiana" (xi). He gives a travelogue of his adventures across the state, telling readers about the "fields of sugarcane, rice, and sweet potatoes in the southern part," and the "majestic pecan and peach orchards in the north" (xi). Lagasse describes the history that created Louisiana and its unique culture and foodways, and he explains how he came to love the people and the food of Louisiana, as he "was struck by the simpleness of life" (xviii). He encourages readers to "experience" this Louisiana. Lagasse is full of praise for his adopted state, and he is an excellent ambassador for its cuisine.

However, Lagasse does not acknowledge the reader, except to say that he hopes "you will come to enjoy the rich and tantalizing dishes . . . of this state" (xix). He focuses on his own travels and joy in meeting people and tasting their food; he even finds "intriguing" the fact that Cajun men cook regularly and "preserve the traditions of the cuisine" (xviii). But his connection with the reader is a tenuous one. He is much more intent on (literally and figuratively) selling the recipes of Louisiana—his own version—as he concludes with these words: "Keep in mind that everyone will tell you that his or her recipe is the best, and well it might be. In the same spirit, I will say the ones in this book are among the best" (xix). If the reader wants to journey along with him, that is fine, but this is a story about Lagasse and his experiences with adapting recipes he has found in his travels.

Bobby Flay's introduction to *Boy Meets Grill* reveals this about his cooking:

> Grilling has always appealed to the "boy" in *me,* and there's no way *I* would abandon the classic burgers *I* remember. But

my menu has grown, and *I* like to slip in the unexpected, as well: clams or mussels steamed in a kettle set on the rack. . . . *I* still love to grill simple food, but *I* add a jolt of bold flavors with seasonings, marinades, and sauces.

I do most of my outdoor cooking during the relaxed weekends *I* spend on Long Island. . . . *I* grill dinner almost every night that *I'm* out there, and often a simple lunch, too, like softshell crabs that *I* turn into a fabulous sandwich [emphasis added]. (1)

In this excerpt from the opening paragraphs of his book, Flay mentions himself twelve times and the reader not at all. He tells what he likes to cook, why he likes to cook it, and how he cooks it. Flay seems to have no interest in his audience, except that they get to know him. His cookbook is a personal promotion, not a how-to-cook-book. Indeed, in a review of the book for Amazon.com, food critic Schuyler Ingle calls it "a chef-as-star cookbook" and wryly mentions that "there's the unspoken suggestion that Bobby Flay invented fire" ("Editorial Reviews").

The introductions to these four cookbooks reveal quite a bit about their authors and their purpose for writing. We have seen that the women are focused on empowering their readers; they serve as cheerleaders for an audience who wants to learn to cook the right way. The men's agenda seems to be to tell about themselves and to get their readers to cook something from the books, but not to learn any specific tasks to enhance their cooking skills. The final author we will examine is the self-taught Rachael Ray. One might expect her to "cash in" on her celebrity, as the men have done, given that she is not a professional chef and that she owes all of her popularity to her shows on the Food Network. Yet she, like the women cookbook authors before her, emphasizes the audience and their interests.

Ray tells her readers that cooking can be fun, simple, and quick. She introduces her *30-Minute Meals* by saying:

The *30-Minute Meal* segments [on the Food Network] are as much about life as they are about food. . . . The *30-Minute Meal* series features someone who looks a lot like you, cooking in a real kitchen that looks a lot like yours, making something that looks really good—something that you know you could do too.

This book does the same thing—it is about can-do cooking, can-do better living. Anyone can cook. . . . Cooking can and should make you feel good about yourself. (19)

Even more than her classically trained sisters, Ray attempts to demystify cooking and make it simple and quick. Indeed, her goal in this, the first of several similar cookbooks, is to teach readers to cook well enough so that they are not tempted to stop to buy dinner on the way home from work:

> Commit yourself to not buying take-out food more than twice this week. Cook the other five nights. Get the hang of it. Change the recipes to reflect your own tastes. . . . Cooking quick and easy recipes night after night will build you a pantry and the confidence to learn to live on your own recipes for the rest of your life. (21)

Like Child and Moulton, Ray encourages her readers to learn the basics so that they can feed themselves well.

Examining the cookbooks completely would take more space than a paper of this type is capable of. However, looking at representative sections and recipes should serve to demonstrate the rhetorical differences in the books.

Throughout *The Way to Cook,* Julia Child writes in a tone that is warm and encouraging, reflecting her stated goal of making cooking more pleasurable (iv). In the introduction to the chapter on soups, she writes: "Imagination and a number of the basic springboards are what this chapter aims to present, with its theme and variations, and its soup bases that act as building blocks. It is my hope that you will draw from it a solid background for making up your own combinations" (3). Child believes that home cooks can learn to do what she does by following her recipes and then experimenting to create their own.

In the soup chapter, as in succeeding ones, she provides "master" recipes, as she calls them, for chicken stock, chowder base, and beef stock, among others. These master recipes are highlighted so that readers can easily locate them and then adapt them to the variations Child lists or to their own tastes. Yet throughout, Child offers hints and special notes right along with her words of encouragement.

The chapter on breads calls the readers' attention to the techniques and tricks for baking breads. Child takes an opportunity to give her opinion about this practice:

> Bread making is for those who love to cook and to work with their hands. There is great satisfaction to be gained from the feel and smell of the dough as it is kneaded and formed, from that wonderful warm aroma of its baking, and finally from the pride of authorship. (35)

But, as we will see, unlike the opinions offered by, for example, Bobby Flay, Child writes not as one who is chronicling her extensive experience as a chef, but rather as one who is attempting to interest others in what she calls "a consuming hobby" (35). Indeed, she ends the introduction by saying that she hopes the reader "will find the solutions to these problems [mushy hamburger buns and soggy pizza crusts] here, starting out with a few hints from an old-time home baker" (35). Child is one of us; she cooks at home, and she wants us to learn to do so as well.

In addition, Child's book is clear and easy to follow. It includes over six hundred full-color photographs so that both novice and experienced cooks can see what they are supposed to do and what dishes should look like, from beginning to end. Sidebars provide special notes, and icons for each chapter denote the master recipes (e.g., something like in the chapter on fish). Although the book includes more than eight hundred recipes, the home cook can find them easily and follow them so that he or she can participate in what Child calls the "pleasures of the table . . . a delightful part of civilized life" (xi).

Likewise, Moulton presents her cookbook in a very reader-friendly way. She tries to help her readers negotiate the recipes by telling them initially, "Please read each recipe in its entirely before you start and then follow it *exactly,* at least the first time you make it. After you've made it once or twice, of course, you're welcome to improve it however you see fit" (xiv). Like Child, Moulton sees herself as a guide to learning to cook; she wants her readers to do as she tells them—not so that they can be like her, but so that they can experience success and then spread their wings to fly on their own. Moulton shares what she has learned from her years as a professional chef to teach readers to cook appetizing and healthy meals at home.

In one of the first recipes in the book, Moulton reveals that she is a student as well. Her recipe for Tonnato-Stuffed Eggs includes this note: "The most important thing to learn from this recipe is how to boil eggs. In fact, as Julia Child taught me, the paradoxically correct method is *not* to boil them" (4). Moulton acknowledges that she has learned from the top chef; her revelation should put her own readers at ease to discover that cooking is a shared experience in which everyone is a student.

Like Child's, Moulton's book is arranged in an easily comprehensible format. Each chapter is devoted to a course in the meal—hors d'oeuvres, pasta, vegetables, and side dishes—and each recipe includes a clearly marked list of ingredients, a headnote, and the procedure. The headnote is in a different color font, indicating that it is not essential, but an interesting addition to the recipe. In some cases, the recipe contains a tip or hint on extra ingredients or procedures (e.g., "seeding jalapenos," "working with raw poultry," or "preparing artichokes"), boxed off by itself as an indication that it is additional, perhaps helpful, information. In all cases, though, Moulton spotlights not herself but the recipes and her sources for them—her parents, friends, and fellow chefs. There are not as many photographs as in Child's book, but the ones that do appear are colorful and detailed, showing readers what the finished dishes will look like and how they might be plated. For Moulton, it is all about getting people to "cook and eat at home" (xii).

In contrast to such warm, encouraging cookbooks by the female chefs, those by the men do little to support the reader's ego. They support the authors' egos quite well, however, as both Lagasse and Flay talk about their restaurants and television shows. But neither man works to give his readers a sense of accomplishment or knowledge. Both books reveal much about their authors, but little about cooking as an activity to cultivate.

Emeril Lagasse's book is notable in the way that it does not attempt to engage the reader. It is woefully bereft of pictures, and the ones that do appear, while culturally interesting, show nothing of the food the reader is trying to cook. This seems like an especially negligent omission, considering that many readers will not be familiar with the cuisine of Louisiana, and color photographs would help them learn to cook.

For example, a staple in Louisiana cooking is roux, the flour and oil mixture essential to many Cajun and Creole dishes. Lagasse gives a fairly comprehensive discussion of how to make a roux, but without pictures the novice cook has no idea what color a blond, medium brown, or dark brown roux should be. Lagasse describes the colors—blond roux, "the color of sandpaper," medium brown, "the color of peanut butter," and dark brown, "the color of chocolate"—but someone who has never seen a roux would have a better idea of the exact color if pictures had been provided. And when Lagasse writes, "Cooking time will vary according to the type of pot used, the heat source (gas or electric), the intensity of heat and the amount of roux that is being prepared" (27), the beginning cook may decide to forget about the recipe completely. This is unfortunate, because a roux is not difficult to prepare, but Lagasse's lack of specificity and encouragement may discourage someone from even trying.

The headnotes to each recipe are concerned not so much with the food or cooking techniques; instead, they discuss Lagasse's preferences, restaurants, and life. He notes that south Louisiana cooks pickle banana peppers, "which is how I like them best. When I was growing up in Fall River, Massachusetts, Dad always pickled his yearly crop" (19). This bit of information does nothing to teach the reader how or why to treat the peppers this way. Likewise, a recipe for a blend of spices to use on meat includes this headnote:

> Every Louisiana kitchen, be it Mama's or the local butcher shop's, is stocked with a personal spice blend. Many of the recipes in this book include some of this spice mix. . . . This seasoning mix is similar to the one in my first book. I like this version for a real and rustic taste. (9)

This information is marginally interesting, but again, it does not assist the reader in learning a basic recipe that he or she can later adapt. It is simply a case of "here's what I like"—and what is a "real and rustic taste"?

When we look at *Bobby Flay's Boy Meets Grill*, we find a rhetoric that calls attention to its author at all times. Flay will help his readers learn to cook, if by "learn," we mean do what he does, and if by "cook," we mean revert to the stereotypically male task of grilling. The title of the book (and similar titles in subsequent books) shows where the spotlight falls: the boy, Flay himself. The book presents an image of Flay as fraternity boy—"grillin' and chillin'"—interestingly foreshadowing current (fall 2005) Food Network episodes in which he does bring fraternity boys to a tailgating cook-off.

In the introduction, titled "A Boy's Introduction to the Grill," Flay writes about himself, leaving readers to make their own decisions with few recommendations, only his likes and dislikes to guide them: "I pre-fer . . . ," "I rely . . . ," "I'm comfortable with . . . ," "I would rather. . . ." In one of his first acknowledgments that he is actually addressing an audience interested in learning to cook, Flay writes: "Because gas grills are easy to ignite . . . you can spend your time preparing the food, not working on the fire—that's what I like to do" (5). This is an interesting revelation considering his earlier admission that his preference for gas grills was born one evening when he was cooking for 250 people and "had forgotten to light the grill!" (viii).

Bobby Flay's Boy Meets Grill is clearly not for an audience that wants to become proficient at grilling. For that, readers would need Steve Raichlen's cookbooks. With over twenty books on the subject, Raichlen is a barbeque expert who explains various grilling or barbequing methods and why each technique is preferable. Perhaps readers find those explanations useful, since his "2.5 million books that detail his grilling methods" have out-sold Flay's (Brown F2).

Boy Meets Grill, while encouraging people to have fun with cooking, provides recipes and stories about Flay, but not much instruction for the cook. Flay takes a task that is elemental and complicates it—not to teach cooks any sort of basics but to highlight recipes from his restaurants' menus or to relive his youth. Grilling–barbecuing–cooking out— whatever it is called—should be simple. It is usually done in the heat of the summer, outdoors, in an attempt to keep the kitchen cool and get everyone out of the house. Yet Flay's ingredient lists are sometimes quite lengthy. Indeed, a recipe for Barbecued Chicken Quesadillas with Grilled Tomato Salsa and Buttermilk Dressing is three pages long, with three separate recipes: one for the dressing, one for the salsa, and one for the quesadillas, which also require barbecue sauce made from a recipe elsewhere in the book. All this to make leftover chicken and melted cheese inside a tortilla. How simple is this for the cook who just wants to get out of the kitchen?

The visual rhetoric of this book also provides a look at what Flay thinks is important. The photographs that accompany the recipes are of two types. First is the black-and-white close-up photo of raw ingredients or equipment: a bunch of asparagus, still rubber-banded together (127), minced ginger (61), or the ignition knob on a grill (32). The second type of photos are shots of Flay, sniffing a bunch of herbs (85), "chillin'" by the grill (117), or dining with (presumably) friends (260). In fact, there are more than twenty-five pictures of Flay himself. In comparing these photos with the ones in Child's or Moulton's books, one may wonder why they are there. These pictures do not help the reader by showing step-by-step preparation or cooking procedures; they do not demonstrate what finished dishes will look like. Instead, they like the recipes and headnotes, promote Bobby Flay rather than the food.

To be sure, there are some thirty pages of full-color pictures of finished dishes. However, as one looks through them, one is struck by the similarity of them all. Since every dish is grilled, the steaks, chicken, and fish, even the desserts, take on a homogenous look. One must read the captions to know exactly what the photos show.

Rachael Ray is not, as we have seen, a professional chef; therefore, her recipes are relatively simple. Yet her rhetoric shows a respect for her readers and a real desire to teach them useful skills. In a biographical note on the back cover, Ray states that "her first love is teaching others to cook," and she gets down to that task right away. She assumes that her readers are those who do not know how to cook or who think that cooking is difficult or time consuming, so she starts right in with encouragement. Although Ray begins each chapter with an anecdote about her family or offers her opinion on current eating trends (such as picking up take-out meals every night), her purpose in these stories is to boost readers' confidence, to let them know that cooking is easy, fun, and a way to establish community with others. She wants people to learn to cook not to feed just their bodies, but their hearts and souls as well.

The first chapter, "30-Minute Pastas," gives recipes for dishes that many people like and that are easy for beginners. This chapter begins with a story about Ray's family—how Ray learned to cook from her mother, who had learned to cook from her father. Ray wants to convince readers that cooking is a skill that can fill their lives with joy, as she writes: "Food is nostalgia. The smell of good, simple food can take you back to all the good times in your life and make you forget all the bad. . . . Place a big bowl of [pasta] in the middle of your kitchen table and see what happens" (28).

Unlike Child or Moulton, Ray appeals to readers who really do not think they can cook, and she gives them the tools to make meals that can take the place of fast food. Because of this slightly different audience, Ray's recipes are simpler and more straightforward. She does not fuss with fancy or expensive ingredients, nor does she ask readers to engage in complicated cooking tasks. Ray encourages her readers not to worry about instruments. She tells them to estimate measurements: 2 tablespoons of oil is twice around the pan; 1/2 cup of red wine becomes "a couple good shots"; 1/4 teaspoon nutmeg equals "a couple shakes." Such methodology allows those who do not have professional equipment to start cooking right away. As they become more proficient, they can buy measuring spoons or garlic presses, but the only equipment Ray specifies that cooks need are a big knife, cutting board, pot, and nonstick frying pan (23). She empowers novice cooks to achieve success with her friendly can-do attitude and her simple but good and filling recipes.

One final analysis can be made by looking at the endorsements or cover copy on the books' back covers. Child's and Lagasse's books have no promotions, but ones found on the other three books are revealing. Moulton's endorsements come from four other chefs, the first one being renowned French chef Jacques Pépin: "From the first moment I cooked alongside Sara in the early '80s at La Tulipe, I knew she was a gifted, dedicated cook." On Ray's book we find acclaim from, presumably, home cooks whom she inspired: "I have not found anyone who could throw together more foods, so quickly, so appealingly, and so deliciously than Rachael." These words of praise for Moulton and Ray attest to their talent and knowledge as both cooks and teachers.

However, when we look at the endorsements on Flay's book, we find that they come not from fellow chefs, not from home cooks who learned something, but from two other male celebrities who have no connection to cooking:

> Bobby Flay is a hot guy, with a hot restaurant, and a hot cookbook. Buy this cookbook and heat up your grill, and get ready to eat some really hot chow.
>
> (James Carville)

> Thanks to Bobby Flay for making my mouth water with recipes that will have me dreaming of that perfect pyramid of glowing briquettes long past the last days of summer.
>
> (Matt Lauer)

The endorsements say nothing about the food or the learning experience; they are all about Flay, his restaurant, his celebrity, and his ability to do the one kind of cooking that men will do at home: cooking over an open fire, just like their primitive ancestors.

This analysis does not claim that the recipes by these male celebrity chefs are not tasty or cannot be created by home cooks. Indeed, I have made many tasty meals from Lagasse's recipes (although Flay's, I must admit, seem much ado about nothing). It is significant to realize, though, that if someone wants to learn to cook, to get the basics and develop a repertoire of recipes that can be adapted, added to, and passed along—as Moulton says, to become "heirlooms"—then one must stick to the women's books. They carry on the modern tradition of teaching, as begun by Fannie Farmer in her 1896 *Boston Cooking-School Cook Book,* and spread by writers such as Irma S. Rombauer and M. F. K. Fisher. There is no doubt that men have influenced the culinary habits of American home cooks; one need only look to classics by great chefs such as James Beard and Craig Claiborne. However, in an age where glitter overwhelms substance and celebrity trumps competence, we might acknowledge that female celebrity chefs are the ones who will provide a link with the past and be, as always, the teachers and nurturers for the future.

Works Cited

Amazon. "Top Sellers List." *Amazon.com*. 1996–2005. 10 Oct. 2005 (http://www.amazon.com).

Barnes and Noble. "Bestsellers: Daily Top 10 Books by Subject: Cooking, Food and Wine." *Barnes and Noble.com* 1997–2005. 13 Oct. 2005 (http://search. barnesandnoble.com/bestsellers/bestsellers.asp?CAT=914300&sort=S& userid=Nr4DHRGBLL).

"Best Selling Cookbooks." *St. Petersburg Times Online* 1 Sept. 2004. 1 Oct. 2005. (http://www.sptimes.com/2004/09/01/news_pf/Taste/Best_selling_ cookbooks.shtml).

"Bio: Bobby Flay." *Food Network.com*. 2005. 9 Oct. 2005 (http://www.foodnetwork. com/food/bobby_flay/article/0,1974,FOOD_9787,00.html).

"Bio: Emeril Lagasse." *Food Network.com*. 2005. 9 Oct. 2005 (http://www. foodnetwork.com/food/emeril_lagasse/article/0,1974,FOOD_9823_1770 157,00.html).

"Bobby Flay's Biography." *StarChefs.com: The Magazine for Culinary Insiders* 1997–2005. 15 Oct. 2005 (http://www.starchefs.com/chefs/BFlay/html/ start.shtml).

Brown, Corie. "Just a Gigantic Rumble in the Belly?" *Los Angeles Times* 7 July 2004: F1–F2.

"Chef Emeril Lagasse's Biography." *StarChefs.com: The Magazine for Culinary Insiders* 1995–2005. 15 Oct. 2005 (http://www.starchefs.com/ELagasse/ html/biography.shtml).

"Chef Julia Child's Biography on StarChefs." *StarChefs.com: The Magazine for Culinary Insiders* 1995–2005. 10 Oct. 2005 (http://www.starchefs.com/ JChild/html/biography.shtml).

Child, Julia. *The Way to Cook*. New York: Knopf, 1989.

Curry, Dale. "Sara to Share Secrets in N.O." [New Orleans] *Times-Picayune* 18 Mar. 2004: F-1, F-4.

Downey, Kevin. "Food Network: Setting a Bigger Table." *Media Life Magazine* 15 Mar. 2005. 9 Oct. 2005 (http://www.medialifemagazine.com/News2005/ mar05/mar14/2_tues/news4tuesday.html).

Flay, Bobby, and Joan Schwartz. *Bobby Flay's Boy Meets Grill*. New York: Hyperion, 1999.

Ingle, Schuyler. "*Bobby Flay's Boy Meets Grill*: Editorial Reviews." *Amazon.com*. 15 Oct. 2005 (http://www.amazon.com/exec/obidos/tg/detail/-/0786864907/ 103-0491296-0267011?v=glance).

Lagasse, Emeril with Marcelle Bienvenu. *Louisiana Real and Rustic*. New York: Morrow, 1996.

Miller, Samantha, and Lisa Kay Greissinger. "Hot Hands." *People Weekly* 13 July 1998: 119–21. *Research Library*. ProQuest. Sims Memorial Library, Southeastern Louisiana University, Hammond, LA. 15 Oct. 2005 (http://www. proquest.com/).

Moulton, Sara. *Sara Moulton Cooks at Home*. New York: Broadway, 2002.

National Cable & Telecommunications Association. "Food Network Fact Sheet." *NCTA.com*. n.d. 9 Oct. 2005 (http://www.ncta.com/guidebook_ pdfs/FoodNetwork.pdf).

Ray, Rachael. *30-Minute Meals*. New York: Lake Isle, 1998.

"Sara Moulton: Biography." *Sara Moulton.com*. 2005. 13 Oct. 2005 (http://www .saramoulton.com/bio.htm).

Simba Information. "Julia Child's Death Heats up Demand for Her Classic Cookbooks." *Book Publishing Report* 6 Sept. 2004: 5. *Business Source Premier*. EBSCO. Sims Memorial Library, Southeastern Louisiana University, Hammond, LA. 9 Oct. 2005 (http://search.epnet.com).

——. "Simba Projects 5.1% Revenue Growth for Cookbooks in 2005." *Book Publishing Report* 25 Apr. 2005: 4. *Business Source Premier*. EBSCO. Sims Memorial Library, Southeastern Louisiana University, Hammond, LA. 9 Oct. 2005 (http://search.epnet.com).

The Song Decoders

Rob Walker

Rob Walker writes the Consumed column for the magazine and is the author of "Buying In: The Secret Dialogue Between What We Buy and Who We Are."

On first listen, some things grab you for their off-kilter novelty. Like the story of a company that has hired a bunch of "musicologists," who sit at computers and listen to songs, one at a time, rating them element by element, separating out what sometimes comes to hundreds of data points for a three-minute tune. The company, an Internet radio service called Pandora, is convinced that by pouring this information through a computer into an algorithm, it can guide you, the listener, to music that you like. The premise is that your favorite songs can be stripped to parts and reverse-engineered.

Some elements that these musicologists (who, really, are musicians with day jobs) codify are technical, like beats per minute, or the presence of parallel octaves or block chords. Someone taking apart Gnarls Barkley's "Crazy" documents the prevalence of harmony, chordal patterning, swung 16ths and the like. But their analysis goes beyond such objectively observable metrics. To what extent, on a scale of 1 to 5, does melody dominate the composition of "Hey Jude"? How "joyful" are the lyrics? How much does the music reflect a gospel influence? And how "busy" is Stan Getz's solo in his recording of "These Foolish Things"? How emotional? How "motion-inducing"? On the continuum of accessible to avant-garde, where does this particular Getz recording fall?

There are more questions for every voice, every instrument, every intrinsic element of the music. And there are always answers, specific numerical ones. It can take 20 minutes to amass the data for a single tune. This has been done for more than 700,000 songs, by 80,000 artists. "The Music Genome Project," as this undertaking is called, is the back end of Pandora.

Pandora was founded in Oakland a decade ago, and for much of the intervening time has lived a precarious existence (the founders spent one three-year stretch working without salaries while they scrambled for investors). But thanks in part to the popularity of the Pandora iPhone app, its fortunes have lately improved. It has attracted 35 million listeners and claims about 65,000 new sign-ups a day (more than half from mobile-device users). About 75 companies are working Pandora into a variety of gizmos and gadgets and Web platforms. The business model relies largely on advertising, and its founder, Tim Westergren, says Pandora will very likely turn its first profit in the fourth quarter of this year.

However things play out for Pandora as a business, its approach is worth understanding if you're interested in the future of listening. It's the "social" theories of music-liking that get most of the attention these days: systems that connect you with friends with similar tastes, or that rely on "collaborative filtering" strategies that cross-match your music-consumption habits with those of like-minded strangers. These popular approaches marginalize traditional gatekeepers; instead of trusting the talent scout, the radio programmer or the music critic, you trust your friends (actual or virtual), or maybe just "the crowd."

Pandora's approach more or less ignores the crowd. It is indifferent to the possibility that any given piece of music in its system might become a hit. The idea is to figure out what you like, not what a market might like. More interesting, the idea is that the taste of your cool friends, your peers, the traditional music critics, big-label talent scouts and the latest influential music blog are all equally irrelevant. That's all cultural information, not musical information. And theoretically at least, Pandora's approach distances music-liking from the cultural information that generally attaches to it.

Which raises interesting questions. Do you really love listening to the latest Jack White project? Do you really hate the sound of Britney Spears? Or are your music-consumption habits, in fact, not merely guided but partly shaped by the cultural information that Pandora largely screens out—like what's considered awesome (or insufferable) by your peers, or by music tastemakers, or by anybody else? Is it really possible to separate musical taste from such social factors, online or off, and make it purely about the raw stuff of the music itself?

Tim Westergren is a familiar type: the musician who was not as successful as he might have been and concluded that the system is flawed because it underrates talented people who deserve a bigger audience. He played in bands that never quite took off and for a time worked as a film-score composer. It was that job—a "methodical, calculating form of composition," he says—that led him to dwell on the way music works and forced him to decode the individual taste of whatever director had hired him. He says he was getting pretty good at this. "So I thought I'd try to codify it," he says.

Rangy and bright-eyed at 43, Westergren comes off more like the head of a fan club than an erstwhile rock star. The only time he seems annoyed is when he's talking about how some unpopular musicians are unfairly overlooked—or how some popular ones are unfairly maligned. Pandora is, in effect, a response to both of those problems.

He founded his company with two tech-and-business-savvy pals in the start-up-friendly year of 1999. Back then it was called Savage Beast Technologies, and the early (not exactly farsighted) business model involved listening kiosks in record stores. Eventually the company got new financing, beefed up the executive team and landed on using its genome as the engine of an Internet radio service "that plays only music you like."

Pandora went online in 2005 and looked much as it does today. When you arrive at the site, you're invited to type in the name of an artist, or a specific song. Let's say you type in "These Foolish Things," by Stan Getz. The Pandora genome looks for something it judges to have a similar infrastructure—like, when I tried recently, "I Don't Know Why," by Don Byas.

This is Pandora's first guess at a song you will like, based on its analysis of the song you picked. You can simply let it play; click a "thumbs down" icon to try another song; or give it a thumbs up if you want Pandora's algorithm to know this was a particularly good choice. You can also click to learn why the song was chosen: you don't get a full breakdown but rather a kind of thumbnail summation. In this case the Byas tune was chosen "because it features swing influences, a leisurely tempo, a tenor-sax head, a tenor-sax solo and acoustic-piano accompaniment."

If you click a lot, the idea is that Pandora's algorithm adjusts, squaring your taste with the genome's database. There are other ways to tweak things—adding more songs to a "station" for the system to scrutinize, creating different stations based on other artists or songs, telling the service not to play a given song for a while. (This happens on a station-specific basis: whatever preferences I express on a station based on "My Sharona" would not affect the songs on, say, my Yanni station.)

Explanation of Profit making

Relying on advertising revenue—visual ads on its site as well as occasional audio ads interspersed between songs on your stations—means that much depends on Pandora's genome doing a good-enough job to keep people listening. (There's also a "premium" ad-free service for $36 a year, and Pandora makes a small commission if you click through its site to buy a song on iTunes or Amazon.com, but it's primarily an ad-driven business.) Its biggest expense is the licensing fee it pays to publishers and performers; the performance fee, paid to an entity called Sound Exchange, which distributes royalties to artists, is equal to something like 50 percent of Pandora's revenue. When you start a station with a specific song, that song isn't the first thing you hear, because this would an entail an "on demand" license, which costs even more.

By way of Pandora's Twitter feed, I issued a call for users who not only listened to the service a lot but also felt that it had had some kind of impact on their listening tastes. Summer Sterling, a 21-year-old senior at Washington and Lee University in Lexington, Va., often starts by typing in well-known bands like the Dixie Chicks, and that has led her to music by groups she had never heard of but now loves, like the Weepies. Stephanie Kessler, a 24-year-old M.B.A. student in St. Louis, started by typing in K T Tunstall and has found her way to Waylon Jennings and David Allan Coe.

Aashay Desai, a 25-year-old computer engineer, has become a "very meticulous" user, building some 30 stations and paying for Pandora's premium service, which offers better sound quality and more features. Aside from his hard rock/metal station, he has a "metalcore" station that's "a little more aggressive," as well as a "polyrhythm metal station" that is probably his "most aggressive." He has also built an R&B station and a trance station; more recently he discovered Django Reinhardt, whom he used as the basis for a gypsy jazz station.

Others, of course, are not impressed by the genome's results. Someone passed along to me a harsh assessment by Bob Lefsetz, whose popular Lefsetz Letter critiques pretty much every aspect of the contemporary music business. "I tried and rejected it," he wrote. "Was flummoxed when a Jackson Browne station I created delivered a Journey song. Huh? . . . Jackson is music for the mind, Journey is music for the MINDLESS!"

Jonathan McEuen told me he heard about Pandora a couple of years ago and started using it immediately, "with the goal of breaking whatever algorithm they had." A devoted music fan and a musician himself, McEuen says he did not believe an online service could understand what sort of music he would like and introduce him to new artists based on some deconstruction of his listening tastes. "You can't just reduce it to a bunch of numbers," he recalls thinking. "This is a romantic, emotional thing," and Pandora's approach to it "can't work."

He has changed his mind. A 28-year-old clinical neuroscience researcher at the University of Pennsylvania, he's a listener who lacks the time to keep up with music news the way he did while amassing hundreds of CDs as a student. Sometimes he runs Pandora as background music; sometimes he's more engaged, using it as a way to learn about contemporary classical and opera—and as a result has become a fan of the music of a young composer named Eric Whitacre. "I don't know how else I would have found out about it," he says. "Except through the exhaustive process of making new friends on the Internet. Which is something I'm kind of loath to do."

What I didn't hear Pandora users talk about was the Genome Project; many didn't really know about it. They cared about the music Pandora served up, period. But I wanted to know what was behind that music. Nolan Gasser was the primary shaper of the lexicon that could reconcile Westergren's genome metaphor with something a computer could evaluate. Gasser, an actual musicologist, wrote a doctoral thesis that dealt with close analyses of Renaissance composition. "I really needed to know what made that music tick," he recalls. That systematic study flowed well into his work with Westergren—although they started with 20th-century pop, not Renaissance vocal music. First every piece is broken down into large-scale aspects of music: melody, harmony, rhythm, form, sound (meaning instrumentation and, if necessary, voice), and in many cases the text, meaning lyrics. Each of these broader categories might have 10, 30, 50 elements.

"We have a number of characteristics for vocals," he continues. "Is it a smooth voice, is it a rough, gravelly voice, is it a nasally voice?" Similar questions are evaluated for every instrument. The upshot was about 250 "genes" for every song in the original pop-rock version of the "genome."

Gasser also helped develop the training mechanisms to make sure the analysts are consistent about more subjective matters—like how "emotionally intense" that Stan Getz solo is. (It's a 4 out of 5, in the genome's view.) The test that candidates take involves being able to pick out, quickly and by ear, harmonic structures, melodic organization and other musical elements. The indoctrination that follows revolves around examples. (You think that vocal gets a 5 on the gravelly scale? Here's Tom Waits. Is it that gravelly?)

181

Recently I sat in as several of Pandora's song deconstructors gathered in a small conference room to talk about Indian music. Pandora listeners have been asking for Indian music for a while, but adding it to the service hasn't been a simple matter. A new genre must arrive in a big batch—about 3,000 pieces of music—because Pandora's algorithm needs lots of choices to be able to recommend something similar-sounding. And all of it has to be pulled apart first. This entails squaring the very different structures of Indian music with Pandora's "genome" data points.

Over the previous six weeks or so, the Pandora analysts listened to 650 Indian pieces, and the session I observed was a refresher course. Steve Hogan, who oversees Pandora's analyst squad, had given a half-dozen of its members the same two songs to analyze. The first was "Raga Ahir Bhairav," recorded by Bismillah Khan in 1955. But the analysts had not been given this cultural information; all they had for the assignment was the music and their ears. Hogan played a snippet and pointed to Kurt Kotheimer, a bass player who often gigs around the Bay Area.

Kotheimer consulted his listening notes: "Flat second, major third, perfect fourth, perfect fifth, major sixth, flat seventh." Everybody nodded: that's the tone set, which helps identify the particular raga, one of 25 new "genes" added to Pandora's algorithm to accommodate this variety of non-Western music. Based on the beat, everyone agreed that this raga was set in Teentaal, with a 16-beat rhythmic cycle often heard in North Indian classical music; it's now in the genome too. But that was the easy part, apparently.

They moved on to vocals, and Alan Lin, a violinist, ticked off the scores he came up with for things like rhythmic intensity and the relative exoticism of the melody scale. "I actually put exotic at 3.5," he said. This prompted Sameer Gupta—a percussionist and an expert on Indian music who was weighing in by speakerphone from New York—to lead a brief discussion of how to think about melody and exoticism in this context. Seven or eight scores related to melody, and then about the same number for harmony. ("A 5 for drone," one analyst announced.) More scores related to form. Tempo. The timbre of the reeds. When Gupta gave his score for riskiness on the percussion—a 3.5—Lin did a sort of fist pump: "Yes!" Evidently he'd scored it the same way, meaning progress toward properly fitting Indian music into the Music Genome Project. Things went on like this for a while. "Even if you have a solo violin with a tabla, you're still going to have monophony," Gupta remarked at one juncture. "I just wanted to point that out." It was hard to believe there was a business riding on this kind of conversation.

But while some of the genes involve expert, subjective judgment, they aren't qualitative in the most traditional sense: there's no rating that allows an analyst to conclude that a vocal or a sax solo is simply lousy. What Pandora's system largely ignores is, in a word, taste. The way that Gasser or Westergren might put this is that it minimizes the influence of other people's taste. Music-liking becomes a matter decided by the listener, and the intrinsic elements of what is heard. Early on, Westergren actually pushed for the idea that Pandora would not even reveal who the artist was until the listener asked. He thought maybe that structure would give users a kind of permission to evaluate music without even the most minimal cultural baggage. "We're so insecure about our tastes," he says.

While his partners talked him out of that approach, Westergren maintains "a personal aversion" to collaborative filtering or anything like it. "It's still a popularity contest," he complains, meaning that for any song to get recommended on a socially driven site, it has to be somewhat known already, by your friends or by other consumers. Westergren is similarly unimpressed by hipster blogs or other theoretically grassroots influencers of musical taste, for their tendency to turn on artists who commit the crime of being too popular; in his view that's just snobbery, based on social jockeying that has nothing to do with music. In various conversations, he defended Coldplay and Rob Thomas, among others, as victims of cool-taste prejudice. (When I ran Bob Lefsetz's dismissal of Pandora by him, he laughed it off, and transitioned to arguing that Journey is, actually, a great band.)

He likes to tell a story about a Pandora user who wrote in to complain that he started a station based on the music of Sarah McLachlan, and the service served up a Celine Dion song. "I wrote back and said, 'Was the music just wrong?' Because we sometimes have data errors," he recounts. "He said, 'Well, no, it was the right sort of thing—but it was Celine Dion.' I said, 'Well, was it the set, did it not flow in the set?' He said, 'No, it kind of worked—but it's Celine Dion.' We had a couple more back-and-forths, and finally his last e-mail to me was: 'Oh, my God, I like Celine Dion.'"

This anecdote almost always gets a laugh. "Pandora," he pointed out, "doesn't understand why that's funny."

By the time the Genome Project got under way, the idea of taking music apart and evaluating it by its acoustic elements was not actually new. "Machine listening" was pioneered in various university settings, often by people who had the exact same problem with collaborative filtering's reliance on social data that Westergren has. Machine listening basically involves teaching computers to assess sound (or really, waveforms representing sound) into something resembling the way that humans hear it, with the goal of eliminating living, breathing listeners from the evaluation process completely.

Like collaborative filtering, machine listening can deal with a lot of data quickly. And when Westergren was trying to raise a second round of financing after the dot-com bust, most everyone involved in the business of music and technology had come to believe that any recommendation system needed to be able to handle millions of songs, instantly. A bunch of musicians sitting around discussing the finer points of drone and monophony wouldn't cut it. "Everybody thought it was ridiculous," Westergren agrees. He gave something like 350 pitches to venture capitalists over three years. "Most investors could not get over this idea that we were using humans." But to Westergren, there were elements of music that machine listening just couldn't capture—like the emotionality of a Getz solo. So yes, he wants listeners to experience new music on the basis of the music and not the influence of other people—but to do it right, people have to analyze the music.

Whatever the algorithmic equation, of course, there's a listener on the other end who is much harder to decode. What you want to hear can depend on your mood, or whether you're listening at work or in a nightclub. Context affects any cultural product, but music is different from, say, books or movies. Even a casual listener hears many thousands of songs; and to love a song is to take it in—whether attentively or as background music—over and over. Mick Jagger was once asked what makes a tune a classic, and the co-author of "(I Can't Get No) Satisfaction" replied, "Repetition." And yet, even the most conservative listener knows the feeling of hearing a hit single once too often. Maybe because music is so ubiquitous, we respond to it almost like food: sometimes we want to try the new restaurant, sometimes the comfort of a familiar favorite dish.

Still, are all these listener-specific factors really enough to explain what music we like, and why? "Music is an inherently social experience," argues David Goodman, the president of *CBS* Interactive Music Group, which includes the popular Last.fm Internet radio service. Last.fm's social-networking model revolves largely around this idea. "The way in which you experience music by sharing, by storytelling, being part of a community. Last.fm is built on what is organic to music."

Ali Partovi, the C.E.O. of iLike, makes a related point. Used as an application on Facebook and similar sites, iLike bills itself as a "social music-discovery service" and claims more than 50 million registered users. There's a huge difference, Partovi argues, between "this computer thinks you'll like this song" and "your friend thinks you'll like this song—even if it's the same song." The problem with a computer reading waveforms is that it "has no common sense," summarizes Mike McCready, a founder of a company called Music Xray, a digital-music business for entertainment companies and artists. "It doesn't take into consideration whether the artist is just starting out or they're at the pinnacle of their career, it doesn't take into consideration what they wore to the Grammys or who they're dating or what they look like or what their age is. You have to factor all of this stuff in."

And why is that? Surely no one consciously says, "My cool friends like the new Jack White, so I'll memorize the lyrics and pretend to like it, too, for sociocultural reasons." Yet the research about how listeners link musical taste (at least at a genre level) and identity is extensive. Surely that's one reason so much of digital music culture is devoted to opportunities to "share" your taste: the endless options for posting playlists, recommending songs, displaying what you are listening to now, announcing your favorite artists.

Maybe the more vivid illustration of social influence on listening habits isn't in what we share but in what we obfuscate. Last.fm, for example, publishes a chart listing the songs that its users most frequently delete from their public listening-stream data. The guilty pleasure Top 10 is dominated by the most radio-ready pop artists—Katy Perry's "I Kissed a Girl," several tracks by Lady Gaga. The service iLike compiles similar data on the most "suppressed" songs its users listen to in secret; Britney Spears figures prominently. Apparently even listeners who can set aside certain cultural information long enough to enjoy something uncool would just as soon their friends didn't know. Maybe even in our most private listening moments, what our peers think matters.

Much attention has been focused in the last few years on studying music-liking at the brain level. Daniel Levitin, a neuroscientist (and musician) has been one of the high-profile thinkers in this area, by way of his popular books "This Is Your Brain on Music" and "The World in Six Songs." One of his central themes is that pretty much all humans are wired to enjoy music, and he says he believes musicality is even important to the evolution of the species.

But when you start talking about individuals, instead of humanity in general, universals are a lot harder to come by. Much depends on culture. The emotions expressed in many of those ragas that Pandora's experts are presently decoding, for instance, are lost on the typical Westerner. Just as we're hard-wired to learn a language, but not to speak English or French, our specific musical understanding, and thus taste, depends on context. If a piece of music sounds dissonant to you, it probably has to do with what sort of music you were exposed to growing up, because you were probably an "expert listener" in your culture's music by about age 6, Levitin writes.

The cliché that our musical tastes are generally refined in our teens and solidify by our early 20s seems largely to be true. For better or worse, peers frequently have a lot to do with that. Levitin recalled to me having moved at age 14 and falling in with a new set of friends who listened to music he hadn't heard before. "The reason I like Queen—and I love Queen—is that I was introduced to Queen by my social group," he says. He's not saying that the intrinsic qualities of the music are irrelevant, and he says Pandora has done some very clever and impressive things in its approach. But part of what we like is, in fact, based on cultural information. "To some degree we might say that personality characteristics are associated with, or predictive of, the kind of music that people like," he has written. "But to a large degree it is determined by more or less chance factors: where you went to school, who you hung out with, what music they happened to be listening to."

Pandora's approach to listening violates at least three pieces of conventional digital-music wisdom: it rejects the supremacy of social-data taste communities; it shrugs off the assumption that contemporary listeners must have instant on-demand access to any single song; and, most striking, it rejects what many observers see as a given, which is that music consumers are fundamentally motivated by access to the most massive pool of songs possible. Slacker.com, a rival Internet-radio service, says its library contains about 2.5 million songs. Spotify, the European music streaming service, expected to be available in the U.S. by early next year, is generating enormous buzz because it offers free, on-demand access to more than 5 million tunes.

Pandora's 700,000-song library sounds puny by comparison. And yet the service has millions of devoted listeners. Why? One answer, perhaps, involves the ways that the genome, quietly, doesn't really screen out sociocultural information. For instance, its algorithms are tweaked by genre, and the inclusion of genes for "influence" ("swing" or "gospel," for example) brings in factors that aren't strictly about sound. And Pandora's algorithm does adjust if, for instance, users routinely thumbs-down a particular song under similar circumstances, meaning the genome's acoustic judgment can at times be trumped by crowd taste. But the biggest cultural decision of all may be the one that also happens to guide Westergren's response to the issue of scale: how, exactly, does a given piece of music get into Pandora's system anyway?

Pandora claims to add about 10,000 songs a month to its library. The "curation" of Pandora, in effect, falls to Michael Zapruder, another musician who has found himself working for a tech company. Zapruder ended up as Pandora's curator because he had a habit of identifying holes in the service's collection.

Eventually he was told to fill all the gaps he could. "I had a field day," he recalls; he'd stroll through record stores, buying every single Johnny Cash CD or every tango disc available, plus anything that looked interesting. He paid attention to users' suggestions. Somebody wrote in to say that Pandora needed to improve its jazz-trombone selection; somebody else complained about the dearth of barbershop-quartet music. He took care of it. He has beefed up the Latin-music and the J-pop catalog. The major acquisition project right now is Afrobeat, because by far the biggest failed search is Fela Kuti. Zapruder is in the midst of this research but knows that as this new batch of music comes online, "we're going to get educated by our listeners."

Every Tuesday he looks at the New Music Tipsheet, which lists a few hundred new tracks in a typical week. He scrutinizes the Billboard and CMJ charts. He hears directly from a wide array of distributors, from indie-focused Revolver Records to big shots like Universal Music Group. In addition to what is simply sent to Pandora (by labels, artists, P.R. firms), the company buys hundreds of CDs a month, as well as electronica and hip-hop downloads, acquired from sites like Beatport. Every month, hundreds of bands send songs, and Zapruder does his best to get onto Pandora what he figures his listeners want to hear. Still, the labor-intensive genome simply can't absorb it all.

Westergren maintains that catalog size receded as a problem at around the 300,000-song mark. Since passing that, he says, the number of "missed" searches has declined markedly, so the great majority of people who come to the site and type in an artist or song name get a proper introduction to the Pandora system. But the more surprising part of Westergren's response is his claim that he isn't worried about compiling the biggest possible catalog. "This may seem counterintuitive," he told me, "but we struggle more with making sure we're adding really good stuff." That sounds like a rather subjective, cultural judgment—shouldn't the listener decide what's good, based purely on the genome's intrinsics-of-music guidance? Well, there's no question that Westergren is a champion of the unheard music that gets marginalized by sociocultural judgments. But even he has standards.

Cultural Literacy Resources from T.E.D.com

School Kill Creativity by Ken Robinson
The World's English Mania by Jay Walker
Endangered Cultures by Wade Davis

Disciplinary Literacies

Disciplinary Literacies: Introduction

Although strategies for revision, invention, arrangement, style and delivery (RAIDS) and considerations of subject, writer, audience and purpose (SWAP) can be used across writing situations, different disciplines can have very different expectations for what literacy products need to be like to be effective. (See Appendix 1 at the end of this book for definitions of RAIDS and SWAP.) The readings we selected for this section serve three major purposes. First, they are meant to familiarize you with some of the ways people think about writing, reading, and researching as literacy activities that allow us to respond to lots of different literacy situations in effective ways. Second, they offer even more invention and arrangement strategies for you to identify and add to your own repertoire. Third, these readings give you a chance to focus on revision as an activity that changes something outside of the text itself.

As you think about how you might focus your own exploration of a disciplinary form of literacy, try to identify what will change as a result of the information you gather. For example, as William Diehl and Larry Mikulecky gather information about how people read and write at work, they revise the idea that school educates people to meet the literacy expectations in most workplaces. As Larry Haun narrates the story of a carpenter's life, he revises the idea that there is no connection between larger cultural changes in technology and the life of individual workers. What will your exploration of disciplinary literacy revise? For what audience? How?

Thinking about invention and arrangement, and asking questions about the revisionary purpose of your writing processes helps you read as a writer and write with the needs of your readers in mind.

Winning Hearts and Minds in War on Plagiarism

Scott Jaschik

Scott Jaschik grew up in Rochester, New York and graduated from Cornell University in 1985. His articles have appeared in numerous publications, such as The New York Times, The Washington Post, The Boston Globe, Campus Watch, *and* Salon. *From 1999 to 2003 he was an editor for* The Chronicle of Higher Education. *Jaschik is a co-founder of* Inside Higher Ed, *an online source for news, commentary, and jobs pertaining to higher education. He is a mentor in the community college fellowship program for the Hechinger Institute on Education and Media. He has received honors for his reporting from* The Washington Monthly *and from* Investigative Reporters and Editors, *a non-profit organization dedicated to improving the quality of investigative reporting. Jaschik currently lives in Washington, DC. In the following article from* Inside Higher Ed, *he profiles one professor's unique approach to teaching students about plagiarism and how to avoid it.*

It's come to this: Writing professors are so desperate for new ways to teach undergraduates about academic integrity that they are assigning them to plagiarize.

That's what Kate Hagopian, an instructor in the first-year writing program at North Carolina State University, does. For one assignment, she gives her students a short writing passage and then a prompt for a standard student short essay. She asks her students to turn in two versions. In one they are told that they must plagiarize. In the second, they

Reprinted by permission from *Inside Higher Ed,* April 7, 2008.

are told not to. The prior night, the students were given an online tutorial on plagiarism and Hagopian said she has become skeptical that having the students "parrot back what we've told them" accomplishes anything. Her hope is that this unusual assignment might change that.

After the students turn in their two responses to the essay prompt, Hagopian shares some with the class. Not surprisingly, the students do know how to plagiarize—but were uncomfortable admitting as much. Hagopian said that the assignment is always greeted with "uncomfortable laughter" as the students must pretend that they never would have thought of plagiarizing on their own. Given the right to do so, they turn in essays with many direct quotes without attribution. Of course in their essays that are supposed to be done without plagiarism, she still finds problems—not so much with passages repeated verbatim, but with paraphrasing or using syntax in ways that were so similar to the original that they required attribution.

When she started giving the assignment, she sort of hoped, Hagopian said, to see students turn in "nuanced tricky demonstrations" of plagiarism, but she mostly gets garden variety copying. But what she is doing is having detailed conversations with her students about what is and isn't plagiarism—and by turning everyone into a plagiarist (at least temporarily), she makes the conversation something that can take place openly.

"Students know I am listening," she said. And by having the conversation in this way—as opposed to reading the riot act—she said she is demonstrating that all plagiarism is not the same, whether in technique, motivation or level of sophistication. There is a difference between "deliberate fraud" and "failed apprenticeship," she said.

Hagopian's approach was among many described at various sessions last week at the *annual meeting of the Conference of College Composition and Communication,* in New Orleans. Writing instructors—especially those tasked with teaching freshmen—are very much on the front lines of the war against plagiarism. As much as other faculty members, they resent plagiarism by their students—and in fact several of the talks featured frank discussion of how betrayed writing instructors feel when someone turns in plagiarized work.

That anger does motivate some to use the software that detects plagiarism as part of an effort to scare students and weed out plagiarists, and there was some discussion along those lines. But by and large, the instructors at the meeting said that they didn't have any confidence that these services were attacking the roots of the problem or finding all of the plagiarism. Several people quipped that if the software really detected all plagiarism, plenty of campuses would be unable to hold classes, what with all of the sessions needed for academic integrity boards.

While there was a group therapy element to some of the discussions, there was also a strong focus on trying new solutions. Freshmen writing instructors after all don't have the option available to other faculty members of just blaming the problem on the failures of those who teach first-year comp.

What to do? New books being displayed in the exhibit hall included several trying to shift the plagiarism debate beyond a matter of pure enforcement. Among them were *Originality, Imitation, and Plagiarism: Teaching Writing in the Digital Age,* just published by the University of Michigan (and *profiled on Inside Higher Ed*), and *Pluralizing Plagiarism: Identities, Contexts, Pedagogies,* released in February by Boynton/Cook.

Like Hagopian, many of those at the meeting said that they are focused on trying to better understand their students, what makes them plagiarize, and what might make them better understand academic integrity. There wasn't much talk of magic bullets, but lots of ideas about ways to better see the issue from a student perspective—and to find ways to use that perspective to promote integrity.

What Students Are Saying

Roy Stamper, associate director of the writing program at N.C. State, gave a presentation about a discussion he followed (for purposes of understanding, not enforcement) on *the Wolf Web,* a student discussion board. Students at N.C. State post anonymously, and while Stamper said he didn't know if all of the students were posting with accuracy about their situations, he still found plenty of truth in what they had to say.

The discussion was kicked off by a student asking for advice about certain term paper companies and whether they sold good work. The student, apparently fearful of how this would make him look, talked about how he was "completely and utterly fried and overloaded" and didn't have enough time. But he also said he didn't want to get caught plagiarizing.

While some of the responses rated various term paper sites, there was also a strong, intense reaction from other students—much of it critical. "The less time you spend posting on here the more time u get to work on your paper," wrote one student. Another student wrote: "It's called college. Grow up and get your shit done."

As other students joined in, offering suggestions on time management, Stamper said he was struck that the argument being put forth against plagiarism wasn't honesty, but efficiency, and that has its dangers too, as was brought home to him by this posting: "I say that if you can get away with doing 30 minutes worth of plagiarism as opposed to a few days of work . . . then you my friend are efficient, and not necessarily a bad person."

Yet another student argued that term paper mills could promote efficiency without turning one into a plagiarist. This student said that he used term papers obtained online to gain ideas, but that because he then rewrites these ideas himself, it's not plagiarism. "My work, with a little help," is how he characterized it.

This prompted an angry outcry from another student, who wrote: "This shit is plagiarism by any definition. If you were caught and turned over to the office of student conduct, your ass would be nailed to the cross."

Stamper said that he shared the anger of that final student (if not the idea that the plagiarist deserved to be compared to Jesus), but that once he got past the anger, he found that his lurking online raised many questions. For instance, Stamper said that while he does not believe being overworked justifies plagiarism, he has found himself wondering about whether an intense workload puts an emphasis for students on efficiency as opposed to quality. "Good writing takes a lot of time and thought. I'm not sure I'm always giving them enough time," he said.

The other thing that the online discussion demonstrated, he said, was that many students do have a strong sense of right and wrong when it comes to plagiarism and the idea that every student born in the last 30 years believes everything online is fair to use is a stereotype. Students clearly are educable, he said, and perhaps the best approach may be peer pressure—the plagiarists on the N.C. State site were clearly embarrassed and looked to justify themselves. Should writing instructors be looking to peer teaching—and specifically peer pressure—as a new tool to promote integrity, Stamper asked.

"Patchwriting" vs. Plagiarism

Several of the speakers discussed ideas related to differentiating plagiarism of the sort that involves buying a term paper or submitting another student's work with more common, and not always intentional, writing behaviors used by many students that meet textbook definitions of plagiarism but that may raise different moral and educational issues. Many cite the work of Rebecca Moore Howard (co-editor of one of the new books on plagiarism and a contributor to another), who is an associate professor of writing and rhetoric at Syracuse University.

Howard talks about "patchwriting" as a common undergraduate technique of grouping together various sources of information, frequently with only minor changes in wording and without appropriate attribution. For her own classes, she uses *a policy* that says such writing will generally lead to a poor grade, but not to sanctions that would go to someone who bought a term paper.

Along these lines, R. Gerald Nelms, an associate professor of composition and rhetoric at Southern Illinois University at Carbondale, spoke of how plagiarism must be seen as "an educational problem that requires an educational response." Much student plagiarism, he said, is unintentional, as students don't know how to take notes, how to summarize ideas, how to attribute ideas or quotes, and what paraphrasing means (and doesn't) with regard to plagiarism.

In a handout, Nelms wrote that patchwriting is "developmental plagiarism," or "behavior that is caused by the effort of the writer not fully integrated into the community for which she or he is trying to write to imitate the behavior of that community." Such plagiarism, he said, shouldn't be viewed as acceptable, but also shouldn't draw punishment. Students who engage in patchwriting need to be taught, he said, not brought up on charges. Nelms recommended a series of teaching subjects for instructors trying to show students how to write original work.

Students need to be taught to take notes, he said in his handout—so notes aren't just direct quotes or synopses, but also include students' reactions or potential use of information. In this way, students are starting to learn how to use information, not just how to repackage it. Similarly, he said in the handout, "integration involves more than citation," and must include efforts to show students how to mix various sources, how to attribute, and how to include original ideas.

"Restorative Justice" for Plagiarists

Christy Zink, an assistant professor of writing at George Washington University, used the controversy over the play *Frozen* to teach her first-year students about plagiarism. The play—about a psychiatrist who examines serial killers—was a Broadway hit, but also led to *charges of plagiarism* against its author by a psychiatrist who said that writings about her career were used without her permission for the drama.

Zink is an advocate of using "restorative justice" to deal with plagiarism. *"Restorative justice"* is an approach to criminal behavior that involves repairing the harm done by an act, but not focusing on punishment for the sake of punishment.

One of Zink's students—even though the course was focused on a discussion of plagiarism issues—plagiarized her work for an assignment. Zink said she was a bit stunned that in such a context, a student would engage in blatant plagiarism (she stressed that this wasn't a borderline case). But the student appealed to Zink's commitment to restorative justice, and said "isn't that why I'm here? To learn from my mistakes?"

While Zink worked out a punishment herself with the student—involving new work and a grade punishment—she also decided to try to apply the restorative justice ideal to the situation by talking to all three sections of the class about the situation (without identifying the student) and seeking their views on what to do. Zink's announcement to her classes that "we have a plagiarist among us" prompted a range of reactions from students.

Zink said that her students were angry at first, but that they then argued that many other considerations should go into consideration of sanctions. To most students, "intentionality matters," Zink said. Students wanted to know if the plagiarism was "an honest mistake" or deliberate. At the same time, given that the class was so focused on plagiarism, the students were doubtful that the student couldn't have known what she was doing was wrong. So the students were both interested in motivation, and not willing to accept any excuse.

The lesson, Zink said, is that while "we need the law," we also need to make decisions on more than just legalistic approaches. As another example, she described very much not wanting to like the play *Frozen,* in part because of the plagiarism issues. But she found herself deeply moved nonetheless.

An Unusual Sort-of Plagiarized Essay About Plagiarism

Catherine Savini, director of the Undergraduate Writing Center at Columbia University, described using an unusual essay to prod students to think in new ways. The essay, *"The Ecstasy of Influence: A Plagiarism,"* appeared in *Harper's* last year. In the work, Jonathan Lethem makes an impassioned plea against traditional concepts of copyright and plagiarism, and he does so with words and phrases that are almost entirely plagiarized—with no credit while making the argument, but a key at the end fessing up to his writing thefts. His technique drew attention and controversy.

Even Lawrence Lessig, the Stanford University law professor who is a prominent critic of copyright restrictions, wrote in to express his discomfort at finding one of his own sentences used in the essay. "The freedom that Lethem depends upon—the freedom to integrate and build upon the work of others—does not need the license the plagiarist takes," Lessig wrote in a letter to the magazine. "The rules against plagiarism, after all, require only that words borrowed be acknowledged as borrowed." (Lessig also applauded the essay's creativity and expressed hope that it would prompt further thought by those who seek to regulate the use of others' works.)

Savini said that this text is at once "dangerous" and provocative for students because it appears to glorify plagiarism and yet goes so far—and copies the work of such noted authors—that students are taken aback. "Is it a model? Is it fodder?"

When she assigned students to write about the essay, many were afraid of a plagiarism trap. "How do I cite Lethem?" was the question she received from many students, anxious about whether citations should go to Lethem, to those whose works he borrowed, both or neither. Students were so puzzled by the situation, Savini said, that many went to unusual lengths to avoid quoting from the essay they were writing about.

Then Savini told the students she wanted them to consider sharing their writing with Lethem. This further challenged students, she said, because they normally don't think about audience in writing, placing their instructors in some other category. Thinking about people as being affected by their writing was another step in viewing writing as more than completing an assignment, Savini said, but as something with ethical issues involved. "It's a difficult leap of the imagination" for many students to think about anyone other than their instructors reading their work, but they need to, she said.

"Suddenly, students were asking questions without easy answers," Savini said, about fairness, about the obligations of authors, and the relationship between authors and readers. "It's a morass I want my students to be in," she said.

Learning the Language
Perri Klass

Perri Klass (1958–) was born to American parents in Trinidad and earned her M.D. from Harvard in 1986, going on to become a pediatrician. She has been writing and publishing widely while pursuing her medical career. Her fiction includes two novels, Recombinations *(1985) and* Other Women's Children *(1990), and a collection of short stories,* I Am Having an Adventure *(1986). She published a collection of autobiographical essays,* A Not Entirely Benign Procedure *(1987) about her experience in medical school. The following selection, "Learning the Language," is excerpted from that book. Klass is sensitive to uses of language and understands how language affects thinking. As you read this essay, think about other special groups who also use language in unique ways.*

"**M**rs. Tolstoy is your basic LOL in NAD, admitted for a soft rule-out MI," the intern announces. I scribble that on my patient list. In other words, Mrs. Tolstoy is a Little Old Lady in No Apparent Distress who is in the hospital to make sure she hasn't had a heart attack (rule out a Myocardial Infarction). And we think it's unlikely that she has had a heart attack (a *soft* rule-out).

If I learned nothing else during my first three months of working in the hospital as a medical student, I learned endless jargon and abbreviations. I started out in a state of primeval innocence, in which I didn't even know that "s̄ CP, SOB, N/V" meant "without chest pain, shortness of breath, or nausea and vomiting." By the end I took the abbreviations so much for granted that I would complain to my

---

Reprinted from *Not an Entirely Benign Procedure* (1987), by permission of the author.

mother the English professor, "And can you believe I had to put down three NG tubes last night?"

"You'll have to tell me what an NG tube is if you want me to sympathize properly," my mother said. NG, nasogastric—isn't it obvious?

I picked up not only the specific expressions but also the patterns of speech and the grammatical conventions; for example, you never say that a patient's blood pressure fell or that his cardiac enzymes rose. Instead, the patient is always the subject of the verb: "He dropped his pressure." "He bumped his enzymes." This sort of construction probably reflects the profound irritation of the intern when the nurses come in the middle of the night to say that Mr. Dickinson has disturbingly low blood pressure. "Oh, he's gonna hurt me bad tonight," the intern might say, inevitably angry at Mr. Dickinson for dropping his pressure and creating a problem.

When chemotherapy fails to cure Mrs. Bacon's cancer, what we say is, "Mrs. Bacon failed chemotherapy."

"Well, we've already had one hit today, and we're up next, but at least we've got mostly stable players on our team." This means that our team (group of doctors and medical students) has already gotten one new admission today, and it is our turn again, so we'll get whoever is admitted next in emergency, but at least most of the patients we already have are fairly stable, that is, unlikely to drop their pressures or in any other way get suddenly sicker and hurt us bad. Baseball metaphor is pervasive. A no-hitter is a night without any new admissions. A player is always a patient—a nitrate player is a patient on nitrates, a unit player is a patient in the intensive care unit, and so on, until you reach the terminal player.

It is interesting to consider what it means to be winning, or doing well, in this perennial baseball game. When the intern hangs up the phone and announces, "I got a hit," that is not cause for congratulations. The team is not scoring points; rather, it is getting hit, being bombarded with new patients. The object of the game from the point of view of the doctors, considering the players for whom they are already responsible, is to get as few new hits as possible.

This special language contributes to a sense of closeness and professional spirit among people who are under a great deal of stress. As a medical student, I found it exciting to discover that I'd finally cracked the code, that I could understand what doctors said and wrote, and could use the same formulations myself. Some people seem to become enamored of the jargon for its own sake, perhaps because they are so deeply thrilled with the idea of medicine, with the idea of themselves as doctors.

I knew a medical student who was referred to by the interns on the team as Mr. Eponym because he was so infatuated with eponymous terminology, the more obscure the better. He never said "capillary pulsations" if he could say "Quincke's pulses." He would lovingly tell over the multinamed syndromes—Wolff-Parkinson-White, Lown-Ganong-Levine, Schönlein-Henoch—until the temptation to suggest Schleswig-Holstein or Stevenson-Kefauver or Baskin-Robbins became irresistible to his less reverent colleagues.

And there is the jargon that you don't ever want to hear yourself using. You know that your training is changing you, but there are certain changes you think would be going a little too far.

The resident was describing a man with devastating terminal pancreatic cancer. "Basically he's CTD," the resident concluded. I reminded myself that I had resolved not to be shy about asking when I didn't understand things. "CTD?" I asked timidly.

The resident smirked at me. "Circling The Drain."

The images are vivid and terrible. "What happened to Mrs. Melville?"

"Oh, she boxed last night." To box is to die, of course.

Then there are the more pompous locutions that can make the beginning medical student nervous about the effects of medical training. A friend of mine was told by his resident, "A pregnant woman with sickle-cell represents a failure of genetic counseling."

Mr. Eponym, who tried hard to talk like the doctors, once explained to me, "An infant is basically a brainstem preparation." The term "brainstem preparation," as used in neurological research, refers to an animal whose higher brain functions have been destroyed so that only the most primitive reflexes remain, like the sucking reflex, the startle reflex, and the rooting reflex.

And yet at other times the harshness dissipates into a strangely elusive euphemism. "As you know, this is a not entirely benign procedure," some doctor will say, and that will be understood to imply agony, risk of complications, and maybe even a significant mortality rate.

The more extreme forms aside, one most important function of medical jargon is to help doctors maintain some distance from their patients. By reformulating a patient's pain and problems into a language that the patient doesn't even speak, I suppose we are in some sense taking those pains and problems under our jurisdiction and also reducing their emotional impact. This linguistic separation between doctors and patients allows conversations to go on at the bedside that are unintelligible to the patient. "Naturally, we're worried about adeno-CA," the intern can say to the medical student, and lung cancer need never be mentioned.

I learned a new language this past summer. At times it thrills me to hear myself using it. It enables me to understand my colleagues, to communicate effectively in the hospital. Yet I am uncomfortably aware that I will never again notice the peculiarities and even atrocities of medical language as keenly as I did this summer. There may be specific expressions I manage to avoid, but even as I remark them, promising myself I will never use them, I find that this language is becoming my professional speech. It no longer sounds strange in my ears—or coming from my mouth. And I am afraid that as with any new language, to use it properly you must absorb not only the vocabulary but also the structure, the logic, the attitudes. At first you may notice these new and alien assumptions every time you put together a sentence, but with time and increased fluency you stop being aware of them at all. And as you lose that awareness, for better or for worse, you move closer and closer to being a doctor instead of just talking like one.

Policing Race and Class

David Cole

iami to Atlanta is 663 miles. If you had a choice, you'd fly.
Those who can't afford air travel often make the trip by
bus, a grueling nineteen-hour ride. On August 27, 1985,
Terrance Bostick, a twenty-eight-year-old black man, was sleeping in
the back seat of a Greyhound bus, on his way from Miami to Atlanta,
when he awoke to find two police officers standing over him. They
were wearing bright green "raid" jackets bearing the Broward County
Sheriff's Office insignia and displaying their badges; one held a gun
in a plastic gun pouch. The bus was stopped at a brief layover in Fort
Lauderdale, and the officers were "working the bus," looking for persons who might be carrying drugs.

Upon waking Bostick, the officers asked for his identification and
ticket. He complied. They then asked to search his bag. Again,
Bostick complied, somewhat inexplicably, because upon opening the
bag, the officers found a pound of cocaine. The officers admitted that
at no time prior to the search did they have any basis for suspecting
Bostick of any criminal activity.

Bus and train sweeps of this kind are a common method of drug
enforcement investigations. Police board buses or trains at intermedi-
ate stops to exploit the fact that the traveler has nowhere to go. In
theory, passengers have a constitutional right to refuse to answer any
questions, and to say no when a police officer asks to search their
luggage. In practice, virtually everybody talks and consents. One
officer testified that he had searched 3,000 bags without once being
refused consent. The tactic works. In West Palm Beach alone, bus
sweeps over a thirteen-month period netted 300 pounds of cocaine,
800 pounds of marijuana, 24 handguns, and 75 suspected drug
"mules." But whether it should be constitutional raises fundamental
questions about the role of race in law enforcement decisionmaking,
and about the courts' responsibility to police the police.

Reprinted from *No Equal Justice: Race and Class in the American Criminal Justice System*
(1999), by permission of New Press.

206

Reasonable People

When prosecutors charged Bostick with drug possession, he challenged the police officer's conduct, and the Florida Supreme Court held it unconstitutional. The court reasoned that Bostick had effectively been "seized" when the officers cornered him at the back of the bus, because at that moment he was not free to leave. The Fourth Amendment forbids the police from seizing individuals without some individualized suspicion that they have committed or are committing a crime, and the police admitted they had none for Bostick. The remedy for such a violation—under the Fourth Amendment's "exclusionary rule"—is that the prosecution may not use evidence obtained by the encounter to establish its case. In addition to holding the evidence inadmissible against Bostick, the Florida Supreme Court broadly condemned "bus sweeps," likening them to methods used by totalitarian states:

> [T]he evidence in this case has evoked images of other days, under other flags, when no man traveled his nation's roads or railways without fear of unwarranted interruption, by individuals who had temporary power in the Government . . . This is not Hitler's Berlin, nor Stalin's Moscow, nor is it white supremacist South Africa. Yet in Broward County, Florida, these police officers approach every person on board buses and trains ("that time permits") and check identification, tickets, ask to search luggage—all in the name of "voluntary cooperation" with law enforcement.

Florida's Attorney General appealed to the U.S. Supreme Court, which agreed to hear the case. In the Supreme Court, Bostick was represented by Donald Ayer, a highly respected Washington lawyer with impeccable conservative credentials. A Republican, Ayer had clerked for Chief Justice William Rehnquist. Shortly before taking Bostick's case, he had stepped down from a position as the Deputy Solicitor General, where he had represented the Reagan administration in some of its most politically charged cases before the Supreme Court. Ayer felt that this was a case of law enforcement going too far, and offered to handle Bostick's case pro bono before the Supreme Court. Ayer convinced Americans for Effective Law Enforcement, a pro-law-enforcement organization that had previously filed eighty-five amicus briefs in the Supreme Court, all supporting the police, to file an amicus brief on Bostick's behalf urging the Court to find an unreasonable seizure in this case.

The principles at stake were fairly basic. The Fourth Amendment prohibits "unreasonable searches and seizures," and the Supreme Court had previously held that a "seizure" is unreasonable without some articulable reason, specific to the individual, for suspecting crime. Seizures come in two varieties: full-scale arrests, which require probable cause that the individual has committed a crime; and brief "stops," which require only a reasonable suspicion that crime is afoot. But all seizures require at least some degree of *individualized* suspicion, and the police had admitted that they had none when they approached Bostick.

Not every encounter between a citizen and a police officer, however, is a "seizure" that must be justified under the Fourth Amendment. Otherwise, police officers would not be able to approach anyone on the street without first having grounds to suspect criminal conduct. In prior cases, the Court had ruled that a police officer "seizes" an individual when "by means of physical force or show of authority, [the officer] has restrained [the citizen's] liberty," and that the relevant question is whether a reasonable person in the citizen's shoes would feel "free to disregard the [officer's] questions and walk away."

Few of us, awakened in the middle of a marathon bus ride by armed police officers standing over us, asking for our identification and requesting to search our bags, would feel free to tell the officers to mind their own business. But the Supreme Court's "reasonable person" apparently has a lot more mettle than the average Joe. The Court had previously ruled, for example, that a traveler approached by police in an airport and asked to show his identification and ticket was not "seized" by the encounter, because a "reasonable person" would feel free to walk away. As long as the police do not convey a message that their requests must be obeyed, the Court ruled, they can approach citizens without any basis for suspicion, interrogate them, ask to see their identification, and request to search their luggage.

But even accepting the dubious proposition that a passenger walking through an airport will feel free to ignore an approaching police officer, Ayer argued, it is quite another thing to say that a reasonable person *in Bostick's place* would have felt free to ignore the two officers who stood above him in the bus aisle, blocking the only way out. Even if Bostick had been able to push his way around the officers and get off the bus, he would have found himself in the middle of rural Florida, far from his destination, and separated from any luggage he'd checked. If he chose to remain on the bus but to refuse to cooperate, he might reasonably have predicted that his conduct would raise police suspicion, and lead to their searching his bags anyway, or worse. The encounter was not truly consensual, as Bostick's conduct demonstrated. Indeed, Ayer argued, no "reasonable person" would agree to a search of a bag that contained a pound of cocaine if he really believed he was free to say no without adverse consequences.

The Supreme Court rejected Ayer's arguments, and reversed the Florida Supreme Court. The proper test, the Court explained, was not whether a reasonable person in Bostick's shoes would have felt free *to leave*—the test the Court had used until Bostick's case—but *to terminate the encounter*. The Court posited that even if he didn't feel free to leave, a "reasonable person" would have felt free to sit there and adamantly refuse to answer the police officer's questions. That Bostick was on a bus may well have restricted his freedom to walk away, but, the Court reasoned, that wasn't the police's fault. The police did not make him get on the bus. They merely found him there. Bostick would have to point to something extraordinary in the *police officer's conduct* to establish that he had been "seized." The mere fact that they had boarded the bus en route, were standing over him, blocking his exit, displaying badges and a gun, and directing questions at him was not enough.

The consequence of *Florida v. Bostick* is that police are free to engage in dragnet-like searches of buses and trains, in settings where it is extremely difficult for any citizen to refuse to cooperate. As long as the police do not effect a "seizure," there are no Fourth Amendment limits whatsoever on whom they approach or what questions they ask. They could routinely direct such inquiries at every person on every bus, train, and for that matter, airplane in America.

By adopting a "reasonable person" standard that is patently fictional, this ruling allows the police to engage in substantial coercion under the rubric of "consent," without any limits on the persons to whom that coercion can be applied. As federal judge Prentice Marshall explained in a separate case, "[i]mplicit in the introduction of the [officer] and the initial questioning is a show of authority to which the average person encountered will feel obliged to stop and respond. Few will feel that they can walk away or refuse an answer." The Court's test assumes the opposite, and finds coercion only where police engage in some coercive conduct above and beyond their inherent authority. For all practical purposes, the Court's test erases the inherently coercive nature of *all* police encounters from the legal calculus for determining whether a Fourth Amendment "seizure" has occurred. As long as police officers use *only* the inherent coercion of their own official identity, they are free to seek citizens' "cooperation" for questioning and searches. In *Bostick* the Court went still further, permitting the police to exploit circumstances that independently constrain citizens' freedom to escape an encounter with the police. The Court's reasonable person fiction has its benefits. It substantially reduces the law enforcement costs that would result were the Fourth Amendment applied to all nonconsensual encounters. By adopting a standard that ignores the coercion inherent even in a situation such as Bostick's, the Court permits the police to engage in a wide range of nonconsensual, coercive intrusions on privacy without any basis for individualized suspicion.

At first glance, this fiction deprives all of us of our Fourth Amendment rights; it equally ignores the coerciveness of police encounters with rich white businessmen and unemployed black teenagers. But this standard will have very different effects on the poor and the wealthy, and on minority and white citizens. First, the police are far more likely to use this unfettered discretion against black teenagers than white executives. In practice, the police are selective about their targets. This is partly a matter of resources; the personnel required to confront all travelers would be extraordinary, and the yield would likely be small, because the vast majority of travelers presumably are not carrying contraband. Selective enforcement may also, however, reflect a savvy political judgment; if the police did in fact inflict such suspicionless treatment on everyone, there would likely be sufficient political will to curtail the practice politically, either by legislation or by community pressure on police departments.

So the police "work the buses" selectively, and because in the Court's view no "seizure" takes place, they need not explain *how* they select their targets. Targets could be selected at random, on the basis of unadulterated hunches, or, more likely, on the basis of unspoken stereotypes and assumptions about the kind of traveler likely to be carrying contraband. There is good reason to believe that minorities in general, and young black men in particular (such as Terrance Bostick), are disproportionately targeted. This tactic is practiced not on airplanes, but on buses and trains, modes of transportation more frequently used by poor and minority travelers. Once on the train, few officers will choose to approach an elderly white woman or a well-dressed businessman over a young black man "roughly dressed." There are few available statistics on the racial breakdown of police stops. Where reported cases discuss bus and train sweeps, however, the defendants are virtually always black or Hispanic. A search of all reported federal bus and train sweep cases from

January 1, 1993, to August 22, 1995, found that, of fifty-five cases in which the defendant's race could be identified, thirty-six were black, eleven were Hispanic, one was Asian, one was Filipino, and six were white. As Justice Thurgood Marshall stated in dissent in *Bostick,* "the basis of the decision to single out particular passengers during a suspicionless sweep is less likely to be inarticulable than unspeakable."

Thus, although the doctrine leaves the police free to target whomever they please, the targets will not be random; by and large they will be young black men. All relevant data—from arrest rates to conviction rates to victim reporting—suggest that young people are more likely to commit crime than old people, men more likely than women, and black people more likely than white people. The disproportionate numbers of young black men in prison and jail—disparities that cannot be explained by discriminatory policing or prosecuting alone—suggest that if police are going to be guided not by individualized suspicion but by more general characteristics, the odds of discovering some evidence of crime will be greater if they stop young black men. By permitting the police to use what is actually quite coercive behavior without any articulable basis for individualized suspicion, the Court's standard encourages the police to act on race-based judgments.

Second, the Court's "objective," one-size-fits-all reasonable person standard fails to take into account that citizens may be differently situated with respect to encounters with the police. It would seem noncontroversial, for example, that a fourteen-year-old child would feel less free to terminate an encounter with a police officer than a fifty-year-old member of Congress, even if the encounters were identical in all other respects. Yet the Supreme Court has held that the reasonable person standard "does not vary with the state of mind of the particular individual being approached," and "calls for consistent application from one police encounter to the next, regardless of the particular individual's response to the actions of the police." Applying that ruling, the District of Columbia Court of Appeals held that the same reasonable person standard applies to a fourteen-year-old child as to an adult.

A citizen's prior experiences with the police are also likely to play a part in how coercive an encounter seems. As the acquittal of O. J. Simpson dramatically illustrated, there is little love lost between the black community and the police in many areas of the nation. A survey of the Los Angeles Police Department found that one-quarter of the 650 *officers* responding agreed that "racial bias (prejudice) on the part of officers toward minority citizens currently exists and contributes to a negative interaction between police and the community," and that "an officer's prejudice toward the suspect's race may lead to the use of excessive force." For a host of reasons, from the disproportionate number of blacks behind bars today, to the historical use of the criminal justice system to maintain racial subordination, to the contemporary treatment of blacks on the streets by many police, the black community has a low level of trust for the criminal justice system, and for the police in particular.

The videotaped beating of Rodney King by officers of the Los Angeles Police Department encapsulated for many blacks the treatment they expect and fear from the police. As California Assemblyman Curtis Tucker was quoted as saying at a subsequent hearing on LAPD practices, "When black people in Los Angeles see a police car approaching, 'They don't know whether justice will be meted out or whether judge, jury and executioner is pulling up behind them.'" Similarly, a black man encountering a police officer in the Bronx today cannot help being affected by the knowledge that police officers there have engaged in a practice of indiscriminate beatings of minority citizens in order to establish their authority. In 1994, the Mollen Commission reported on widespread police corruption and brutality in the Bronx. One officer testified that he was called "the Mechanic," because "I used to tune people up," a "police word for beatin' up people." He testified that the beating was widespread:

Q. Did you beat people up who you arrested?
A. No. We just beat people up in general. If they're on the street, hanging around drug locations. Just—It was a show of force.
Q. Why were these beatings done?
A. To show who was in charge. We were in charge, the police.

The officer admitted that most of the victims were black and Hispanic, although he denied that the attacks were racially motivated. He conceded that the neighborhood residents hated the police, saying, "You'd hate the police too, if you lived there."

The Mollen Commission found that police corruption, brutality, and violence were present in every high-crime precinct with an active narcotics trade that it studied, all of which have predominantly minority populations. It found disturbing patterns of police corruption and brutality, including stealing from drug dealers, engaging in unlawful searches, seizures, and car stops, dealing and using drugs, lying in order to justify unlawful searches and arrests and to forestall complaints of abuse, and indiscriminate beating of innocent and guilty alike. The commission found that police officers and supervisors often accepted lying and brutality as necessary aspects of the job, in part because of what they perceived to be unrealistic legal constraints, and in part because of the police officers' "Us vs. Them" mentality, particularly in minority communities.

Similar practices were ongoing in Philadelphia, as Arthur Colbert, a black college student from Michigan, learned first-hand in 1991 when he made the mistake of getting lost in North Philadelphia while looking for his date. Two police officers looking for a drug dealer named Hakim pulled Colbert over, put him in a police van, and took him to an abandoned house, where they repeatedly accused him of being Hakim. Colbert showed them his Temple University ID and his driver's license, but they were not deterred. The officers hit him with their flashlights and a two-by-four. When Colbert still would not admit to being Hakim, one officer put his gun to Colbert's head and said, "If you don't tell us what we want to know, I'm going to blow your head away. You have three seconds." He cocked the gun's hammer and began to count down: "Three . . . two . . . one." But there wasn't anything Colbert could tell them, because he wasn't Hakim, and had never even heard of Hakim. The officers ultimately let him go without charges.

This was only one of many such stories uncovered in a corruption investigation in Philadelphia, which found a pattern of misconduct directed at the predominantly poor black neighborhood of North Philadelphia. In the early 1990s, a group of police officers there engaged in a widespread practice of beating and robbing citizens, planting evidence, and lying to support false convictions. The investigation's disclosures led to several criminal convictions of the police officers, and reversals of over fifty criminal convictions obtained on the strength of the officers' testimony.

Stories of black men being stopped by the police for no apparent reason other than the color of their skin are so common that they are not even considered news, and often get reported only when the victims happen to be celebrities or the confrontation is captured on film. In 1988, Joe Morgan, former All-Star second baseman for the Cincinnati Reds, was at Los Angeles International Airport waiting for a flight to Tucson. According to Morgan and an eyewitness, a police officer approached Morgan while he was making a phone call, said he was conducting a drug investigation, asked for his identification, and accused him of traveling with another person suspected of dealing drugs. Morgan objected, and turned to get his identification from his luggage, forty feet away. The officer grabbed him from behind, forced him to the floor, handcuffed him, put his hand over Morgan's mouth and nose, and led him off to a small room, where the police ascertained that Morgan was not traveling with the suspected drug dealer after all. The police maintained that Morgan had been hostile throughout the encounter, and that he had been forced to the floor only after he started swinging his arms. Even by the police officer's own account, however, the only basis for approaching Morgan in the first place was that another black man, stopped as a suspected drug dealer, had told the officers that he was traveling with a man that "looked like himself." As a result, the officers were on the lookout for a black man, and Joe Morgan fit that description.

In 1989, former police officer Don Jackson was doing a news story about police abuse against black men in Long Beach, California, when he was pulled over by the police on Martin Luther King, Jr., Boulevard, allegedly for straddling lanes. When he asked why he was being stopped, an officer pushed him through a plate glass store window. NBC captured the incident on film. In 1992, the ABC newsmagazine "20/20" conducted an experiment, sending out two groups of young men—one white, the other black—on successive evenings in Los Angeles. They drove in identical cars and took identical routes at identical times. The black group was stopped and questioned by police on several occasions in one evening, while the white group saw police cars pass them by sixteen times without showing any interest.

In 1990, the Massachusetts Attorney General's Civil Rights Division issued a report condemning the Boston Police Department for a practice of subjecting black citizens to unconstitutional stops and searches. The report recounted more than fifty such incidents in 1989 and 1990. The incidents followed the Boston Police Department's announcement of a policy of searching on sight "known gang members" in Roxbury, a predominantly black neighborhood in Boston. A deputy superintendent admitted that he had instructed his officers to "stop and frisk any known gang members in a gang location where there has been high-crime problems . . . , and if there are other kids with the gangs that are not known to us, that we will search them too for the protection of my officers." The report also discussed widespread complaints that the Boston Police Department had responded to the killing of a white woman, Carol Stuart, by engaging in unconstitutional stops, searches, and interrogations of young black men. Carol Stuart was in fact killed by her husband, Charles Stuart, a white man, who then falsely claimed that a black man had killed his wife.

As a result of such experiences, and the recounting of these and countless similar tales within the black community, black citizens, and particularly young black men, are likely to feel considerably less comfortable than members of other demographic groups in their encounters with police officers. Those practices were the backdrop for the encounter between the Broward County officials and Terrance Bostick, just as they are the backdrop for any encounter between a police officer and a black citizen. As Judge Julia Cooper Mack of the District of Columbia Court of Appeals put it in another case, "no reasonable innocent black male (with any knowledge of American history) would feel free to ignore or walk away from a drug interdiction team." Yet the Supreme Court did not even mention Bostick's race.

The Court's use of a uniform reasonable-person standard effectively sanctions *greater* coercion against those more vulnerable to police authority. By failing to consider the citizen's prior experiences with the police in determining whether a "seizure" has occurred, the Court permits the police to employ, on average, more coercion against black persons than against whites. The history of police practices against black citizens means that the same police conduct will be more threatening when directed against a black man than when directed against a white man. The objective standard builds that inequality into the criminal justice system, and sanctions it under the rubric of applying the same standard to all.

The effect is to tolerate a double standard. Most citizens will not be approached by a police officer for questioning unless the officer has some objective grounds for suspecting that they are involved in criminal activity. Our freedom to walk the streets is protected, in other words, by the constitutional requirement of probable cause. But young black men will routinely be subjected to police stops, not rising to the legal formality of "seizures," simply because they are young black men. At the same time, the police will be able to apply more coercion to black citizens than to whites in such "noncoercive" encounters, because the Court's legal standard presumes that we all have the same set of experiences vis-à-vis the police, and that none of us has any reason to feel coerced by an "ordinary" police encounter. As a result, the Court has it both ways—it protects the rights of some, but avoids the cost of extending the same protections equally to all.

The Truth Wears Off: Is There Something Wrong With the Scientific Method?

Jonah Lehrer

O n September 18, 2007, a few dozen neuroscientists, psychia-
trists, and drug-company executives gathered in a hotel conference room in Brussels to hear some startling news. It had to
do with a class of drugs known as atypical or second-generation
antipsychotics, which came on the market in the early nineties. The
drugs, sold under brand names such as Abilify, Seroquel, and Zyprexa,
had been tested on schizophrenics in several large clinical trials, all of
which had demonstrated a dramatic decrease in the subjects' psychiatric
symptoms. As a result, second-generation antipsychotics had become
one of the fastest-growing and most profitable pharmaceutical classes.
By 2001, Eli Lilly's Zyprexa was generating more revenue than Prozac.
It remains the company's top-selling drug.

But the data presented at the Brussels meeting made it clear that
something strange was happening: the therapeutic power of the drugs
appeared to be steadily waning. A recent study showed an effect that
was less than half of that documented in the first trials, in the early
nineteen-nineties. Many researchers began to argue that the expensive
pharmaceuticals weren't any better than first-generation antipsychotics,
which have been in use since the fifties. "In fact, sometimes they now
look even worse," John Davis, a professor of psychiatry at the University of Illinois at Chicago, told me.

Before the effectiveness of a drug can be confirmed, it must be
tested and tested again. Different scientists in different labs need to
repeat the protocols and publish their results. The test of replicability,
as it's known, is the foundation of modern research. Replicability is
how the community enforces itself. It's a safeguard for the creep of
subjectivity. Most of the time, scientists know what results they want,

---

Reprinted from The *New Yorker,* December 13, 2010, by permission of the author.

and that can influence the results they get. The premise of replicability is that the scientific community can correct for these flaws.

But now all sorts of well-established, multiply confirmed findings have started to look increasingly uncertain. It's as if our facts were losing their truth: claims that have been enshrined in textbooks are suddenly unprovable. This phenomenon doesn't yet have an official name, but it's occurring across a wide range of fields, from psychology to ecology. In the field of medicine, the phenomenon seems extremely widespread, affecting not only antipsychotics but also therapies ranging from cardiac stents to Vitamin E and antidepressants: Davis has a forthcoming analysis demonstrating that the efficacy of antidepressants has gone down as much as threefold in recent decades.

For many scientists, the effect is especially troubling because of what it exposes about the scientific process. If replication is what separates the rigor of science from the squishiness of pseudoscience, where do we put all these rigorously validated findings that can no longer be proved? Which results should we believe? Francis Bacon, the early-modern philosopher and pioneer of the scientific method, once declared that experiments were essential, because they allowed us to "put nature to the question." But it appears that nature often gives us different answers.

Jonathan Schooler was a young graduate student at the University of Washington in the nineteen-eighties when he discovered a surprising new fact about language and memory. At the time, it was widely believed that the act of describing our memories improved them. But, in a series of clever experiments, Schooler demonstrated that subjects shown a face and asked to describe it were much less likely to recognize the face when shown it later than those who had simply looked at it. Schooler called the phenomenon "verbal overshadowing."

The study turned him into an academic star. Since its initial publication, in 1990, it has been cited more than four hundred times. Before long, Schooler had extended the model to a variety of other tasks, such as remembering the taste of a wine, identifying the best strawberry jam, and solving difficult creative puzzles. In each instance, asking people to put their perceptions into words led to dramatic decreases in performance.

But while Schooler was publishing these results in highly reputable journals, a secret worry gnawed at him: it was proving difficult to replicate his earlier findings. "I'd often still see an effect, but the effect just wouldn't be as strong," he told me. "It was as if verbal overshadowing, my big new idea, was getting weaker." At first, he assumed that he'd made an error in experimental design or a statistical miscalculation. But he couldn't find anything wrong with his research. He then concluded that his initial batch of research subjects must have been unusually susceptible to verbal overshadowing. (John Davis, similarly, has speculated that part of the drop-off in the effectiveness of antipsychotics can be attributed to using subjects who suffer from milder forms of psychosis which are less likely to show dramatic improvement.) "It wasn't a very satisfying explanation," Schooler says. "One of my mentors told me that my real mistake was trying to replicate my work. He told me doing that was just setting myself up for disappointment."

Schooler tried to put the problem out of his mind; his colleagues assured him that such things happened all the time. Over the next few years, he found new research questions, got married and had kids. But his replication problem kept on getting worse. His first attempt at replicating the 1990 study, in 1995, resulted in an effect that was thirty per cent smaller. The next year, the size of the effect shrank another thirty per cent. When other labs repeated Schooler's experiments, they got a similar spread of data, with a distinct downward trend. "This was profoundly frustrating," he says. "It was as if nature gave me this great result and then tried to take it back." In private, Schooler began referring to the problem as "cosmic habituation," by analogy to the decrease in response that occurs when individuals habituate to particular stimuli. "Habituation is why you don't notice the stuff that's always there," Schooler says. "It's an inevitable process of adjustment, a ratcheting down of excitement. I started joking that it was like the cosmos was habituating to my ideas. I took it very personally."

Schooler is now a tenured professor at the University of California at Santa Barbara. He has curly black hair, pale green eyes, and the relaxed demeanor of someone who lives five minutes away from his favorite beach. When he speaks, he tends to get distracted by his own digressions. He might begin with a point about memory, which reminds him of a favorite William James quote, which inspires a long soliloquy on the importance of introspection. Before long, we're looking at pictures from Burning Man on his iPhone, which leads us back to the fragile nature of memory.

Although verbal overshadowing remains a widely accepted theory—it's often invoked in the context of eyewitness testimony, for instance—Schooler is still a little peeved at the cosmos. "I know I should just move on already," he says. "I really should stop talking about this. But I can't." That's because he is convinced that he has stumbled on a serious problem, one that afflicts many of the most exciting new ideas in psychology.

One of the first demonstrations of this mysterious phenomenon came in the early nineteen-thirties. Joseph Banks Rhine, a psychologist at Duke, had developed an interest in the possibility of extrasensory perception, or E.S.P. Rhine devised an experiment featuring Zener cards, a special deck of twenty-five cards printed with one of five different symbols: a card was drawn from the deck and the subject was asked to guess the symbol. Most of Rhine's subjects guessed about twenty per cent of the cards correctly, as you'd expect, but an undergraduate named Adam Linzmayer averaged nearly fifty per cent during his initial sessions, and pulled off several uncanny streaks, such as guessing nine cards in a row. The odds of this happening by chance are about one in two million. Linzmayer did it three times.

Rhine documented these stunning results in his notebook and prepared several papers for publication. But then, just as he began to believe in the possibility of extrasensory perception, the student lost his spooky talent. Between 1931 and 1933, Linzmayer guessed at the identity of another several thousand cards, but his success rate was now barely above chance. Rhine was forced to conclude that the student's "extra-sensory perception ability has gone through a marked decline." And Linzmayer wasn't the only subject to experience such a drop-off: in nearly every case in which Rhine and others documented E.S.P. the effect dramatically diminished over time. Rhine called this trend the "decline effect."

Schooler was fascinated by Rhine's experimental struggles. Here was a scientist who had repeatedly documented the decline of his data; he seemed to have a talent for finding results that fell apart. In 2004, Schooler embarked on an ironic imitation of Rhine's research: he tried to replicate this failure to replicate. In homage to Rhine's interests, he decided to test for a parapsychological phenomenon known as precognition. The experiment itself was straightforward: he flashed a set of images to a subject and asked him or her to identify each one. Most of the time, the response was negative—the images were displayed too quickly to register. Then Schooler randomly selected half of the images to be shown again. What he wanted to know was whether the images that got a second showing were more likely to have been identified the first time around. Could subsequent exposure have somehow influenced the initial results? Could the effect become the cause?

The craziness of the hypothesis was the point: Schooler knows that precognition lacks a scientific explanation. But he wasn't testing extrasensory powers; he was testing the decline effect. "At first, the data looked amazing, just as we'd expected," Schooler says. "I couldn't believe the amount of precognition we were finding. But then, as we kept on running subjects, the effect size"—a standard statistical measure—"kept on getting smaller and smaller." The scientists eventually tested more than two thousand undergraduates. "In the end, our results looked just like Rhine's," Schooler said. "We found this strong paranormal effect, but it disappeared on us."

The most likely explanation for the decline is an obvious one: regression to the mean. As the experiment is repeated, that is, an early statistical fluke gets cancelled out. The extrasensory powers of Schooler's subjects didn't decline—they were simply an illusion that vanished over time. And yet Schooler has noticed that many of the data sets that end up declining seem statistically solid—that is, they contain enough data that any regression to the mean shouldn't be dramatic. "These are the results that pass all the tests," he says. "The odds of them being random are typically quite remote, like one in a million. This means that the decline effect should almost never happen. But it happens all the time! Hell, it's happened to me multiple times." And this is why Schooler believes that the decline effect deserves more attention: its ubiquity seems to violate the laws of statistics. "Whenever I start talking about this, scientists get very nervous," he says. "But I still want to know what happened to my results. Like most scientists, I assumed that it would get easier to document my effect over time. I'd get better at doing the experiments, at zeroing in on the conditions that produce verbal overshadowing. So why did the opposite happen? I'm convinced that we can use the tools of science to figure this out. First, though, we have to admit that we've got a problem."

In 1991, the Danish zoologist Anders Møller, at Uppsala University, in Sweden, made a remarkable discovery about sex, barn swallows, and symmetry. It had long been known that the asymmetrical appearance of a creature was directly linked to the amount of mutation in its genome, so that more mutations led to more "fluctuating asymmetry." (An easy way to measure asymmetry in humans is to compare the length of the fingers on each hand.) What Møller discovered is that female barn swallows were far more likely to mate with male birds that had long, symmetrical feathers. This suggested that the picky females were using symmetry as a proxy for the quality of male genes. Møller's paper, which was published in *Nature*, set off a frenzy of research. Here was an easily measured, widely applicable indicator of genetic quality, and females could be shown to gravitate toward it. Aesthetics was really about genetics.

In the three years following, there were ten independent tests of the role of fluctuating asymmetry in sexual selection, and nine of them found a relationship between symmetry and male reproductive success. It didn't matter if scientists were looking at the hairs on fruit flies or replicating the swallow studies—females seemed to prefer males with mirrored halves. Before long, the theory was applied to humans. Researchers found, for instance, that women preferred the smell of symmetrical men, but only during the fertile phase of the menstrual cycle. Other studies claimed that females had more orgasms when their partners were symmetrical, while a paper by anthropologists at Rutgers analyzed forty Jamaican dance routines and discovered that symmetrical men were consistently rated as better dancers.

Then the theory started to fall apart. In 1994, there were fourteen published tests of symmetry and sexual selection, and only eight found a correlation. In 1995, there were eight papers on the subject, and only four got a positive result. By 1998, when there were twelve additional investigations of fluctuating asymmetry, only a third of them confirmed the theory. Worse still, even the studies that yielded some positive result showed a steadily declining effect size. Between 1992 and 1997, the average effect size shrank by eighty per cent.

And it's not just fluctuating asymmetry. In 2001, Michael Jennions, a biologist at the Australian National University, set out to analyze "temporal trends" across a wide range of subjects in ecology and evolutionary biology. He looked at hundreds of papers and forty-four meta-analyses (that is, statistical syntheses of related studies), and discovered a consistent decline effect over time, as many of the theories seemed to fade into irrelevance. In fact, even when numerous variables were controlled for—Jennions knew, for instance, that the same author might publish several critical papers, which could distort his analysis—there was still a significant decrease in the validity of the hypothesis, often within a year of publication. Jennions admits that his findings are troubling, but expresses a reluctance to talk about them publicly. "This is a very sensitive issue for scientists," he says. "You know, we're supposed to be dealing with hard facts, the stuff that's supposed to stand the test of time. But when you see these trends you become a little more skeptical of things."

What happened? Leigh Simmons, a biologist at the University of Western Australia, suggested one explanation when he told me about his initial enthusiasm for the theory: "I was really excited by fluctuating asymmetry. The early studies made the effect look very robust." He decided to conduct a few experiments of his own, investigating symmetry in male horned beetles. "Unfortunately, I couldn't find the effect," he said. "But the worst part was that when I submitted these null results I had difficulty getting them published. The journals only wanted confirming data. It was too exciting an idea to disprove, at least back then." For Simmons, the steep rise and slow fall of fluctuating asymmetry is a clear example of a scientific paradigm, one of those intellectual fads that both guide and constrain research: after a new paradigm is proposed, the peer-review process is tilted toward positive results. But then, after a few years, the academic incentives shift—the paradigm has become entrenched—so that the most notable results are now those that disprove the theory.

Jennions, similarly, argues that the decline effect is largely a product of publication bias, or the tendency of scientists and scientific journals to prefer positive data over null results, which is what happens when no effect is found. The bias was first identified by the statistician Theodore Sterling, in 1959, after he noticed that ninety-seven per cent of all published psychological studies with statistically significant data found the effect they were looking for. A "significant" result is defined as any data point that would be produced by chance less than five per cent of the time. This ubiquitous test was invented in 1922 by the English mathematician Ronald Fisher, who picked five per cent as the boundary line, somewhat arbitrarily, because it made pencil and slide-rule calculations easier. Sterling saw that if ninety-seven per cent of psychology studies were proving their hypotheses, either psychologists were extraordinarily lucky or they published only the outcomes of successful experiments. In recent years, publication bias has mostly been seen as a problem for clinical trials, since pharmaceutical companies are less interested in publishing results that aren't favorable. But it's becoming increasingly clear that publication bias also produces major distortions in fields without large corporate incentives, such as psychology and ecology.

While publication bias almost certainly plays a role in the decline effect, it remains an incomplete explanation. For one thing, it fails to account for the initial prevalence of positive results among studies that never even get submitted to journals. It also fails to explain the experience of people like Schooler, who have been unable to replicate their initial data despite their best efforts. Richard Palmer, a biologist at the University of Alberta, who has studied the problems surrounding fluctuating asymmetry, suspects that an equally significant issue is the selective reporting of results—the data that scientists choose to document in the first place. Palmer's most convincing evidence relies on a statistical tool known as a funnel graph. When a large number of studies have been done on a single subject, the data should follow a pattern: studies with a large sample size should all cluster around a common value—the true result—whereas those with a smaller sample size should exhibit a random scattering, since they're subject to greater sampling error. This pattern gives the graph its name, since the distribution resembles a funnel.

The funnel graph visually captures the distortions of selective reporting. For instance, after Palmer plotted every study of fluctuating asymmetry, he noticed that the distribution of results with smaller sample sizes wasn't random at all but instead skewed heavily toward positive results. Palmer has since documented a similar problem in several other contested subject areas. "Once I realized that selective reporting is everywhere in science, I got quite depressed," Palmer told me. "As a researcher, you're always aware that there might be some nonrandom patterns, but I had no idea how widespread it is." In a recent review article, Palmer summarized the impact of selective reporting on his field: "We cannot escape the troubling conclusion that some—perhaps many—cherished generalities are at best exaggerated in their biological significance and at worst a collective illusion nurtured by strong a-priori beliefs often repeated."

Palmer emphasizes that selective reporting is not the same as scientific fraud. Rather, the problem seems to be one of subtle omissions and unconscious misperceptions, as researchers struggle to make sense of their results. Stephen Jay Gould referred to this as the "shoehorning" process. "A lot of scientific measurement is really hard," Simmons told me. "If you're talking about fluctuating asymmetry, then it's a matter of minuscule differences between the right and left sides of an animal. It's millimetres of a tail feather. And so maybe a researcher knows that he's measuring a good male"—an animal that has successfully mated—"and he knows that it's supposed to be symmetrical. Well, that act of measurement is going to be vulnerable to all sorts of perception biases. That's not a cynical statement. That's just the way human beings work."

One of the classic examples of selective reporting concerns the testing of acupuncture in different countries. While acupuncture is widely accepted as a medical treatment in various Asian countries, its use is much more contested in the West. These cultural differences have profoundly influenced the results of clinical trials. Between 1966 and 1995, there were forty-seven studies of acupuncture in China, Taiwan, and Japan, and every single trial concluded that acupuncture was an effective treatment. During the same period, there were ninety-four clinical trials of acupuncture in the United States, Sweden, and the U.K., and only fifty-six per cent of these studies found any therapeutic benefits. As Palmer notes, this wide discrepancy suggests that scientists find ways to confirm their preferred hypothesis, disregarding what they don't want to see. Our beliefs are a form of blindness.

John Ioannidis, an epidemiologist at Stanford University, argues that such distortions are a serious issue in biomedical research. "These exaggerations are why the decline has become so common," he says. "It'd be really great if the initial studies gave us an accurate summary of things. But they don't. And so what happens is we waste a lot of money treating millions of patients and doing lots of follow-up studies on other themes based on results that are misleading." In 2005, Ioannidis published an article in the *Journal of the American Medical Association* that looked at the forty-nine most cited clinical-research studies in three major medical journals. Forty-five of these studies reported positive results, suggesting that the intervention being tested was effective. Because most of these studies were randomized controlled trials—the "gold standard" of medical evidence—they tended to have a significant impact on clinical practice, and led to the spread of treatments such as hormone replacement therapy for menopausal women and daily low-dose aspirin to prevent heart attacks and strokes. Nevertheless, the data Ioannidis found were disturbing: of the thirty-four claims that had been subject to replication, forty-one per cent had either been directly contradicted or had their effect sizes significantly downgraded.

The situation is even worse when a subject is fashionable. In recent years, for instance, there have been hundreds of studies on the various genes that control the differences in disease risk between men and women. These findings have included everything from the mutations responsible for the increased risk of schizophrenia to the genes underlying hypertension. Ioannidis and his colleagues looked at four hundred and thirty-two of these claims. They quickly discovered that the vast majority had serious flaws. But the most troubling fact emerged when he looked at the test of replication: out of four hundred and thirty-two claims, only a single one was consistently replicable. "This doesn't mean that none of these claims will turn out to be true," he says. "But, given that most of them were done badly, I wouldn't hold my breath."

According to Ioannidis, the main problem is that too many researchers engage in what he calls "significance chasing," or finding ways to interpret the data so that it passes the statistical test of significance—the ninety-five-percent boundary invented by Ronald Fisher. "The scientists are so eager to pass this magical test that they start playing around with the numbers, trying to find anything that seems worthy," Ioannidis says. In recent years, Ioannidis has become increasingly blunt about the pervasiveness of the problem. One of his most cited papers has a deliberately provocative title: "Why Most Published Research Findings Are False."

The problem of selective reporting is rooted in a fundamental cognitive flaw, which is that we like proving ourselves right and hate being wrong. "It feels good to validate a hypothesis," Ioannidis said. "It feels even better when you've got a financial interest in the idea or your career depends upon it. And that's why, even after a claim has been systematically disproven"—he cites, for instance, the early work on hormone replacement therapy, or claims involving various vitamins—"you still see some stubborn researchers citing the first few studies that show a strong effect. They really want to believe that it's true."

That's why Schooler argues that scientists need to become more rigorous about data collection before they publish. "We're wasting too much time chasing after bad studies and underpowered experiments," he says. The current "obsession" with replicability distracts from the real problem, which is faulty design. He notes that nobody even tries to replicate most science papers—there are simply too many. (According to *Nature,* a third of all studies never even get cited, let alone repeated.) "I've learned the hard way to be exceedingly careful," Schooler says. "Every researcher should have to spell out, in advance, how many subjects they're going to use, and what exactly they're testing, and what constitutes a sufficient level of proof. We have the tools to be much more transparent about our experiments."

In a forthcoming paper, Schooler recommends the establishment of an open-source database, in which researchers are required to outline their planned investigations and document all their results. "I think this would provide a huge increase in access to scientific work and give us a much better way to judge the quality of an experiment,"

Schooler says. "It would help us finally deal with all these issues that the decline effect is exposing."

Although such reforms would mitigate the dangers of publication bias and selective reporting, they still wouldn't erase the decline effect. This is largely because scientific research will always be shadowed by a force that can't be curbed, only contained: sheer randomness. Although little research has been done on the experimental dangers of chance and happenstance, the research that exists isn't encouraging.

In the late nineteen-nineties, John Crabbe, a neuroscientist at the Oregon Health and Science University, conducted an experiment that showed how unknowable chance events can skew tests of replicability. He performed a series of experiments on mouse behavior in three different science labs: in Albany, New York; Edmonton, Alberta; and Portland, Oregon. Before he conducted the experiments, he tried to standardize every variable he could think of. The same strains of mice were used in each lab, shipped on the same day from the same supplier. The animals were raised in the same kind of enclosure, with the same brand of saw-dust bedding. They had been exposed to the same amount of incandescent light, were living with the same number of littermates, and were fed the exact same type of chow pellets. When the mice were handled, it was with the same kind of surgical glove, and when they were tested it was on the same equipment, at the same time in the morning.

The premise of this test of replicablity, of course, is that each of the labs should have generated the same pattern of results. "If any set of experiments should have passed the test, it should have been ours," Crabbe says. "But that's not the way it turned out." In one experiment, Crabbe injected a particular strain of mouse with cocaine. In Portland the mice given the drug moved, on average, six hundred centimetres more than they normally did; in Albany they moved seven hundred and one additional centimetres. But in the Edmonton lab they moved more than five thousand additional centimetres. Similar deviations were observed in a test of anxiety. Furthermore, these inconsistencies didn't follow any detectable pattern. In Portland one strain of mouse proved most anxious, while in Albany another strain won that distinction.

The disturbing implication of the Crabbe study is that a lot of extraordinary scientific data are nothing but noise. The hyperactivity of those coked-up Edmonton mice wasn't an interesting new fact—it was a meaningless outlier, a by-product of invisible variables we don't understand. The problem, of course, is that such dramatic findings are also the most likely to get published in prestigious journals, since the data are both statistically significant and entirely unexpected. Grants get written, follow-up studies are conducted. The end result is a scientific accident that can take years to unravel.

This suggests that the decline effect is actually a decline of illusion. While Karl Popper imagined falsification occurring with a single, definitive experiment—Galileo refuted Aristotelian mechanics in an afternoon—the process turns out to be much messier than that. Many scientific theories continue to be considered true even after failing numerous experimental tests. Verbal overshadowing might exhibit the decline effect, but it remains extensively relied upon within the field. The same holds for any number of phenomena, from the disappearing benefits of second-generation antipsychotics to the weak coupling ratio exhibited by decaying neutrons, which appears to have fallen by more than ten standard deviations between 1969 and 2001. Even the law of gravity hasn't always been perfect at predicting real-world phenomena. (In one test, physicists measuring gravity by means of deep boreholes in the Nevada desert found a two-and-a-half-percent discrepancy between the theoretical predictions and the actual data.) Despite these findings, second-generation antipsychotics are still widely prescribed, and our model of the neutron hasn't changed. The law of gravity remains the same.

Such anomalies demonstrate the slipperiness of empiricism. Although many scientific ideas generate conflicting results and suffer from falling effect sizes, they continue to get cited in the textbooks and drive standard medical practice. Why? Because these ideas seem true. Because they make sense. Because we can't bear to let them go. And this is why the decline effect is so troubling. Not because it reveals the human fallibility of science, in which data are tweaked and beliefs shape perceptions. (Such shortcomings aren't surprising, at least for scientists.) And not because it reveals that many of our most exciting theories are fleeting fads and will soon be rejected. (That idea has been around since Thomas Kuhn.) The decline effect is troubling because it reminds us how difficult it is to prove anything. We like to pretend that our experiments define the truth for us. But that's often not the case. Just because an idea is true doesn't mean it can be proved. And just because an idea can be proved doesn't mean it's true. When the experiments are done, we still have to choose what to believe.

Disciplinary Literacies

Creativity and Play by Tim Brown
How Ideas Trump Crisis by Alex Tarbarrok

http://www.ted.com/talks/lang/eng/eric_whitacre_a_virtual_choir_2_000_voices_strong.html

Remixing/Technological Literacies

Remixing/Technological Literacies: Introduction

The readings in this section explore the ways that we communicate with things other than essays and common words. They also challenge us to rethink our ideas about "text" in ways that include nontraditional forms of literacy. Music, visuals, video, multimodal blogs and instant messaging all offer ways to expand our audiences and exercise other forms of creativity.

As you read these essays, keep thinking about invention, arrangement, and revision, but also think about delivery. As you and your class discuss possible topics and media for your remix assignment, think about what sorts of messages, information and insights from your previous work might be best shared with others in a new media. Why share that information? Why in that medium? Thinking about delivery also pushes you to consider how to get the final project to your audience. Will you need an electronic delivery system for an audience far away from your geographic location? What form(s) could delivery take? Can you create material artifacts like paintings or do something like write a play and invite your audience to your classroom for a show?

Thinking about delivery raises all kinds of good opportunities for discussions about audience, resources, and how to make decisions about what messages are best communicated in what types of media.

For Some, the Blogging Never Stops

Katie Hafner and Tim Gnatek

Katie Hafner has a degree in German literature from the University of California, San Diego and a degree in journalism from Columbia University. She is currently a technology reporter for The New York Times *and a contributing editor for* Newsweek. *She has also published articles in* Business Week, Esquire, The New Republic, The New York Times Magazine, Wired, *and* Working Woman. *She has written four books:* Cyberpunk: Outlaws and Hackers on the Computer Frontier *(co-author, 1991);* The House at the Bridge: A Story of Modern Germany *(1995);* Where Wizards Stay Up Late: The Origins of the Internet *(co-author, 1996); and* The Well: A Story of Love, Death & Real Life in the Seminal Online Community *(2001). She lives in Marin County, California. Tim Gnatek, who contributed reporting for the following selection, has a degree in journalism from Columbia University and in 2003 and 2004 won the Wired Magazine Award for New Media Journalism.*

To celebrate four years of marriage, Richard Wiggins and his wife, Judy Matthews, recently spent a week in Key West, Fla. Early on the morning of their anniversary, Ms. Matthews heard her husband get up and go into the bathroom. He stayed there for a long time.

"I didn't hear any water running, so I wondered what was going on," Ms. Matthews said. When she knocked on the door, she found him

Reprinted from the *New York Times,* May 27, 2004, by permission of the New York Times Company.

seated with his laptop balanced on his knees, typing into his Web log, a collection of observations about the technical world, over a wireless link.

Blogging is a pastime for many, even a livelihood for a few. For some, it becomes an obsession. Such bloggers often feel compelled to write several times daily and feel anxious if they don't keep up. As they spend more time hunkered over their computers, they neglect family, friends and jobs. They blog at home, at work and on the road. They blog openly or sometimes, like Mr. Wiggins, quietly so as not to call attention to their habit.

"It seems as if his laptop is glued to his legs 24/7," Ms. Matthews said of her husband.

The number of bloggers has grown quickly, thanks to sites like blogger.com, which makes it easy to set up a blog. Technorati, a blog-tracking service, has counted some 2.5 million blogs.

Of course, most of those millions are abandoned or, at best, maintained infrequently. For many bloggers, the novelty soon wears off and their persistence fades.

Sometimes, too, the realization that no one is reading sets in. A few blogs have thousands of readers, but never have so many people written so much to be read by so few. By Jupiter Research's estimate, only 4 percent of online users read blogs.

Indeed, if a blog is likened to a conversation between a writer and readers, bloggers like Mr. Wiggins are having conversations largely with themselves.

Mr. Wiggins, 48, a senior information technologist at Michigan State University in East Lansing, does not know how many readers he has; he suspects it's not many. But that does not seem to bother him.

"I'm just getting something off my chest," he said.

Nor is he deterred by the fact that he toils for hours at a time on his blog for no money. He gets satisfaction in other ways. "Sometimes there's an 'I told you so' aspect to it," he said. Recent ruminations on wigblog.blogspot.com have focused on Gmail, Google's new e-mail service. Mr. Wiggins points with pride to Wigblog posts that voiced early privacy concerns about Gmail.

Perhaps a chronically small audience is a blessing. For it seems that the more popular a blog becomes, the more some bloggers feel the need to post.

Tony Pierce started his blog three years ago while in search of a distraction after breaking up with a girlfriend. "In three years, I don't think I've missed a day," he said. Now Mr. Pierce's blog (www.tonypierce.com/blog/bloggy.htm), a chatty diary of Hollywood, writing and women in which truth sometimes mingles with fiction, averages 1,000 visitors a day.

Where some frequent bloggers might label themselves merely ardent, Mr. Pierce is more realistic. "I wouldn't call it dedicated, I would call it a problem," he said. "If this were beer, I'd be an alcoholic."

Mr. Pierce, who lives in Hollywood and works as a scheduler in the entertainment industry, said blogging began to feel like an addiction when he noticed that he would rather be with his computer than with his girlfriend—for technical reasons.

"She's got an iMac, and I don't like her computer," Mr. Pierce said. When he is at his girlfriend's house, he feels "antsy." "We have little fights because I want to go home and write my thing," he said.

Mr. Pierce described the rush he gets from what he called "the fix" provided by his blog. "The pleasure response is twofold," he said. "You can have instant gratification; you're going to hear about something really good or bad instantly. And if I feel like I've written something good, it's enjoyable to go back and read it."

"And," he said, "like most addictions, those feelings go away quickly. So I have to do it again and again."

Joseph Lorenzo Hall, 26, a graduate student at the School of Information Management and Systems at the University of California at Berkeley who has studied bloggers, said that for some people blogging has supplanted e-mail as a way to procrastinate at work.

People like Mr. Pierce, who devote much of their free time to the care and feeding of their own blogs and posting to other blogs, do so largely because it makes them feel productive even if it is not a paying job.

The procrastination, said Scott Lederer, 31, a fellow graduate student with Mr. Hall, has a collective feel to it. "You feel like you're participating in something important, because we're all doing it together," he said.

Jeff Jarvis, president of Advance.net, a company that builds Web sites for newspapers and magazines, and a blogging enthusiast, defended what he called one's "obligation to the blog."

"The addictive part is not so much extreme narcissism," Mr. Jarvis said. "It's that you're involved in a conversation. You have a connection to people through the blog."

Some compulsive bloggers take their obligation to extremes, blogging at the expense of more financially rewarding tasks.

Mr. Wiggins has missed deadline after deadline at Searcher, an online periodical for which he is a paid contributor.

Barbara Quint, the editor of the magazine, said she did all she could to get him to deliver his columns on time. Then she discovered that Mr. Wiggins was busily posting articles to his blog instead of sending her the ones he had promised, she said. "Here he is working all night on something read by five second cousins and a dog, and I'm willing to pay him," she said.

Ms. Quint has grown more understanding of his reasons, if not entirely sympathetic. "The Web's illusion of immortality is sometimes more attractive than actual cash," she said.

Jocelyn Wang, a 27-year-old marketing manager in Los Angeles, started her blog, a chronicle of whatever happens to pop into her head (www.jozjozjoz.com), 18 months ago as an outlet for boredom.

Now she spends at least four hours a day posting to her blog and reading other blogs. Ms. Wang's online journal is now her life. And the people she has met through the blog are a large part of her core of friends.

"There is no real separation in my life," she said. Like Mr. Wiggins, Ms. Wang blogs while on vacation. She stays on floors at the Hotel Nikko in San Francisco with access to a free Internet connection. ("So I can blog," she explains.)

Blogging for a cause can take on a special urgency. Richard Khoe, a political consultant in Washington who in his spare time helps run a pro-John Kerry group called Run Against Bush, posts constantly to the blog embedded in the group's Web site (www.runagainstbush.org). He blogs late into the night, although he knows that the site still attracts relatively few visitors.

"Sometimes you get really particular with the kind of link you want, so you search a little more, then a little more, then you want to see what other people are saying about that link you chose," he said. "And before you know it, some real time has passed."

Others find they are distracted to the point of neglectfulness. Tom Lewis, 35, a project manager for a software firm in western Massachusetts who has a photo blog (tomdog.buzznet.com/user), has occasionally shown up "considerably late" for events and has put off more than a few work-related calls to tend to his blog.

Mr. Jarvis characterizes the blogging way of life as a routine rather than an obsession. "It's a habit," he said. "What you're really doing is telling people about something that they might find interesting.

When that becomes part of your life, when you start thinking in blog, it becomes part of you."

The constant search for bloggable moments is what led Gregor J. Rothfuss, a programmer in Zurich, to blog to the point of near-despair. Bored by his job, Mr. Rothfuss, 27, started a blog that focused on technical topics.

"I was trying to record all thoughts and speculations I deemed interesting," he said. "Sort of creating a digital alter ego. The obsession came from trying to capture as much as possible of the good stuff in my head in as high fidelity as possible."

For months, Mr. Rothfuss said, he blogged at work, at home, late into the night, day in and day out until it all became a blur—all the while knowing, he added, "that no one was necessarily reading it, except for myself."

When traffic to the blog, greg.abstract.ch started to rise, he began devoting half a day every day and much of the weekend to it. Mr. Rothfuss said he has few memories of that period in his life aside from the compulsive blogging.

He was saved from the rut of his online chronicle when he traveled to Asia. The blog became more of a travelogue. Then Mr. Rothfuss switched jobs, finding one he enjoyed, and his blogging grew more moderate.

He still has the blog, but posts to it just twice a week, he said, "as opposed to twice an hour." He feels healthier now. "It's part of what I do now, it's not what I do," he said.

Suffering from a similar form of "blog fatigue," Bill Barol, a free-lance writer in Santa Monica, Calif., simply stopped altogether after four years of nearly constant blogging.

"It was starting to feel like work, and it was never supposed to be a job," Mr. Barol said. "It was supposed to be an anti-job."

Even with some 200 visitors to his blog each day, he has not posted to his blog since returning from a month of travel.

Still, Mr. Barol said, he does not rule out a return to blogging someday.

"There is this seductive thing that happens, this kind of snowball-rolling-down-a-hill thing, where the sheer momentum of several years' posting becomes very keenly felt," he said. "And the absence of posting feels like—I don't know, laziness or something."

I Think, Therefore IM

Jennifer Lee

*Jennifer Lee (1976–) was born in New York City. She grad-
uated from Harvard University in 1999 with a degree in
mathematics and economics. While at Harvard she spent a
year at Beijing University on a fellowship studying international relations. Lee has received a scholarship from the
Asian American Journalism Association and has interned at*
The Boston Globe, The New York Times, Newsday, The
Wall Street Journal, *and* The Washington Post. *She joined
the staff of* The New York Times *in 2001 as a technology
reporter and began writing for the Metro section the next
year. The following selection on instant-messaging language
originally appeared in the* Times *in September 2002.*

Each September Jacqueline Harding prepares a classroom presentation on the common writing mistakes she sees in her students'
work.

Ms. Harding, an eighth-grade English teacher at Viking Middle
School in Guernee, Ill., scribbles the words that have plagued generations of schoolchildren across her whiteboard:

There. Their. They're.
Your. You're.
To. Too. Two.
Its. It's.

This September, she has added a new list: u, r, ur, b4, wuz, cuz, 2.

When she asked her students how many of them used shortcuts
like them in their writing, Ms. Harding said, she was not surprised
when most of them raised their hands. This, after all, is their online

lingua franca: English adapted for the spitfire conversational style of Internet instant messaging.

Ms. Harding, who has seen such shortcuts creep into student papers over the last two years, said she gave her students a warning: "If I see this in your assignments, I will take points off."

"Kids should know the difference," said Ms. Harding, who decided to address this issue head-on this year. "They should know where to draw the line between formal writing and conversational writing."

As more and more teenagers socialize online, middle school and high school teachers like Ms. Harding are increasingly seeing a breezy form of Internet English jump from e-mail into schoolwork. To their dismay, teachers say that papers are being written with shortened words, improper capitalization and punctuation, and characters like &, $ and @.

Teachers have deducted points, drawn red circles and tsk-tsked at their classes. Yet the errant forms continue. "It stops being funny after you repeat yourself a couple of times," Ms. Harding said.

But teenagers, whose social life can rely as much these days on text communication as the spoken word, say that they use instant-messaging shorthand without thinking about it. They write to one another as much as they write in school, or more.

"You are so used to abbreviating things, you just start doing it unconsciously on schoolwork and reports and other things," said Eve Brecker, 15, a student at Montclair High School in New Jersey.

Ms. Brecker once handed in a midterm exam riddled with instant-messaging shorthand. "I had an hour to write an essay on *Romeo and Juliet*," she said. "I just wanted to finish before my time was up. I was writing fast and carelessly. I spelled 'you' 'u.'" She got a C.

Even terms that cannot be expressed verbally are making their way into papers. Melanie Weaver was stunned by some of the term papers she received from a 10th-grade class she recently taught as part of an internship. "They would be trying to make a point in a paper, they would put a smiley face in the end," said Ms. Weaver, who teaches at Alvernia College in Reading, Pa. "If they were presenting an argument and they needed to present an opposite view, they would put a frown."

As Trisha Fogarty, a sixth-grade teacher at Houlton Southside School in Houlton, Maine, puts it, today's students are "Generation Text."

Almost 60 percent of the online population under age 17 uses instant messaging, according to Nielsen/NetRatings. In addition to cellphone text messaging, Weblogs and e-mail, it has become a popular means of flirting, setting up dates, asking for help with homework and keeping in contact with distant friends. The abbreviations are a natural outgrowth of this rapid-fire style of communication.

"They have a social life that centers around typed communication," said Judith S. Donath, a professor at the Massachusetts Institute of Technology's Media Lab who has studied electronic communication. "They have a writing style that has been nurtured in a teenage social milieu."

Some teachers see the creeping abbreviations as part of a continuing assault of technology on formal written English. Others take it more lightly, saying that it is just part of the larger arc of language evolution.

"To them it's not wrong," said Ms. Harding, who is 28. "It's acceptable because it's in their culture. It's hard enough to teach them the art of formal writing. Now we've got to overcome this new instant-messaging language."

Ms. Harding noted that in some cases the shorthand isn't even shorter. "I understand 'cuz,' but what's with the 'wuz'? It's the same amount of letters as 'was,' so what's the point?" she said.

Deborah Bova, who teaches eighth-grade English at Raymond Park Middle School in Indianapolis, thought her eyesight was failing several years ago when she saw the sentence "B4 we perform, ppl have 2 practice" on a student assignment.

"I thought, 'My God, what is this?'" Ms. Bova said. "Have they lost their minds?"

The student was summoned to the board to translate the sentence into standard English: "Before we perform, people have to practice." She realized that the students thought she was out of touch. "It was like 'Get with it, Bova,'" she said. Ms. Bova had a student type up a reference list of translations for common instant-messaging expressions. She posted a copy on the bulletin board by her desk and took another one home to use while grading.

Students are sometimes unrepentant.

"They were astonished when I began to point these things out to them," said Henry Assetto, a social studies teacher at Twin Valley High School in Elverson, Pa. "Because I am a history teacher, they did not think a history teacher would be checking up on their grammar or their spelling," said Mr. Assetto, who has been teaching for 34 years.

But Montana Hodgen, 16, another Montclair student, said she was so accustomed to instant-messaging abbreviations that she often read right past them. She proofread a paper last year only to get it returned with the messaging abbreviations circled in red.

"I was so used to reading what my friends wrote to me on Instant Messenger that I didn't even realize that there was something wrong," she said. She said her ability to separate formal and informal English declined the more she used instant messages. "Three years ago, if I had seen that, I would have been 'What is that?'"

The spelling checker doesn't always help either, students say. For one, Microsoft Word's squiggly red spell-check lines don't appear beneath single letters and numbers such as u, r, c, 2 and 4. Nor do they catch words which have numbers in them such as "l8r" and "b4" by default.

Teenagers have essentially developed an unconscious "accent" in their typing, Professor Donath said. "They have gotten facile at typing and they are not paying attention."

Teenagers have long pushed the boundaries of spoken language, introducing words that then become passe with adult adoption. Now teenagers are taking charge and pushing the boundaries of written language. For them, expressions like "oic" (oh I see), "nm" (not much), "jk" (just kidding) and "lol" (laughing out loud), "brb" (be right back), "ttyl" (talk to you later) are as standard as conventional English.

"There is no official English language," said Jesse Sheidlower, the North American editor of the *Oxford English Dictionary.* "Language is spread not because anyone dictates any one thing to happen. The decisions are made by the language and the people who use the language."

Some teachers find the new writing style alarming. "First of all, it's very rude, and it's very careless," said Lois Moran, a middle school English teacher at St. Nicholas School in Jersey City.

"They should be careful to write properly and not to put these little codes in that they are in such a habit of writing to each other," said Ms. Moran, who has lectured her eighth-grade class on such mistakes.

Others say that the instant-messaging style might simply be a fad, something that students will grow out of. Or they see it as an opportunity to teach students about the evolution of language.

"I turn it into a very positive teachable moment for kids in the class," said Erika V. Karres, an assistant professor at the University of North Carolina at Chapel Hill who trains student teachers. She shows students how English has evolved since Shakespeare's time. "Imagine Langston Hughes's writing in quick texting instead of 'Langston writing,'" she said. "It makes teaching and learning so exciting."

Other teachers encourage students to use messaging shorthand to spark their thinking processes. "When my children are writing first drafts, I don't care how they spell anything, as long as they are writing," said Ms. Fogarty, the sixth-grade teacher from Houlton, Maine. "If this lingo gets their thoughts and ideas onto paper quicker, the more power to them." But during editing and revising, she expects her students to switch to standard English.

Ms. Bova shares the view that instant-messaging language can help free up their creativity. With the help of students, she does not even need the cheat sheet to read the shorthand anymore.

"I think it's a plus," she said. "And I would say that with a + sign."

Finding One's Own Space in Cyberspace

Amy Bruckman

Amy Bruckman teaches in the College of Computing at Georgia Tech, having completed a Ph.D. in the Epistemology and Learning Group at the MIT Media Lab. While still a graduate student, Bruckman founded two virtual communities, MediaMOO (for media researchers) and MOOSE Crossing (for children), the latter the subject of her dissertation. In the article from Technology Review *reprinted here, she describes the new rules emerging as people form societies that exist only when people are online together.*

The week the last Internet porn scandal broke, my phone didn't stop ringing: "Are women comfortable on the Net?" "Should women use gender neutral names on the Net?" "Are women harassed on the Net?" Reporters called from all over the country with basically the same question. I told them all: your question is ill-formed. "The Net" is not one thing. It's like asking: "Are women comfortable in bars?" That's a silly question. Which woman? Which bar?

The summer I was 18, I was the computer counselor at a summer camp. After the campers were asleep, the counselors were allowed out, and would go bar hopping. First everyone would go to Maria's, an Italian restaurant with red-and-white-checkered tablecloths. Maria welcomed everyone from behind the bar, greeting regular customers by name. She always brought us free garlic bread. Next we'd go to the Sandpiper, a disco with good dance music. The Sandpiper seemed excitingly adult—it was a little scary at first, but then I loved it. Next, we went to the Sportsman, a leather motorcycle bar that I found

Reprinted from *Technology Review 99, no. 1* (1996), by permission of Massachusetts Institute of Technology.

absolutely terrifying. Huge, bearded men bulging out of their leather vests and pants leered at me. I hid in the corner and tried not to make eye contact with anyone, hoping my friends would get tired soon and give me a ride back to camp.

Each of these bars was a community, and some were more comfortable for me than others. The Net is made up of hundreds of thousands of separate communities, each with its own special character. Not only is the Net a diverse place, but "women" are diverse as well—there were leather-clad women who loved the Sportsman, and plenty of women revel in the fiery rhetoric of Usenet's alt.flame. When people complain about being harassed on the Net, they've usually stumbled into the wrong online community. The question is not whether "women" are comfortable on "the Net," but rather, what types of communities are possible? How can we create a range of communities so that everyone— men and women—can find a place that is comfortable for them?

If you're looking for a restaurant or bar, you can often tell without even going in: Is the sign flashing neon or engraved wood? Are there lots of cars parked out front? What sort of cars? (You can see all the Harleys in front of the Sportsman from a block away.) Look in the window: How are people dressed? We are accustomed to diversity in restaurants. People know that not all restaurants will please them, and employ a variety of techniques to choose the right one.

It's a lot harder to find a good virtual community than it is to find a good bar. The visual cues that let you spot the difference between Maria's and the Sportsman from across the street are largely missing. Instead, you have to "lurk"—enter the community and quietly explore for a while, getting the feel of whether it's the kind of place you're looking for. Although published guides exist, they're not always very useful—most contain encyclopedic lists with little commentary or critical evaluation, and by the time they're published they're already out of date. Magazines like *NetGuide* and *Wired* are more current and more selective, and therefore more useful, but their editorial bias may not fit with your personal tastes.

Commonly available network-searching tools are also useful. The World Wide Web is filled with searching programs, indexes, and even indexes of indexes ("meta-indexes"). Although browsing with these tools can be a pleasant diversion, it is not very efficient, and searches for particular pieces of information often end in frustration. If you keep an open mind, however, you may come across something good.

Shaping an Online Society

But what happens if, after exploring and asking around, you still can't find an online environment that suits you? Don't give up: start your own! This doesn't have to be a difficult task. Anyone can create a new newsgroup in Usenet's "alt" hierarchy or open a new chat room on America Online. Users of Unix systems can easily start a mailing list. If you have a good idea but not enough technical skill or the right type of Net access, there are people around eager to help. The more interesting question is: How do you help a community to become what you hope for? Here, I can offer some hard-won advice.

In my research at the MIT Media Lab (working with Professor Mitchel Resnick), I design virtual communities. In October of 1992, I founded a professional community for media researchers on the Internet called MediaMOO. Over the past three years, as MediaMOO has grown to 1,000 members from 33 countries, I have grappled with many of the issues that face anyone attempting to establish a virtual community. MediaMOO is a "multi-user dungeon" or MUD—a virtual world on the Internet with rooms, objects, and people from all around the world. Messages typed in by a user instantly appear on the screens of all other users who are currently in the same virtual "room." This real-time interaction distinguishes MUDs from Usenet newsgroups, where users can browse through messages created many hours or days before. The MUD's virtual world is built in text descriptions. MOO stands for MUD object-oriented, a kind of MUD software (created by Pavel Curtis of the Xerox Palo Alto Research Center and Stephen White, now at InContext Systems) that allows each user to write programs to define spaces and objects.

The first MUDS, developed in the late 1970s, were multiplayer fantasy games of the dungeons-and-dragons variety. In 1989, a graduate student at Carnegie Mellon University named James Aspnes decided to see what would happen if you took away the monsters and the magic swords but instead let people extend the virtual world. People's main activity went from trying to conquer the virtual world to trying to build it, collaboratively.

Most MUDs are populated by undergraduates who should be doing their homework. I thought it would be interesting instead to bring together a group of people with a shared intellectual interest: the study of media. Ideally, MediaMOO should be like an endless reception for a conference on media studies. But given the origin of MUDs as violent games, giving one an intellectual and professional atmosphere was a tall order. How do you guide the evolution of who uses the space and what they do there?

A founder/designer can't control what the community ultimately becomes—much of that is up to the users—but can help shape it. The personality of the community's founder can have a great influence on what sort of place it becomes. Part of what made Maria's so comfortable for me was Maria herself. She radiated a warmth that made me feel at home.

Similarly, one of the most female-friendly electronic communities I've visited is New York City's ECHO (East Coast Hang Out) bulletin board, run by Stacy Horn. Smart, stylish, and deliberately outrageous, Horn is role model and patron saint for the ECHO-ites. Her outspoken but sensitive personality infuses the community, and sends a message to women that it's all right to speak up. She added a conference to ECHO called "WIT" (women in telecommunications), which one user describes as "a warm, supportive, women-only, private conference where women's thoughts, experiences, wisdom, joys, and despairs are shared." But Horn also added a conference called "BITCH," which the ECHO-ite calls "WIT in black leather jackets. All-women, riotous and raunchy."

Horn's high-energy, very New York brand of intelligence establishes the kind of place ECHO is and influences how everyone there behaves. When ECHO was first established, Horn and a small group of her close friends were the most active people on the system. "That set the emotional tone, the traditional style of posting, the unwritten rules about what it's OK to say," says Marisa Bowe, an ECHO administrator for many years. "Even though Stacy is too busy these days to post very much, the tone established in the early days continues," says Bowe, who is now editor of an online magazine called *Word*.

Beyond the sheer force of a founder's personality, a community establishes a particular character with a variety of choices on how to operate. One example is to set a policy on whether to allow participants to remain anonymous. Initially, I decided that members of MediaMOO should be allowed to choose: they could identify themselves with their real names and e-mail addresses, or remain anonymous. Others questioned whether there was a role for anonymity in a professional community.

As time went on, I realized they were right. People on Media-MOO are supposed to be networking, hoping someone will look up who they really are and where they work. Members who are not willing to share their personal and professional identities are less likely to engage in serious discussion about their work, and consequently about media in general. Furthermore, comments from an anonymous entity are less valuable because they are unsituated—"I believe X" is less meaningful to a listener than "I am a librarian with eight years of experience who lives in a small town in Georgia, and I believe X." In theory, anonymous participants could describe their professional experiences and place their comments in that context; in practice it tends not to happen that way. After six months, I proposed that we change the policy to require that all new members be identified. Despite the protests of a few vocal opponents, most people thought that this was a good idea, and the change was made.

Each community needs to have its own policy on anonymity. There's room for diversity here too: some communities can be all-anonymous, some all-identified, and some can leave that decision up to each individual. An aside: right now on the Net no one is either really anonymous or really identified. It is easy to fake an identity; it is also possible to use either technical or legal tools to peer behind someone else's veil of anonymity. This ambiguous state of affairs is not necessarily unfortunate: it's nice to know that a fake identity that provides a modicum of privacy is easy to construct, but that in extreme cases such people can be tracked down.

Finding Birds of a Feather

Another important design decision is admissions policy. Most places on the Net have a strong pluralistic flavor, and the idea that some people might be excluded from a community ruffles a lot of feathers. But exclusivity is a fact of life. MIT wouldn't be MIT if everyone who wanted to come was admitted. Imagine if companies had to give jobs to everyone who applied! Virtual communities, social clubs, universities, and corporations are all groups of people brought together for a purpose. Achieving that purpose often requires that there be some way to determine who can join the community

A key decision I made for MediaMOO was to allow entry only to people doing some sort of "media research." I try to be loose on the

definition of "media"—writing teachers, computer network adminis-
trators, and librarians are all working with forms of media—but strict
on the definition of "research." At first, this policy made me uncomfortable. I would nervously tell people, "It's mostly a self-selection
process. We hardly reject anyone at all!" Over time, I've become more
comfortable with this restriction, and have enforced the requirements
more stringently. I now believe my initial unease was naive.

Even if an online community decides to admit all comers, it does
not have to let all contributors say anything they want. The existence
of a moderator to filter postings often makes for more focused and
civil discussion. Consider Usenet's two principal newsgroups dealing
with feminism—alt.feminism and soc.feminism. In alt.feminism,
anyone can post whatever they want. Messages in this group are filled
with the angry words of angry people; more insults than ideas are ex-
changed. (Titles of messages found there on a randomly selected day
included "Women & the workplace (it doesn't work)" and "What is a
feminazi?") The topic may nominally be feminism, but the discussion
itself is not feminist in nature.

The huge volume of postings (more than 200 per day, on average)
shows that many people enjoy writing such tirades. But if I wanted to
discuss some aspect of feminism, alt.feminism would be the last place
I'd go. Its sister group, soc.feminism, is moderated—volunteers read
messages submitted to the group and post only those that pass muster.
Moderators adhere to soc.feminism's lengthy charter, which explains
the criteria for acceptable postings—forbidding ad hominem attacks,
for instance.

Moderation of a newsgroup, like restricting admission to a MUD,
grants certain individuals within a community power over others.
If only one group could exist, I'd have to choose the uncensored
alt.feminism to the moderated soc.feminism. Similarly, if MediaMOO
were the only virtual community or MIT the only university, I'd argue
that they should be open to all. However, there are thousands of universities and the Net contains hundreds of thousands of virtual communities, with varying criteria for acceptable conduct. That leaves room for
diversity: some communities can be moderated, others unmoderated.
Some can be open to all, some can restrict admissions.

The way a community is publicized—or not publicized—also influences its character. Selective advertising can help a community
achieve a desired ambiance. In starting up MediaMOO, for example,

we posted the original announcement to mailing lists for different aspects of media studies—not to the general-purpose groups for discussing MUDs on Usenet. MediaMOO is now rarely if ever deliberately advertised. The group has opted not to be listed in the public, published list of MUDs on the Internet. Members are asked to mention MediaMOO to other groups only if the majority of members of that group would probably be eligible to join MediaMOO.

New members are attracted by word of mouth among media researchers. To bring in an influx of new members, MediaMOO typically "advertises" by organizing an online discussion or symposium on some aspect of media studies. Announcing a discussion group on such topics as the techniques for studying behavior in a virtual community, or strategies for using computers to teach writing, attracts the right sort of people to the community and sets a tone for the kinds of discussion that take place there. That's much more effective than a more general announcement of MediaMOO and its purpose.

In an ideal world, virtual communities would acquire new members entirely by self-selection: people would enter an electronic neighborhood only if it focused on something they cared about. In most cases, this process works well. For example, one Usenet group that I sometimes read—sci.aquaria—attracts people who are really interested in discussing tropical fishkeeping. But self-selection is not always sufficient. For example, the challenge of making MediaMOO's culture different from prevailing MUD culture made self-selection inadequate. Lots of undergraduates with no particular focus to their interests want to join MediaMOO. To preserve MediaMOO's character as a place for serious scholarly discussions, I usually reject these applications. Besides, almost all of the hundreds of other MUDs out there place no restrictions on who can join. MediaMOO is one of the few that is different.

Emotionally and politically charged subject matter, such as feminism, makes it essential for members of a community to have a shared understanding of the community's purpose. People who are interested in freshwater and saltwater tanks can coexist peacefully in parallel conversations on sci.aquaria. However, on alt.feminism, people who want to explore the implications of feminist theory, and those who want to question its basic premises, don't get along quite so well. Self-selection alone is not adequate for bringing together a group to discuss a hot topic. People with radically differing views may wander in innocently,

or barge in deliberately—disrupting the conversation through igno-
rance or malice.

Such gate crashing tends to occur more frequently as the community grows in size. For example, some participants in the Usenet
group alt.tasteless decided to post a series of grotesque messages to the
thriving group rec.pets.cats, including recipes for how to cook cat. A
small, low-profile group may be randomly harassed, but that's less
likely to happen.

In the offline world, membership in many social organizations is
open only to those who are willing and able to pay the dues. While it
may rankle an American pluralistic sensibility, the use of wealth as a
social filter has the advantages of simplicity and objectivity: no one's
personal judgment plays a role in deciding who is to be admitted. And
imposing a small financial hurdle to online participation may do more
good than harm. Token fees discourage the random and pointless
postings that dilute the value of many newsgroups. One of the first
community networks, Community Memory in Berkeley, Calif., found
that charging a mere 25 cents to post a message significantly raised the
level of discourse, eliminating many trivial or rude messages.

Still, as the fee for participation rises above a token level, this
method has obvious moral problems for a society committed to equal
opportunity. In instituting any kind of exclusionary policy, the
founder of a virtual community should first test the key assumption
that alternative, nonexclusionary communities really do exist. If they
do not, then less restrictive admissions policies may be warranted.

Building on Diversity

Anonymity policy, admissions requirements, and advertising strategy
all contribute to a virtual community's character. Without such methods of distinguishing one online hangout from another, all would tend
to sink to the least common denominator of discourse—the equivalent of every restaurant in a town degenerating into a dive. We need
better techniques to help members of communities develop shared expectations about the nature of the community, and to communicate
those expectations to potential new members. This will make it easier
for people to find their own right communities.

Just as the surest way to find a good restaurant is to exchange tips
with friends, word of mouth is usually the best way to find out about

virtual communities that might suit your tastes and interests. The best published guides for restaurants compile comments and ratings from a large group of patrons, rather than relying on the judgment of any one expert. Approaches like this are being explored on the Net. Yezdi Lashkari, cofounder of Agents Inc., designed a system called "Webhound" that recommends items of interest on the World Wide Web. To use Webhound, you enter into the system a list of web sites you like. It matches you with people of similar interests, and then recommends other sites that they like. Not only do these ratings come from an aggregate of many opinions, but they also are matched to your personal preferences.

Webhound recommends just World Wide Web pages, but the same basic approach could help people find a variety of communities, products, and services that are likely to match their tastes. For example, Webhound grew out of the Helpful Online Music Recommendation Service (HOMR), which recommends musical artists. A subscriber to this service—recently renamed Firefly—first rates a few dozen musical groups on a scale from "the best" to "pass the earplugs"; Firefly searches its database for people who have similar tastes, and uses their list of favorites to recommend other artists that might appeal to you. The same technique could recommend Usenet newsgroups, mailing lists, or other information sources. Tell it that you like to read the Usenet group "rec.arts.startrek.info," and it might recommend "alt.tv.babylon-5"—people who like one tend to like the other. While no such tool yet exists for Usenet, the concept would be straightforward to implement.

Written statements of purpose and codes of conduct can help communities stay focused and appropriate. MediaMOO's stated purpose, for example, helps set its character as an arena for scholarly discussion. But explicit rules and mission statements can go only so far. Elegant restaurants don't put signs on the door saying "no feet on tables" and fast food restaurants don't post signs saying "feet on tables allowed." Subtle cues within the environment indicate how one is expected to behave. Similarly, we should design regions in cyberspace so that people implicitly sense what is expected and what is appropriate. In this respect, designers of virtual communities can learn a great deal from architects.

Vitruvius, a Roman architect from the first century B.C., established the basic principle of architecture as commodity (appropriate function), firmness (structural stability), and delight. These principles translate into the online world, as William Mitchell, dean of MIT's School of Architecture and Planning, points out in his book *City of Bits: Space, Place, and the Infobahn.*

Architects of the twenty-first century will still shape, arrange and connect spaces (both real and virtual) to satisfy human needs. They will still care about the qualities of visual and ambient environments. They will still seek commodity, firmness, and delight. But commodity will be as much a matter of software functions and interface design as it is of floor plans and construction materials. Firmness will entail not only the physical integrity of structural systems, but also the logical integrity of computer systems. And delight? Delight will have unimagined new dimensions.

Marcos Novak of the University of Texas at Austin is exploring some of those "unimagined dimensions" with his notion of a "liquid architecture" for cyberspace, free from the constraints of physical space and building materials. But work of this kind on the merging of architecture and software design is regrettably rare; if virtual communities are buildings, then right now we are living in the equivalent of thatched huts. If the structure keeps out the rain—that is, if the software works at all—people are happy.

More important than the use of any of these particular techniques, however, is applying an architect's design sensibility to this new medium. Many of the traditional tools and techniques of architects, such as lighting and texture, will translate into the design of virtual environments. Depending on choice of background color and texture, type styles, and special fade-in effects, for instance, a Web page can feel playful or gloomy, futuristic or old-fashioned, serious or fun, grown-up or child-centered. The language of the welcoming screen, too, conveys a sense of the community's purpose and character. An opening screen thick with the jargon of specialists in, say, genetic engineering, might alert dilettantes that the community is for serious biologists.

As the Net expands, its ranks will fill with novices—some of whom, inevitably, will wander into less desirable parts of cybertown. It is important for such explorers to appreciate the Net's diversity—to realize, for example, that the newsgroup alt.feminism does not constitute the Internet's sole contribution to feminist debate. Alternatives exist.

I'm glad there are places on the Net where I'm not comfortable. The world would be a boring place if it invariably suited any one person's taste. The great promise of the Net is diversity. That's something we need to cultivate and cherish. Unfortunately, there aren't yet enough good alternatives—too much of the Net is like the Sportsman and too little of it is like Maria's. Furthermore, not enough people are aware that communities can have such different characters.

People who accidentally find themselves in the Sportsman, alt.feminism, or alt.flame, and don't find the black leather or fiery insults to their liking, should neither complain about it nor waste their time there—they should search for a more suitable community. If you've stumbled into the wrong town, get back on the bus. But if you've been a long-time resident and find the community changing for the worse—that's different. Don't shy away from taking political action within that community to protect your investment of time: speak up, propose solutions, and build a coalition of others who feel the same way you do.

With the explosion of interest in networking, people are moving from being recipients of information to creators, from passive subscribers to active participants and leaders. Newcomers to the Net who are put off by harassment, pornography, and just plain bad manners should stop whining about the places they find unsuitable and turn their energies in a more constructive direction: help make people aware of the variety of alternatives that exist, and work to build communities that suit their interests and values.

Remixing/Technological Literacies

Culture in the Arab World by Shereen El Feki
Laws that Choke Creativity by Larry Lesig
Chris Jordan Pictures Some Shocking Stats by Chris
Jordan

Wesch Web 2.0: The Machine is Us/ing Us - http://www.youtube
.com/watch?v=6gmP4nk0EOE

Revising Literacies

Revising Literacies: Introduction

Your ideas about literacy have probably changed as you have worked through this book. In this section, we present some essays in which writers talk with us about how their views of literacy have changed and/or how literacy has helped them make a change. Remember to think about invention, arrangement, revision and delivery as you read. Although chances are you have discussed style throughout the semester, at this point think about how the style the writer uses helps or hinders these texts' revisionary purposes.

As you prepare to compose your final project, think about what significant changes have occurred in your ideas about literacy, in your literacy practices, in your understanding of how literacy will affect your life in the future. How might what you have learned become part of one of the larger conversations about literacy you have been introduced to this semester? What invention, arrangement, revision, style and delivery choices do you have to make? How can you use some of the new strategies you have learned this semester to create a paper that engages your new learning?

We invite you to think about revision as an invention strategy that facilitates reflection as you become even more aware of your own literacies and their places in the world.

Writing Is my Passion

bell hooks

bell hooks (1952–), the pseudonym of Gloria Watkins, was born in Kentucky. She received a B.A. from Stanford University and a Ph.D. from the University of California, Santa Cruz. An advocate for African-American women in the feminist movement as well as a critic of the white male–dominated U.S. power structure, hooks has taught at Oberlin College and Yale University. Her books include Ain't I a Woman: Black Women and Feminism *(1981),* Feminist Theory: From Margin to Center *(1984),* Talking Back: Thinking Feminist, Thinking Black *(1989),* Yearning: Race, Gender, and Cultural Politics *(1990),* Breaking Bread: Insurgent Black Intellectual Life *(1992),* Black Looks: Race and Representation *(1992),* Outlaw Culture *(1994),* Teaching to Transgress: Education as the Practice of Freedom *(1994),* Reel to Real: Race, Sex, and Class at the Movies *(1996), and* Remembering Rapture *(1999). The following selection is a chapter from* Wounds of Passion: A Writing Life *(1997).*

Writing is my passion. Words are the way to know ecstasy. Without them life is barren. The poet insists *Language is a body of suffering and when you take up language you take up the suffering too.* All my life I have been suffering for words. Words have been the source of the pain and the way to heal.

Struck as a child for talking, for speaking out of turn, for being out of my place. Struck as a grown woman for not knowing when to shut up, for not being willing to sacrifice words for desire. Struck by writing a book that disrupts. There are many ways to be hit. Pain is

Reprinted from *Wounds of Passion: a Writing Life* (1997), by permission of the author.

the price we pay to speak the truth. *Language is a body of suffering and when you take up language you take up the suffering too.*

Nothing is as simple as it seems, so much is neither good nor bad, but always a blend of truths. In the household of my childhood, that place where I was held prisoner, there was no doubt in anyone's mind that I would write, that I would become a writer, magician of words, one who suffers well. *She works hard in the name of love. She who is able to sacrifice.*

Nothing is as simple as it seems. No one in the house of my childhood doubts my power to create. I learn doubt when I leave home. I learn to doubt my intelligence, my creativity in the integrated world—at college and in the arms of talented men. They try and teach me to fear a woman's word, to doubt whether her words can ever be as good, as perfect as any man's sound. No wonder then there is something in me that clings to childhood—to the girl who loved Emily Dickinson, writer, thinker, dreamer of worlds. In the shadow of her presence, I am without doubt. I know I can become a writer.

She stayed with him much longer than she should have. Her staying was never a way to cling to love. She feared losing the discipline to write. She entered a committed relationship so soon, so young to devote herself to writing. So much in the world distracted her from words. So much made life seem crazy. At times she dreamed of returning home. Despite all the madness of home, she had always found a place to read, contemplate life, and write there.

She is right. Nothing is as simple as it seems. You would think all those fancy colleges she went to so far away from home would have made it easy to write. Baba used to asked her How can you live so far away from your people. At home she doubted her capacity to love, to be intimate, to make friends even. Introverted and awkward she doubted so much about herself but never her ability to imagine, to write.

No one really says how it will be. When we try to leave behind all the limits of race and gender and class, to transcend them, to get to the heart of the matter. No one really says how painful it will be—that just when you think you are moving forward in life some new thing, another barrier surfaces that just stops you in your tracks. For all that goes wrong in my life with Mack, I have had shelter here, a sanctuary for that part of me that was destined to write, to make a life in words.

Language is a body of suffering and when you take up language you take up the suffering too.

Nobody ever talked to us about how we would become these new women and men transformed by feminist movement. All the cultural revolutions created by black liberation and sexual liberation and women's liberation, and yet there is still no map—nothing that will guide us safely to mutual love and respect. We lose our way. One thing is certain—we can never turn back.

After all our feminist victory, there is still a grave silence about the issue of whether women can be in love relationships with men and truly develop as writers. I believe my relationship with Mack strengthens me as a thinker and a writer. I used to say that we were better at giving each other the space to be independent than we were at being together. I grew stronger as a writer at all times, even during times when we were in crisis. Writing was my refuge and my rescue.

She believed for so long that if she left their relationship she might cease to write. After all she became a disciplined published writer there in the shadows of their love. To depart from that love might mean to depart from writing. She could imagine living without him. She could not imagine living without words. And so she remained.

They all wanted to know *Why did you stay with him so long.* I am weary explaining. Doesn't everyone realize that nothing is as simple as it seems. Our relationship falling apart is no one's fault. Everybody wants somebody to blame. I wanted to make sense of the pain. The ways I was hurt in this relationship and the ways I hurt were only one fragment of a larger piece. When I left home, I thought I was leaving hurt behind. I did not even imagine that there were ways to be hurt in the world outside home. When you are confined to a small segregated area across the tracks, away from so much going on in the larger world, innocence is still possible. Measured against the pain in the world, home seemed a safe haven, both the home I left and the home I had made with Mack.

To explain things she says: Every terrorist regime in the world uses isolation to break the human spirit. It is not difficult for her to see that women writers, especially black women writers, are isolated. She can count the ones whose work is recognized. She can see for herself how many die alone, unloved, their work forgotten. She can see for herself how many remain invisible. She can see how many go mad.

Haunted by the fear of madness, I am deeply convinced that the world is not a safe place for me. I remain reluctant to move, to change, to go anywhere. I need company to move outside the home. That was the way it was growing up. A girl was never left alone. When I came to college I realized I had never been alone not even for a day. Whenever we left the house as girls we were escorted. In private I love to be alone. In public I prefer company.

They were always so together the two of them. They did everything together. No wonder then it was surprising that they could not work together in the same room. In private they were alone, they were silent. In private they were devoted to work.

Women sacrifice for words. They suffer and they die. The poet Audre Lorde visits our house. She sits and flirts on our Victorian deep red couch. She has just autographed a copy of my favorite poem "Litany for Survival." Her words say everything there is to say about the perils the exploited and the oppressed face coming to voice. She goes straight to the heart of the matter: *When we are loved we are afraid love will vanish / when we are alone we are afraid love will never return / and when we speak we are afraid our words will not be heard not welcome / but when we are silent we are still afraid.*

Professions for Women

Virginia Woolf

Virginia Woolf (1882–1941) was born in London. She was educated at home by her father, a well-known writer and scholar. As a young woman, she became a member of the Bloomsbury Group of writers and artists in London. In 1912, she wed author and publisher Leonard Woolf, another member of the Bloomsbury Group; together they set up Hogarth Press, which published much of her work. Woolf, who suffered from depression throughout her life, committed suicide in her late fifties. Woolf's publications include the novels Mrs. Dalloway *(1925),* To the Lighthouse *(1927), and* The Waves *(1931) and the essay collections* A Room of One's Own *(1920) and* The Death of the Moth and Other Essays *(1948). Known for her impressionistic, stream-of-consciousness style, Woolf is a dominant force in English literature. This essay, written as a speech that Woolf presented to the Women's Service League in 1931, presents Woolf's view of employment hurdles facing women.*

When your secretary invited me to come here, she told me that your Society is concerned with the employment of women and she suggested that I might tell you something about my own professional experiences. It is true I am a woman; it is true I am employed; but what professional experiences have I had? It is difficult to say. My profession is literature; and in that profession there are fewer experiences for women than in any other, with the exception of the stage—fewer, I mean, that are peculiar to women. For the road was cut many years ago—by Fanny Burney, by Aphra Behn,

Reprinted from *The Death of the Moth and Other Essays* (1942, 1970), by permission of Houghton Mifflin Harcourt.

by Harriet Martineau, by Jane Austen, by George Eliot—many famous women, and many more unknown and forgotten, have been before me, making the path smooth, and regulating my steps. Thus, when I came to write, there were very few material obstacles in my way. Writing was a reputable and harmless occupation. The family peace was not broken by the scratching of a pen. No demand was made upon the family purse. For ten and sixpence one can buy paper enough to write all the plays of Shakespeare—if one has a mind that way. Pianos and models, Paris, Vienna and Berlin, masters and mistresses, are not needed by a writer. The cheapness of writing paper is, of course, the reason why women have succeeded as writers before they have succeeded in the other professions.

But to tell you my story—it is a simple one. You have only got to figure to yourselves a girl in a bedroom with a pen in her hand. She had only to move that pen from left to right—from ten o'clock to one. Then it occurred to her to do what is simple and cheap enough after all—to slip a few of those pages into an envelope, fix a penny stamp in the corner, and drop the envelope into the red box at the corner. It was thus that I became a journalist; and my effort was rewarded on the first day of the following month—a very glorious day it was for me—by a letter from an editor containing a cheque for one pound ten shillings and sixpence. But to show you how little I deserve to be called a professional woman, how little I know of the struggles and difficulties of such lives, I have to admit that instead of spending that sum upon bread and butter, rent, shoes and stockings, or butcher's bills, I went out and bought a cat—a beautiful cat, a Persian cat, which very soon involved me in bitter disputes with my neighbors.

What could be easier than to write articles and to buy Persian cats with the profits? But wait a moment. Articles have to be about something. Mine, I seem to remember, was about a novel by a famous man. And while I was writing this review, I discovered that if I were going to review books I should need to do battle with a certain phantom. And the phantom was a woman, and when I came to know her better I called her after the heroine of a famous poem, "The Angel in the House." It was she who used to come between me and my paper when I was writing reviews. It was she who bothered me and wasted my time and so tormented me that at last I killed her. You who come of a younger and happier generation may not have heard of her—you may not know what I mean by the Angel in the House. I will describe her as shortly as I can. She was intensely sympathetic. She was immensely charming. She was utterly unselfish. She excelled in the difficult arts of family life. She sacrificed herself daily. If there was chicken, she took the leg; if there was a draught she sat in it—in short she was so constituted that she never had a mind or a wish of her own, but preferred to sympathize always with the minds and wishes of others. Above all—I need not say it—she was pure. Her purity was supposed to be her chief beauty—her blushes, her great grace. In those days—the last of Queen Victoria—every house had its Angel. And when I came to write I encountered her with the very first words. The shadow of her wings fell on my page; I heard the rustling of her skirts in the room. Directly, that is to say, I took my pen in hand to review that novel by a famous man, she slipped behind me and whispered: "My dear, you are a young woman. You are writing about a book that has been written by a man. Be sympathetic; be tender; flatter; deceive; use all the arts and wiles of our sex. Never let anybody guess that you have a mind of your own. Above all, be pure." And she made as if to guide my pen. I now record the one act for which I take some credit to myself, though the credit rightly belongs to some excellent ancestors of mine who left me a certain sum of money—shall we say five hundred pounds a year?—so that it was not necessary for me to depend solely on charm for my living. I turned upon her and caught her by the throat. I did my best to kill her. My excuse, if I were to be had up in a court of law, would be that I acted in self-defence. Had I not killed her she would have killed me. She would have plucked the heart out of my writing. For, as I found, directly I put pen to paper, you cannot review even a novel without having a mind of your own, without expressing what you think to be the truth about human relations, morality, sex. And all these questions, according to the Angel in the House, cannot be dealt with freely and openly by women; they must charm, they must conciliate, they must—to put it bluntly—tell lies if they are to succeed. Thus, whenever I felt the shadow of her wing or the radiance of her halo upon my page, I took up the inkpot and flung it at her. She died hard. Her fictitious nature was of great assistance to her. It is far harder to kill a phantom than a reality. She was always creeping back when I thought I had despatched her. Though I flatter myself that I killed her in the end, the struggle was severe; it took much time that had better have been spent upon learning Greek grammar; or in roaming the world in search of adventures. But it was a real experience; it was an experience that was bound to befall all women writers at that time. Killing the Angel in the House was part of the occupation of a woman writer.

But to continue my story. The Angel was dead; what then remained? You may say that what remained was a simple and common object—a young woman in a bedroom with an inkpot. In other words, now that she had rid herself of falsehood, that young woman had only to be herself. Ah, but what is "herself"? I mean, what is a woman? I assure you, I do not know. I do not believe that you know. I do not believe that anybody can know until she has expressed herself in all the arts and professions open to human skill. That indeed is one of the reasons why I have come here—out of respect for you, who are in process of showing us by your experiments what a woman is, who are in process of providing us, by your failures and successes, with that extremely important piece of information.

But to continue the story of my professional experiences. I made one pound ten and six by my first review; and I bought a Persian cat with the proceeds. Then I grew ambitious. A Persian cat is all very well, I said; but a Persian cat is not enough. I must have a motor car. And it was thus that I became a novelist—for it is a very strange thing that people will give you a motor car if you will tell them a story. It is a still stranger thing that there is nothing so delightful in the world as telling stories. It is far pleasanter than writing reviews of famous novels. And yet, if I am to obey your secretary and tell you my professional experiences as a novelist, I must tell you about a very strange experience that befell me as a novelist. And to understand it you must try first to imagine a novelist's state of mind. I hope I am not giving away professional secrets if I say that a novelist's chief desire is to be as unconscious as possible. He has to induce in himself a state of perpetual lethargy. He wants life to proceed with the utmost quiet and regularity. He wants to see the same faces, to read the same books, to do the same things day after day, month after month, while he is writing, so that nothing may break the illusion in which he is living—so that nothing may disturb or disquiet the mysterious nosings about, feelings round, darts, dashes and sudden discoveries of that very shy and illusive spirit, the imagination. I suspect that this state is the same both for men and women. Be that as it may, I want you to imagine me writing a novel in a state of trance. I want you to figure to yourself a girl sitting with a pen in her hand, which for minutes, and indeed for hours, she never dips into the inkpot. The image that comes to my mind when I think of this girl is the image of a fisherman lying sunk in dreams on the verge of a deep lake with a rod held out over the water. She was letting her imagination sweep unchecked round every rock and cranny of the world that lies submerged in the depths of our unconscious being. Now came the experience, the experience that I believe to be far commoner with women writers than with men. The line raced through the girl's fingers. Her imagination had rushed away. It had sought the pools, the depths, the dark places where the largest fish slumber. And then there was a smash. There was an explosion. There was foam and confusion. The imagination had dashed itself against something hard. The girl was roused from her dream. She was indeed in a state of the most acute and difficult distress. To speak without figure she had thought of something, something about the body, about the passions which it was unfitting for her as a woman to say. Men, her reason told her, would be shocked. The consciousness of what men will say of a woman who speaks the truth about her passions had roused her from her artist's state of unconsciousness. She could write no more. The trance was over. Her imagination could work no longer. This I believe to be a very common experience with women writers—they are impeded by the extreme conventionality of the other sex. For though men sensibly allow themselves great freedom in these respects, I doubt that they realize or can control the extreme severity with which they condemn such freedom in women.

These then were two very genuine experiences of my own. These were two of the adventures of my professional life. The first—killing the Angel in the House—I think I solved. She died. But the second, telling the truth about my own experiences as a body, I do not think I solved. I doubt that any woman has solved it yet. The obstacles against her are still immensely powerful—and yet they are very difficult to define. Outwardly, what is simpler than to write books? Outwardly, what obstacles are there for a woman rather than for a man? Inwardly, I think, the case is very different: she has still many ghosts to fight, many prejudices to overcome. Indeed it will be a long time still, I think, before a woman can sit down to write a book without finding a phantom to be slain, a rock to be dashed against. And if this is so in literature, the freest of all professions for women, how is it in the new professions which you are now for the first time entering?

Those are the questions that I should like, had I time, to ask you. And indeed, if I have laid stress upon these professional experiences of mine, it is because I believe that they are, though in different forms, yours also. Even when the path is nominally open—when there is nothing to prevent a woman from being a doctor, a lawyer, a civil servant—there are many phantoms and obstacles, as I believe, looming in her way. To discuss and define them is, I think, of great value and importance; for thus only can the labour be shared, the difficulties be solved. But besides this, it is necessary also to discuss the ends and the aims for which we are fighting, for which we are doing battle with these formidable obstacles. Those aims cannot be taken for granted; they must be perpetually questioned and examined. The whole position, as I see it—here in this hall surrounded by women practicing for the first time in history I know not how many different professions—is one of extraordinary interest and importance. You have won rooms of your own in the house hitherto exclusively owned by men. You are able, though not without great labor and effort, to pay the rent. You are earning your five hundred pounds a year. But this freedom is only a beginning; the room is your own, but it is still bare. It has to be furnished; it has to be decorated; it has to be shared. How are you going to furnish it, how are you going to decorate it? With whom are you going to share it, and upon what terms? These, I think, are questions of the utmost importance and interest. For the first time in history you are able to ask them; for the first time you are able to decide for yourselves what the answers should be. Willingly would I stay and discuss those questions and answers—but not tonight. My time is up; and I must cease.

A Letter to America

Margaret Atwood

Margaret Atwood (1939–), born in Ottawa, Canada, attended the University of Toronto, Radcliffe, and Harvard. At a young age she decided to become a writer, and she has published a remarkable list of novels, poetry, and essays, along with forays into other genres such as children's stories and television scripts. She is best known, however, for her novels: The Edible Woman *(1969),* Surfacing *(1972),* Lady Oracle *(1976),* Life Before Man *(1979),* Bodily Harm *(1982),* The Handmaid's Tale *(1985),* Cat's Eye *(1989),* The Robber Bride *(1994),* Alias Grace *(1996),* The Blind Assassin *(2000),* Oryx and Crake *(2003), which was shortlisted for the Giller Prize and the Man Booker Prize,* The Penelopiad *(2005), and* The Tent *(2006). In this letter published in the* International Herald Tribune, *Atwood expresses her deep concerns regarding the direction of United States' domestic and foreign policy in the first years of the twenty-first century.*

Dear America:
This is a difficult letter to write, because I'm no longer sure who you are.

Some of you may be having the same trouble. I thought I knew you: We'd become well acquainted over the past 55 years. You were the Mickey Mouse and Donald Duck comic books I read in the late 1940s. You were the radio shows—Jack Benny, Our Miss Brooks. You were the music I sang and danced to: the Andrews Sisters, Ella Fitzgerald, the Platters, Elvis. You were a ton of fun.

Reprinted from the *Globe and Mail*, March 28, 2003, by permission of the author.

You wrote some of my favorite books. You created Huckleberry Finn, and Hawkeye, and Beth and Jo in *Little Women,* courageous in their different ways. Later, you were my beloved Thoreau, father of environmentalism, witness to individual conscience; and Walt Whitman, singer of the great Republic; and Emily Dickinson, keeper of the private soul. You were Hammett and Chandler, heroic walkers of mean streets; even later, you were the amazing trio, Hemingway, Fitzgerald, and Faulkner, who traced the dark labyrinths of your hidden heart. You were Sinclair Lewis and Arthur Miller, who, with their own American idealism, went after the sham in you, because they thought you could do better.

You were Marlon Brando in *On The Waterfront,* you were Humphrey Bogart in *Key Largo,* you were Lillian Gish in *Night of the Hunter.* You stood up for freedom, honesty and justice; you protected the innocent. I believed most of that. I think you did, too. It seemed true at the time.

You put God on the money, though, even then. You had a way of thinking that the things of Caesar were the same as the things of God: that gave you self-confidence. You have always wanted to be a city upon a hill, a light to all nations, and for a while you were. Give me your tired, your poor, you sang, and for a while you meant it.

We've always been close, you and us. History, that old entangler, has twisted us together since the early 17th century. Some of us used to be you; some of us want to be you; some of you used to be us. You are not only our neighbors: In many cases—mine, for instance—you are also our blood relations, our colleagues, and our personal friends. But although we've had a ringside seat, we've never understood you completely, up here north of the 49th parallel.

We're like Romanized Gauls—look like Romans, dress like Romans, but aren't Romans—peering over the wall at the real Romans. What are they doing? Why? What are they doing now? Why is the haruspex eyeballing the sheep's liver? Why is the soothsayer wholesaling the Bewares?

Perhaps that's been my difficulty in writing you this letter: I'm not sure I know what's really going on. Anyway, you have a huge posse of experienced entrail-sifters who do nothing but analyze your every vein and lobe. What can I tell you about yourself that you don't already know?

This might be the reason for my hesitation: embarrassment, brought on by a becoming modesty. But it is more likely to be embarrassment of another sort. When my grandmother—from a New England background—was confronted with an unsavory topic, she would change the subject and gaze out the window. And that is my own inclination: Mind your own business.

But I'll take the plunge, because your business is no longer merely your business. To paraphrase Marley's Ghost, who figured it out too late, mankind is your business. And vice versa: When the Jolly Green Giant goes on the rampage, many lesser plants and animals get trampled underfoot. As for us, you're our biggest trading partner: We know perfectly well that if you go down the plug-hole, we're going with you. We have every reason to wish you well.

I won't go into the reasons why I think your recent Iraqi adventures have been—taking the long view—an ill-advised tactical error. By the time you read this, Baghdad may or may not look like the craters of the Moon, and many more sheep entrails will have been examined. Let's talk, then, not about what you're doing to other people, but about what you're doing to yourselves.

You're gutting the Constitution. Already your home can be entered without your knowledge or permission, you can be snatched away and incarcerated without cause, your mail can be spied on, your private records searched. Why isn't this a recipe for widespread business theft, political intimidation, and fraud? I know you've been told all this is for your own safety and protection, but think about it for a minute. Anyway, when did you get so scared? You didn't used to be easily frightened.

You're running up a record level of debt. Keep spending at this rate and pretty soon you won't be able to afford any big military adventures. Either that or you'll go the way of the USSR: lots of tanks, but no air conditioning. That will make folks very cross. They'll be even crosser when they can't take a shower because your short-sighted bulldozing of environmental protections has dirtied most of the water and dried up the rest. Then things will get hot and dirty indeed.

You're torching the American economy. How soon before the answer to that will be, not to produce anything yourselves, but to grab stuff other people produce, at gunboat-diplomacy prices? Is the world going to consist of a few megarich King Midases, with the rest being serfs, both inside and outside your country? Will the biggest business sector in the United States be the prison system? Let's hope not.

If you proceed much further down the slippery slope, people around the world will stop admiring the good things about you.

They'll decide that your city upon the hill is a slum and your democracy is a sham, and therefore you have no business trying to impose your sullied vision on them. They'll think you've abandoned the rule of law. They'll think you've fouled your own nest.

The British used to have a myth about King Arthur. He wasn't dead, but sleeping in a cave, it was said; in the country's hour of greatest peril, he would return. You, too, have great spirits of the past you may call upon: men and women of courage, of conscience, of prescience. Summon them now, to stand with you, to inspire you, to defend the best in you. You need them.

White Privilege: Unpacking the Invisible Knapsack

Peggy McIntosh

Peggy McIntosh is Associate Director of the Wellesley College Center for Research for Women.
Reprinted by permission of the author. This essay is excerpted from her working paper. "White Privilege and Male Privilege: A Personal Account of Coming to See Correspondences Through Work in Women's Studies."

Through work to bring materials from Women's Studies into the rest of the curriculum, I have often noticed men's unwillingness to grant that they are overprivileged, even though they may grant that women are disadvantaged. They may say they will work to improve women's status, in the society, the university, or the curriculum, but they can't or won't support the idea of lessening men's. Denials, which amount to taboos, surround the subject of advantages, which men gain from women's disadvantages. These denials protect male privilege from being fully acknowledged, lessened or ended.

Thinking through unacknowledged male privilege as a phenomenon, I realized that since hierarchies in our society are interlocking, there was most likely a phenomenon of white privilege, which was similarly denied and protected. As a white person, I realized I had been taught about racism as something which puts others at a disadvantage, but had been taught not to see one of its corollary aspects, white privilege which puts me at an advantage.

I think whites are carefully taught not to recognize white privilege, as males are taught not to recognize male privilege. So I have begun in an untutored way to ask what it is like to have white privilege. I have come to see white privilege as an invisible package of unearned assets

Reprinted by permission from the S.E.E.D. Project.

which I can count on cashing in each day, but about which I was "meant" to remain oblivious. White privilege is like an invisible weightless knapsack of special provisions, maps, passports, codebooks, visas, clothes, tools and blank checks.

Describing white privilege makes one newly accountable. As we in Women's Studies work to reveal male privilege and ask men to give up some of their power, so one who writes about having white privilege must ask, "Having described it what will I do to lessen or end it?"

After I realized the extent to which men work from a base of unacknowledged privilege, I understood that much of their oppressiveness was unconscious. Then I remembered the frequent charges from women of color that white women whom they encounter are oppressive. I began to understand why we are justly seen as oppressive, even when we don't see ourselves that way. I began to count the ways in which I enjoy unearned skin privilege and have been conditioned into oblivion about its existence.

My schooling gave me no training in seeing myself as an oppressor, as an unfairly advantaged person or as a participant in a damaged culture. I was taught to see myself as an individual whose moral state depended on her individual moral will. My schooling followed the pattern my colleague Elizabeth Minnich has pointed out: whites are taught to think of their lives as morally neutral, normative, and average, and also ideal, so that when we work to benefit others, this is seen as work which will allow "them" to be more like "us."

I decided to try to work on myself at least by identifying some of the daily effects of white privilege on my life. I have chosen those conditions which I think in my case *attach somewhat more to skin-color privilege* than to class, religion, ethnic status, or geographical location, though of course all these other factors are intricately intertwined. As far as I can see, my African American co-workers, friends and acquaintances with whom I come into daily or frequent contact in this particular time, place and line of work cannot count on most of these conditions.

1. I can if I wish arrange to be in the company of people of my race most of the time.
2. If I should need to move, I can be pretty sure of renting or purchasing housing in an area, which I can afford and in which I would want to live.
3. I can be pretty sure that my neighbors in such a location will be neutral or pleasant to me.
4. I can go shopping alone most of the time, pretty well assured that I will not be followed or harassed.

273

5. I can turn on the television or open to the front page of the paper and see people of my race widely represented.

6. When I am told about our national heritage or about "civilization," I am shown that people of my color made it what it is.

7. I can be sure that my children will be given curricular materials that testify to the existence of their race.

8. If I want to, I can be pretty sure of finding a publisher for this piece on white privilege.

9. I can go into a music shop and count on finding the music of my race represented, into a supermarket and find the staple foods which fit with my cultural traditions, into a hairdresser's shop and find someone who can cut my hair.

10. Whether I use checks, credit cards or cash, I can count on my skin color not to work against the appearance of my financial reliability.

11. I can arrange to protect my children most of the time from people who might not like them.

12. I can swear, or dress in secondhand clothes, or not answer letters, without having people attribute these choices to the bad morals, the poverty, or the illiteracy of my race.

13. I can speak in public to a powerful male group without putting my race on trial.

14. I can do well in a challenging situation without being called a credit to my race.

15. I am never asked to speak for all the people of my racial group.

16. I can remain oblivious of the language and customs of persons of color who constitute the world's majority without feeling in my culture any penalty for such oblivion.

17. I can criticize our government and talk about how much I fear its policies and behavior without being seen as a cultural outsider.

18. I can be pretty sure that if I ask to talk to "the person in charge," I will be facing a person of my race.

19. If a traffic cop pulls me over or if the IRS audits my tax return, I can be sure I haven't been singled out because of my race.

20. I can easily buy posters, post-cards, picture books, greeting cards, dolls, toys, and children's magazines featuring people of my race.

21. I can go home from most meetings of organizations I belong to feeling somewhat tied in, rather than isolated, out-of-place, out-numbered, unheard, held at a distance, or feared.

22. I can take a job with an affirmative action employer without having coworkers on the job suspect that I got it because of race.

23. I can choose public accommodation without fearing that people of my race cannot get in or will be mistreated in the place I have chosen.

24. I can be sure that if I need legal or medical help my race will not work against me.

25. If my day, week or year is going badly, I need not ask of each negative episode or situation whether it has racial overtones.
26. I can choose blemish cover or bandages in "flesh" color and have them more or less match my skin.

I repeatedly forgot each of the realizations on this list until I wrote it down. For me white privilege has turned out to be an elusive and fugitive subject. The pressure to avoid it is great, for in facing it I must give up the myth of meritocracy. If these things are true, this is not such a free country; one's life is not what one makes it; many doors open for certain people through no virtues of their own.

In unpacking this invisible backpack of white privilege, I have listed conditions of daily experience which I once took for granted. Nor did I think of any of these perquisites as bad for the holder. I now think that we need a more finely differentiated taxonomy of privilege, for some these varieties are only what one would want for everyone in a just society, and others give license to be ignorant, oblivious, arrogant and destructive.

I see a pattern running through the matrix of white privilege, a pattern of assumptions which were passed on to me as a white person. There was one main piece of cultural turf; it was my own turf, and I was among those who could control the turf. *My skin color was an asset for any move I was educated to want to make.* I could think of myself as belonging in major ways, and of making social systems work for me. I could freely disparage, fear, neglect, or be oblivious to anything outside of the dominant cultural forms. Being of the main culture, I could also criticize it fairly freely.

In proportion as my racial group was being confident, comfortable, and oblivious, other groups were likely being made unconfident, uncomfortable, and alienated. Whiteness protected me from many kinds of hostility, distress, and violence, which I was being subtly trained to visit in turn upon people of color.

For this reason, the word "privilege" now seems to be misleading. We usually think of privilege as being a favored state, whether earned or conferred by birth or luck. Yet some of the conditions I have described here work to systematically over empower certain groups. Such privilege simply *confers dominance* because of one's race or sex.

I want, then, to distinguish between earned strength and unearned power conferred systematically. Power from unearned privilege can look like strength when it is in fact permission to escape or to dominate. But not all of the privileges on my list are inevitably damaging. Some, like the expectation that neighbors will be decent to you, or that your race will not count against you in court, should be the norm in a just society. Others, like the privilege to ignore less powerful people, distort the humanity of the holders as well as the ignored groups.

We might at least start by distinguishing between positive advantages which we can work to spread, and negative types of advantages which, unless rejected, will always reinforce our present hierarchies. For example, the feeling that one belongs within the human circle, as Native Americans say, should not be seen as a privilege for a few. Ideally it is an *unearned entitlement*. At present, since only a few have it, it is an *unearned advantage* for them. This paper results from a process of coming to see that some of the power which I originally saw as attendant on being a human being in the U.S. consisted in *unearned advantage* and *conferred dominance*.

I have met very few men who are truly distressed about systemic, unearned male advantage and conferred dominance. And so one question for me and others like me is whether we will be like them or whether we will get truly distressed, even outraged about unearned race advantage and conferred dominance and if so, what will we do to lessen them. In any case, we need to do more work in identifying how they actually affect our daily lives. Many, perhaps most of our white students in the U.S. think that racism doesn't affect them because they are not people of color, they do not see "whiteness" as a racial identity. In addition, since race and sex are not the only advantaging systems at work, we need similarly to examine the daily experience of having age advantage, or ethnic advantage, or physical ability, or advantage related to nationality, religion or sexual orientation.

Difficulties and dangers surrounding the task of finding parallels are many. Since racism, sexism and heterosexism are not the same, the advantaging associated with them should not be seen as the same. In addition, it is hard to disentangle aspects of unearned advantage which rest more on social class, economic class, race, religion, sex and ethnic identity than on other factors. Still, all of the oppressions are interlocking, as the Combahee River Collective Statement of 1977 continues to remind us eloquently.

One factor seems clear about all of the interlocking oppressions. They take both active forms which we can see and embedded forms which as a member of the dominant group one is not taught to see. In

276

my class and place, I did not see myself as a racist because I was taught to recognize racism only in individual acts of meanness by members of my group, never in the invisible systems conferring unsought racial dominance on my group from birth.

Disapproving of the systems won't be enough to change them. I was taught to think that racism could end if white individuals changed their attitudes. (But) a "white" skin in the United States opens many doors for whites whether or not we approve of the way dominance has been conferred on us. Individual acts can palliate, but cannot end, these problems.

To redesign social systems we need first to acknowledge their colossal unseen dimensions. The silences and denials surrounding privilege are the key political tool here. They keep the thinking about equality or equity incomplete, protecting unearned advantage and conferred dominance by making these taboo subjects. Most talk by whites about equal opportunity seems to me now to be about equal opportunity to try to get into a position of dominance while denying that systems of dominance exist.

It seems to me that obliviousness about white advantage, like obliviousness about male advantage, is kept strongly inculturated in the United States so as to maintain the myth of meritocracy, the myth that democratic choice is equally available to all. Keeping most people unaware that freedom of confident action is there for just a small number of people props up those in power, and serves to keep power in the hands of the same groups that have most of it already.

Though systemic change takes many decades, there are pressing questions for me and I imagine for some others like me if we raise our daily consciousness on the perquisites of being light-skinned. What will we do with such knowledge? As we know from watching men, it is an open question whether we will choose to use unearned advantage to weaken hidden systems of advantage and whether we will use any of our arbitrarily-awarded power to reconstruct power systems on a broader base.

Reflection on My EFL Experiences

Ramesh Kumar Pokharel

L earning a foreign language is like exploring a foreign land; one will be directionless and may be lost in the exploration as one makes efforts to learn foreign language. It is not easy to learn or teach foreign language. However, an appropriate teaching approach or technique can facilitate learning of foreign language, and, thus, it can be taught or learned comfortably if good and effective skills are applied. Here, I will make an attempt to reflect on my experiences as a second language learner about how the language was taught and how I would teach differently if I were in the position of teacher in that context.

I learned English as a foreign language, or academic language. I began learning English with the alphabets in Grade 4. English was taught extensively but not intensively from Grade 4 to undergraduate level as a compulsory subject, resulting in poor outcomes. Research has shown that intensive learning or teaching of any language, rather, has better impact on learning. At school, learning or teaching English language mainly concentrated on teaching vocabulary and grammar rules with special emphasis on prescriptive grammar. Later on at higher secondary school and university-level courses, it was believed that language learning did not only involve learning vocabulary and grammar rules, it was associated with culture that gets reflected in literature. So literary texts were much focused on teaching English language. But still the traditional and discarded approach of the grammar translation method was used in teaching language and literature instead of oral structural method.

Reprinted from *TESOL Journal* 21, March 2011, by permission of Teachers of English to Speakers of Other Languages, Inc.

Learning a language effectively, in fact, involves learning four language skills simultaneously (speaking, writing, reading, and listening), and it can be sustainable and long-lasting only if the four language skills are learned/taught in balance. But we did not have the environment for learning these language skills; there was no opportunity for speaking and listening at all, and some writing and reading would be done only limitedly. For writing, some exercises would be done from the textbooks, and no free or creative writing was encouraged. Though reading was limited to reading textbooks only, there was little more focus on writing and reading than in speaking and listening.

The teachers would focus on rote learning: We would learn the grammar rules and vocabulary by heart without knowing how the words are used in context. I remember I could do grammar exercise correctly, but still I had problems writing an essay on my own. Whether rote learning is a good or bad thing I don't know, but I felt like learning a passage or a story or a poem by heart sometimes helped me understand the content, vocabulary, and grammatical structure of the sentences used in the context that definitely enabled me to reproduce similar expression in my writings. I learned to use the vocabulary and sentence structure subsequently. More important was that learning the vocabulary, grammar rules, and even sentences as used in the text built my self-confidence as if I knew it and I could use the language well. But when I was asked to memorize long passages, lines of poetry, or long lists of vocabulary and grammar rules by heart, it would be troublesome. At the same time, I would have self-satisfaction if I could do so.

If I were in the position of teacher in this context, I would contextualize the teaching of language with the life of the learners by creating lifelike situations in examples and tests. I would make them read many books on the literature in the target language because I do believe that learning language structure can best be done from reading literature as language is used in context in literary text. I would try to teach all language skills with equal focus because learning a language means, in fact, learning all language skills. I would discard the grammar translation method and create oral structural situations for the learners to practice their speaking skill. Likewise, to develop writing and listening skills together with reading and speaking, I would create a lifelike context for writing assignments and make them write more and more because I believe that writing makes one exact and polished. For listening practice, I would provide them opportunity to listen to dialogues in different contexts because they would learn what sorts of utterances are produced in what context.

Overall, I would balance the four skills and provide opportunities for authentic language learning.

Revising Literacies

The Hole in The Wall Project by Sugata Mitra
Nurturing Creativity by Elizabeth Gilbert

http://www.youtube.com/watch?v=NL1GopyXT_g

Appendix I: RAIDS

You have probably used some common pre-writing strategies like brainstorming, freewriting, journaling, mapping, or clustering in the past. These strategies can be effective in some writing situations. In writing situations that ask you to incorporate readings and the insights about writing that come from those readings, however, it is best to have some invention strategies that help you read as a writer. At Michigan State University, we have developed an innovative way to put reading and writing in relationship with one another so that as you read you develop richer, more flexible and more effective approaches to succeeding in a variety of composing situations. Like all inquiry-based approaches to knowledge building, ours begins with a series of questions. You will use these questions both when you read and when you write. The questions ask you to think about five of the major components of literacy: Invention, Arrangement, Revision, Style and Delivery. If you scramble the first letter of each of these elements of literacy you get the word RAIDS, an easy way to remember all five. Here are the questions (the sub-questions that appear in parentheses are examples of things to ask if you are having trouble getting started with the larger questions):

Invention

What is invention? (What cognitive, social, and other activities did the writer/writers have to engage in to create the text?)

What's being invented? (What attitudes, beliefs, practices, ideas, etc. emerge from the text? If you get stuck, ask yourself what you know, think, feel, as a result of engaging with the text. What ideas, feelings, beliefs, etc. have changed as a result of your reading?)

Arrangement

What's being arranged? (What's being put in relationship with what? What ideas are being put in relationship with one another? What people, cultural practices, etc. are being put in relationship with one another?)

What is arrangement? (How are things being put in relationship with one another? What organizational plans are at work (e.g. inductive, deductive, narrative, categorical)?

Revision

What's being revised? (What ideas, attitudes, practices, etc. could change if people adopted the ideas, beliefs, attitudes, practices, etc. suggested by the text?)

What is revision? (What strategies are used specifically to make these changes occur? Note: There are usually some strategies that are used both for invention and for revision.)

Style

What style is most prevalent in the text (e.g. high, middle, low, popular, scholarly, etc.)?

How does the style help the writer(s) relate to audience?

How does the style affect the ethos of the writer and the message(s)?

Delivery

What mode of delivery is used to present the text? (Remember that more than one mode may have been used. For example, if the text appears in an online course management site you may need to ask questions or do a bit of research to identify the other ways it has been delivered.)

How does the mode of delivery affect writer/reader relationships?

How does the mode of delivery affect the ethos of the writer and the message?

SWAP

Analyzing writing situations that you are given to respond to and composing writing situations of your own is easier if you begin by thinking about four of the major elements that become factors across most situations that call for a written response of some kind (whether visual, verbal, multimodal, etc.). Thinking about Subject, Writer, Audience and Purpose will start the process.

Subject: the major topics, issues, time period etc. that your readers/viewers will be presented with

Writer: the ethos of the author(s) of the text

Audience: the person or people who will view the text(s) created by the writer

Purpose: the focus for revision

SWAP is really about understanding the relationships between and among subject, writer, audience and purpose. For example, you might select subjects because you have a certain audience and you know that that audience will be interested in the subject. On the other hand, the audience may have prescribed the subject and your main job is to relate that subject strongly to a purpose, for example proving that you have studied and know the material about that subject. As you grow more familiar and comfortable with SWAP, remember that they can be most beneficial to composers who think about the elements of SWAP as existing in relationship with one another.